MW00414875

How to Talk to
Parents About Autism

How to Talk to Parents About Autism

Roy Q. Sanders

W W. Norton & Company
New York • London

For information about permission to
reproduce selections from this book, write to
Permissions, W. W. Norton & Company, Inc.,
500 Fifth Avenue, New York, NY 10110

Production Manager: Leeann Graham
Manufacturing by Quebecor World, Fairfield Graphics

Library of Congress Cataloging-in-Publication Data

Sanders, Roy Q.
How to talk to parents about autism / Roy Q. Sanders — 1st ed.
    p. cm. — (A Norton professional book)
Includes bibliographical references and index.
ISBN 978-0-393-70529-4 (pbk.)
    1. Autism in children.   2. Parents of autistic children.
3. Physician and patient.   4. Communication in medicine.
I. Title.
RJ506.A9S354   2008
618.92'85882—dc22

W. W. Norton & Company, Inc., 500 Fifth Avenue, New York, N.Y. 10110
www.wwnorton.com

W. W. Norton & Company, Ltd., Castle House, 75/76 Wells St.
London W1T 3QT

1   3   5   7   9   0   8   6   4   2

This book is dedicated to my family—
Charlie, Frankie, and McCrae—
and to all the families who allow me into
their lives everyday. You are my teachers.

Table of Contents

Acknowledgments

I would like especially to thank Lynn Donham for her incredible patience, insightful prodding, and eloquent prose. There would be no book without her partnership. I would also like to thank my friend Jessica Landisman-Williams for her editing and encouragement. Deborah Malmud provided the idea and the opportunity to make this book a reality, and for that I am grateful. Thanks also to Rhonda Venable, PhD, Lisa Sacco, PsyD, Arden Dingle, MD, and Paige Pierce. I would like to thank Charlie for his love, patience, and support. Lastly, I want to thank our boys Frankie and McCrae, who inspire me to be the best person, parent, and physician I am capable of being.

How to Talk to Parents About Autism

PART 1

INTRODUCTION

Introduction

The most recent epidemiologic data from the Centers for Disease Control suggest that 1 in every 150 children has some form of autism. Autism Spectrum Disorder (ASD) is a neurodevelopmental disorder that is characterized by pervasive developmental problems that must include impairments in social engagement, difficulties with language use, and fixations often associated with repetitive behaviors accompanied by rigidity. However, symptoms often vary from child to child. Parents of children diagnosed with autism often feel overwhelmed. They experience a range of feelings that may include denial, wishful thinking, and desperation. Sometimes they pursue unproven or useless treatments and interventions.

This book will help professionals who consult with parents understand autism's symptoms, while providing proactive guidance. I hope this guidance will give parents the knowledge to understand more fully the problems associated with autism and make decisions that help their child develop to be as fully happy and engaged as possible. To work effectively with parents and understand parents' concerns, professionals must know the defining characteristics and symptoms of autism. Diagnosis and early interventions are only the beginning.

We cannot underestimate the stress on families affected by ASD. Perhaps the professional's most important response is to connect parents to other families who have a child with this disorder. Professionals help in many critical ways, but oftentimes another parent feels like the only secure lifeline in a sea of disappointments and confusing choices.

I know this confusion, because my oldest son was diagnosed with ASD. I know a parent's anger and agitation at professionals as well as the comfort from another family going through the same struggles. When Frankie was diagnosed at 15 months, I was sad and incredibly angry. Oddly, irrationally, I was most angry with the pediatrician who finally gave us a diagnosis. For months I had known that something was wrong, and because of my own work and training, I knew it was autism and possibly worse. Nonetheless, I did not want to fully acknowledge the extent of his disability. I kept hoping that I was misreading the signs and symptoms.

After a day of testing and waiting, the pediatrician finally came in to talk with us. We were tired and anxious. She outlined very clearly all of the test results and the findings from the team's observations. Then she said something about autism.

At first I didn't understand what she was saying, and I asked her "Are you saying he is autistic?" She said something to the effect that yes, he met the criteria for that diagnosis with some atypical symptoms, and that additionally he had other developmental delays.

I asked, "Do you mean that he is mentally retarded?" She said that it was "possible" but too early to determine. I was furious. I felt like I had been kicked in the stomach. I don't know if it was her approach or her message, but I wanted to strike back, to act out the anger and hurt that I have rarely felt in my life.

On the way home that evening the car was quiet. My mind was reeling, thinking about what we would do. The life I had imagined for my son and our family was now clearly impossible. I was unaware of the depth of my denial. I did not know what to say.

I wanted to talk with someone who had answers, someone who could give me a roadmap—tell me where to go, what to do, and what to expect. When we were finally able to connect with other families, it was a blessing. They knew better than anyone where to go, what to ask, what to expect, and even more, what to demand.

I believe most parents experience many of the same feelings and thoughts when their child is first diagnosed. They usually don't know where to look for answers, what to ask, or worse, *who* to ask.

So the purpose of this book is to give the professional who is facing a family that has been given the diagnosis of autism for their child, a place to start. I base my advice on my experience as a parent of a child with ASD and intellectual disabilities and as a child psychiatrist who sees and treats autistic children every day. I hope this book will be a useful guide to enlarge professionals' understanding and ability to assist children with autism and the families who love them.

CHAPTER ONE

How to Talk with Parents When Autism Is First Diagnosed

While no one, including highly trained professionals, is objective about his or her children, no parent should be discounted. Not long after we received our diagnosis the parent of a child with disabilities told me to remember, "You are the expert on Frankie." What an amazing concept! She reminded me that the professionals were experts in their fields but my role as a parent was to be the expert on my son.

Never forget that parents are the experts on their child. This is the number one rule when dealing with families of children affected by any disease or disability, and it is true with autism spectrum disorder (ASD). It is true the first time you see a child with his or her family, and it will be true as long as you see them. Parents want help for their child. They want answers, but they also want and need to be listened to and respected. Your respect and validation may be as important as any information and advice you provide to parents. Because autistic symptoms and needs can be so individual, helping professionals contribute most when they empower parents to understand and trust their experience with their child.

The First Visit

When I sit down with a family for the first time *I ask them to tell me the story of their child.* Parents are far more capable of offering me an exact picture of the difficulties than I am of eliciting those problems by asking a standard set of questions. Although the standard set of questions is important in order to verify a diagnosis or determine particular symptoms or their severity, this should come *after* listening to the parents' conception of the issues.

The picture that emerges from simply letting the parent tell the story with gentle guidance is the story of the unique child in front of you. No other child will be just like this child. No other child will experience the exact same difficulties as this child. Listening to the parents' story does not take a long time, and it sets the stage for a collaborative experience that will ultimately be satisfying to you as the professional, and to the child's family.

Determine and Address Parents' Concerns

During your visits with the family you must listen to their specific concerns and try to address them. Few things frustrate parents more than to clearly outline their concerns and have them ignored or dismissed.

Parents may ask "What is the diagnosis?" or "Will he ever be able to live on his own?" There is often no quick answer to the concern raised, and many times there may be no answer at all. It's tempting to avoid acknowledging this. At times, neither of these questions is easy to answer. But these and other questions require a response even if you must say, "I am not sure" or "I don't know."

Whether you first see a child with ASD when he or she is very young or after years of difficulties, varying diagnoses and interventions, the questions parents have are often the same.

What to Say to Parents

- *You are the expert on your child. Every child is different, and your observations and judgments are important.* Parents usually fail to recognize that they are the experts on their children. Professionals generally do not acknowledge parents' expertise and may even dismiss parents' observations or conclusions. As a professional I believe that it is essential that we understand that parents know their child best and are the experts. Saying this lets parents know they are a valued part of the team; in turn, they will give you information and understanding that you would not have otherwise.

- *This is not your fault.* Parents often feel that it is their fault that their child has problems. Many times they have been told that they are the problem. Sometimes the parents will blame each other for the problems their child experiences. Grandparents, siblings, friends, coworkers, even passersby will imply a parent has caused the problems now recognized as ASD. We can reassure parents that they did not cause this. You can reassert that ASD is a complicated brain disorder with physical causes.

- *It's normal to be scared, overwhelmed, angry, or disbelieving about the diagnosis.* The first time parents actually hear the words *autism* or *autism spectrum disorder* their brains may literally shut down from the sheer emotional impact of what they are hearing. They will often be frightened or inexplicably angry. They may not believe that the diagnosis is correct. Professionals must acknowledge to parents they are working with the emotions they may experience. You can say simply, "I know you may be frightened, overwhelmed, or angry about this diagnosis. I also know that it may be difficult to believe or accept. I am here to listen to your concerns and try to answer your questions."

- *The information, guidance, and support you receive should strengthen your understanding and ability to care for your child, not undermine it.* Once a child is diagnosed with ASD and the family starts to look for answers and interventions, they are often bombarded with information and strategies for intervention, some of which are helpful, and some of which are not. Stress to parents that what professionals tell them should help them be better parents and strengthen their ability to parent. If the information or guidance takes them out of the parenting role or dismisses their contribution to the care and progress of their child it is not good information or guidance and they should dismiss it.

- *Autism affects your whole family—it's all connected. Keeping your family whole will help your child.* Families whose child has ASD are at high risk for separation and divorce. Having a child with autism can set the child's siblings against parents or against one another. Extended family may become estranged or even overinvolved. Tell parents about stressors on the family, the whole family, and emphasize the need for outside support or counseling from professionals such as social workers, counselors, or religious leaders. Parents need to know that it is okay to ask for help and by doing so, they can really help their child thrive.

- *Your health and well-being as a parent, a spouse, and an individual is essential to your ability to care for your child. Caring for your child means caring for yourself.* Parents forget to take care of themselves. They become so overwhelmed by the diagnosis and the enormity of all that's required to get help for their child that they may literally forget to eat, rest, or at times even breathe. In *Kitchen Table Wisdom* (1997), Rachel Naomi Remen reminds us that flight attendants direct airline passengers to put on their oxygen mask first *before* they assist a child. It is important to remind parents to take care of themselves by eating, exercising, taking time off, relaxing, and talking with friends and family so that they can do their best in caring for their child with ASD and others who depend on them.

- *Tell me about the support you have in place now.* Asking parents about the support they currently have is very important. It is important because it validates the need for support and helps the parents to start thinking about whom they can rely on or turn to for help with what needs to be done. Parents can be embarrassed by their need or so overwhelmed they cannot begin to think about what to do next. Asking this question starts them to thinking about that next thing they can do.

- *Tell me what concerns you most right now.* Finding out the most pressing concerns is one of the most important things you can do in a first visit. You can begin to set priorities and plan how to address the problems the family faces. Parents know you have heard them and that their concerns will be addressed. After you listen to their concerns, write them down and begin an instruction sheet for parents for after they leave the office the first time. When parents leave my office with this list of "To do's" before the next visit, I make sure their concerns are addressed on that list. Examples of tasks and activities that may appear on a to-do list include: visiting the Autism Society of America's website (see Appendix A); signing up for a local listserv of families living with ASD; making an appointment with a developmental pediatrician; contacting a family therapist; contacting a local early intervention program for children with developmental delays; arranging for an evaluation by a speech therapist; and arranging for an evaluation by an occupational therapist.

Questions Parents May Ask

- *What is the diagnosis?* If you are the first professional a family has seen this may be the question that most concerns them. If you have a clear idea of the diagnosis then present it as simply as you can. Use nonclinical or everyday terms as much as possible in a conversational style. Don't lecture. Pause now and then to ask parents if what you are telling them is clear, or ask "Does that make sense?" However, many times you may not have a clear understanding of the diagnosis at the first visit. You may know that the child meets the criteria for ASD but you may know little else. You may need to send the child for more comprehensive testing and evaluation. Parents may find it difficult to wait for the final opinion on the diagnosis and it is important to acknowledge that waiting is tough. You can and should give parents interventions they can begin right away, depending on the child's problems, in addition to giving them the steps to take to try and get a clear diagnosis. For example, if a child has language problems refer the parents to a speech therapist; if there are problems with motor development refer them to an occupational therapist and a physical therapist; if there are problems with behavior help them to find a behavioral specialist. If the child is younger than 3 years old, connect the family to a local early childhood intervention program that can assess and address needs. These systems also help the families start applying for any services and entitlements available through state and local governments. All federal entitlements are administered through state government. If the child is older than 3 years tell them to contact their local school's special education department to begin an assessment of appropriate educational intervention. Families can take all these steps even before an official diagnosis is made.

- *What is autism?* It is best to keep the answer as simple and as nonclinical as possible. I tell parents that autism is a complicated brain disorder with many different causes. First, the person with autism has problems interacting with other people socially. Second, he or she has problems with language. Some people may be completely unable to communicate. Others speak but have problems with language or other forms of communication. Finally, the person with autism gets stuck on activities, topics, or behaviors, and can be quite single-minded in pursuit of these interests. These are the three main categories of autism symptoms and are present in all of the different kinds of autism that make up ASD. Simply stated they are problems with social engagement, difficulties with language use, and fixations often associated with repetitive behaviors accompanied by rigidity.

- *What are signs my child may be autistic?* The first symptom most often noticed is a lack or loss of speech, or some other oddness or difference in speech or language that is often difficult to describe. Of course there are usually other signs that predate the language problems. Most children who will be diagnosed with ASD fail to make eye contact with most people. They seem to have little desire for engagement with other children and many times even the adults in their life. They may resist being held or hugged. At times they stiffen or arch when touched. They may have difficulty with any changes in routine and can become agitated at even the smallest variation in how they are dressed, fed, changed, or bathed. They do not "play" like other children but will engage in repetitive play without imagination. These are some of the early signs that arouse concern. Many of these signs appear before age 2 and some before 12 months.

- *When do symptoms appear?* For most children, symptoms of ASD are clearly apparent by 2 years old. Many clinicians argue that symptoms are present in most children as early as 6 months of age. But some children seem to develop normally until 18 months to 2 to 3 years old and regress to a point where they develop the symptoms of ASD described above: social problems, language problems, and restrictive/rigid interests. Many parents say they have known something was wrong from the beginning. Professionals talking with families should handle this question carefully. One family may have always known something was wrong and never felt they got the validation necessary to begin interventions. This family needs to be validated and their anger and grief recognized. Other families may have lived in denial about their child's problems and are grief-stricken and guilty that they did not recognized signs earlier. These families need reassurance and help to move on to the necessary interventions to make things better. As a professional it is important to tease out what is behind their questions and then choose the best response.

- *How do you know if my child has autism?* The answer to this question will depend on your professional experience and your field of expertise. If you are a seasoned clinician who has worked with many children with ASD you can rely on your clinical judgment and the recognition that this child is like many other children you have seen in the past diagnosed with this disorder. If you are a professional who has worked with only a few children with ASD your answer might be that you rely on experts whom you know and trust. If the diagnosis is unclear (even if you are a seasoned clinician), you might tell the parents that you are not sure that the child has ASD but will help them sort out the diagnosis by a referral to other specialists, and perhaps even suggest psychological testing to clarify the diagnosis as much as possible.

- *How do you know we have the right diagnosis?* You can tell parents that you know you have the right diagnosis when the diagnosis is verifiable by different experts at separate times in different situations, perhaps even using different styles of evaluation to come to the same conclusion. It is generally accepted that a definitive diagnosis reached by a trained and experienced clinician using the Autism Diagnostic Interview—Revised (ADI; 3rd edition) or the Autism Diagnostic Observational Schedule (ADOS-G), both of which are evaluative instruments with known validity, is verification of the "right" diagnosis or misdiagnosis.

- *Can autism be misdiagnosed?* ASD can be misdiagnosed. Many times in a rush to place a label or sometimes to avoid placing a different label, a clinician will diagnose a child with ASD who may merit another diagnosis altogether. I have seen children misdiagnosed with ASD who simply had expressive or receptive language disorders. Children with psychotic illness or childhood schizophrenia can be misdiagnosed with ASD. This is also true for children with reactive attachment disorder, severe posttraumatic stress disorder, major depression, thyroid disease, moderate to severe intellectual disability, and many other disorders that can be confused with ASD. When talking with families tell them you will work to make sure the diagnosis you ultimately make is the one most appropriate for their child. This is important because it will help to define the appropriate interventions.

- *Are there different kinds of autism?* The simple answer for parents is "yes." That is why we talk about autism as a "spectrum" of disorders. We will discuss this more completely in the next chapter, but during the first visit you can talk with parents about some of the different ways the problems we outlined above may appear. Some types of ASD have different initial presentations. Some are different because we know the cause, and we distinguish them on that basis. In my experience parents usually ask this question because they have seen other children labeled with autism and their child is different. It is important to reassure the parents about the wide range of ways of social and language problems and restricted interests can present and that their child is one example.

- *How common is it? Is there an epidemic?* Currently the data supports that about 1 in every 100 to 150 people has some form of ASD. Those statistics are certainly an increase from previous numbers just a few years ago that suggested autism was only as common as 1 in every 4,000 people. Whether there is an epidemic is a hotly debated. I would honestly tell parents that I don't know if there is an epidemic. The science is unclear whether there is an actual increase in the number of people with ASD or if there is only an increase in the number of people being *diagnosed* with the disorder. It could be that as clinicians become better able to recognize the problems associated with the disorder and more parents and teachers become aware of the problem, more children and even adults are being identified with ASD. Possibly there is a real increase in the number of people with the disorder, and something about the environment, our genetics, our lifestyle, or other unknown factors that is leading to an increase in the diagnosis.

- *What causes autism?* For most forms of ASD no one knows for sure what causes the disorder. Some forms offer a clearer picture of causality. We know that exposure to certain viruses or infections before birth leads to a higher incidence of ASD. Other genetic disorders and chromosomal abnormalities have a high association with an ASD diagnosis. Brain injury from trauma or infection can also lead to symptoms consistent with this diagnosis. At this point in our understanding the best answer for parents is that no one really knows the cause of ASD. There are probably multiple causes. It is important to be very clear about the limits of our knowledge to equip parents who may be told that there is a specific cause of ASD with an intervention that leads to a cure.

- *Can it be cured?* Again the short answer for parents is "no." There is no cure for ASD. There are people who promise a cure, and they assert that there are particular causes for the disorder that, if addressed, specifically lead to a cure. Currently nothing in the accepted scientific literature points to a cure or complete elimination of the symptoms. But there are social and educational programs that seem to make a big difference in the ability of people with the disorder to function. I do believe that it is important to look at those options for intervention (we discuss these interventions in a later chapter). I tell parents that there is no cure, but there are things that will help and we will explore those together. I warn them about anyone who claims to know the cause or to have a cure. My experience has been that such people are usually selling something very costly that is not covered by insurance. Families are seldom in a position to pay those costs easily. When they try it usually leads to a situation where they have fewer resources later to take care of their child with ASD or other members of their family.
- *Will my other children have autism, too?* Because there are certain types of ASD related to genetic disorders and there is a growing awareness of the role multiple genes play in the disorder, if a family has one child with ASD it is more likely they may have another. As part of the workup you should include a referral to a human geneticist. A human genetics counselor in consultation with a human geneticist will best be able to counsel the parents on their specific reproductive issues related to ASD.
- *Does autism affect boys and girls differently?* Boys and girls are

not affected differently by ASD but more boys than girls are diagnosed with most types of ASD. Some causes of this disorder only affect girls and others only affect boys. It is unclear why more boys than girls have this diagnosis. In general boys are more vulnerable to organic difficulties; girls have the protection of two X chromosomes while boys only have one. Ongoing research addresses these differences and their possible meaning, especially related to the possible causes and interventions for ASD.

- *Will my child be able to live on her own, have a job, and a relationship?* Parents worry about what life will be like for their child. When a child is young he or she is so full of promise. There are endless possibilities. Raising the specter of a lifelong disability immediately demolishes many dreams parents have for their child. They want to know what dreams they may still hold. This is a difficult question to answer. There will be no clear answers when you first see a child. It is important, however, to acknowledge parents' fears about the future and their grief about the dreams that may not come true. With some parents you can begin to explore an attitude of hoping for the best but planning for the worst. I have found this to be a helpful paradigm for our family and others.

Our Experience

When we first started raising concerns about our son Frankie's progress at 9 months old, doctors dismissed our concerns. Our pediatrician and other professionals told us we were overanxious parents. In particular, I was told that as a pediatric psychiatrist who worked with developmentally disabled children, I knew too much and was looking for something to be wrong.

Although I came into all of these discussions armed with my observations and ready to challenge their opinions, after the first several visits I came away convinced that I was overreacting, so I did not push for more interventions. I lulled myself into denial, hoping against hope that I *was* truly overreacting. This pattern continued for another six months until the pediatrician finally sent us to a developmental pediatrician at a highly respected child development center.

We did not have any one professional to answer our questions after Frankie's diagnosis, but our questions were answered over time by all of the different professionals we worked with to help Frankie begin his process of habilitation and development. It is important for professionals working with families where a child has been diagnosed with ASD to remember to save time to answer questions. It may be important to set aside time specifically to address concerns. Many times the questions and concerns come in layers, as parents assimilate earlier information and are ready to hear more. Other times the protective denial is so great the information does not penetrate. Invite families to have the discussions when they are ready. Ask them to bring supportive family or friends who can listen to the information, too. Do not hesitate to allow families to take notes or record what you are saying. Remember that much of the information you are giving feels routine and obvious to you, but it is new to the families. Your support and the information you provide directly or through referrals is part of the safety net for the family you are seeing at one of their most vulnerable times.

Despite our early frustrations with feeling as if we were not being heard, I do not know how we would have survived without all of the professionals who helped us through those early months and years of trying to find a way for Frankie and our family.

CHAPTER TWO

How to Talk about Different Kinds of Autism and Other Labels

Depending on your profession, you may see a child with an ASD when he or she is very young or after years of difficulties, varying diagnoses, and interventions. So often, even in older children, diagnoses are bounced around all the time. While parents may be clearly told, "Your child is on the autism spectrum," they may also hear other diagnoses such as pervasive developmental disorder, autism, Asperger's disorder, mental retardation, sensory integration dysfunction, attention deficit hyperactivity disorder, obsessive compulsive disorder, and others, all of which are supposed to apply to their child. Some of these labels are part of what is called the autism spectrum. Others are names for problems that often coexist in children and adults with ASD.

Some children are diagnosed with an ASD after being diagnosed with another underlying disorder such as Down syndrome, Fragile X syndrome, cerebral palsy, neurofibromatosis, tuberous sclerosis, velo-cardio facial syndrome, or other neurological or genetic disorders known to be associated with an ASD. Sometimes the diagnosis of an

ASD and a subsequent evaluation of the disorder lead to a child being diagnosed with one of these other disorders as well.

Many parents whose children are diagnosed with ASD become frustrated by being unable to have a single label or name that explains all the problems that comprise their child's presentation. These children are a diverse group whose symptoms present in a widely variable fashion. Parents may see that their child is very different from other children with the same diagnosis. As a professional talking to parents, remember that presentations vary but there are always three core concerns in ASD: problems with social engagement, difficulties with language use, and fixations often associated with rigid, repetitive behaviors.

A child labeled today as having ASD may look very different from the child diagnosed in the 1970s, when autism was still described using Leo Kanner's terminology (Kanner was the physician who first described the disorder; Kanner, 1940). Over time, understanding of this group of disorders has expanded, and the criteria for inclusion on the spectrum has expanded as well. Children who once had no particular label at all and whose symptoms were not easily categorized are now labeled as part of this spectrum because they have similar but not identical features to those children who were originally described in the 1940s. This inclusion has led to the development of a greater understanding of these children and more helpful interventions. The professional community is now in the process of sorting out all of the different etiologies of this complex of symptoms. Eventually there will be a better classification system. For now we have the system described below with all the confusion it can cause for parents and professionals working with these children.

For parents and many professionals, naming the problem gives them a solid place to stand amid the chaos, fears, and uncertainty of their experience. A name or label seems to say, "You are not alone. Others have experienced this before. There are ways to help your child." A name or label gives parents a way to explain their child to family members, teachers, and others. The label is also many times the key to getting much-needed services for a child. Without a label there is often no way to get a particular therapy, placement, or other supports. Agencies and professionals that provide these services use the labels to justify the costs of the services. The diagnosis says, "This is a medical problem," and "Your child is not to blame" for his or her behavior or disabilities. "He or she deserves help."

At the same time, labels can be frightening to parents who don't yet understand the spectrum of children who share the same diagnosis. Many times the labels imply a possible future the parents do not want to face. Parents often focus on their worst apprehensions. As a professional working with children with ASD it is important to recognize and talk about the power of the label in just this way. Acknowledging these important feelings about labels helps parents to understand their frustration when the labels are unclear or less descriptive, or when they are frightening and loaded with connotations that may or may not be accurate.

Sometimes it is difficult to find the right label. As professionals we walk a tightrope of trying to diagnose a child with the most appropriate label, while not inappropriately labeling a child in a way that might cause harm. Because diagnosis of all ASD is still made by matching a list of descriptive symptoms to a child's behavior, there is a lot of room for subjective judgment. Many times we may feel compelled to label something in order to give the parents or others involved in the child's life a diagnosis to help with all of the issues described above. This rush to label, however, may ultimately do a disservice to the child, the family, and helping professionals who seek to gain knowledge about the disorder.

Accurate labels and accurate diagnoses are critical to a true understanding of this disorder's causes and origins, as well as valid, scientifically based treatment options for children, whether or not they meet the criteria for ASD.

If you are seeing a child whose problems you are unsure exactly how to classify or if you cannot determine into which diagnostic categories that child's problems may fall, it is best to forgo a specific label and refer the parents to another specialist. When talking with the parents, you should acknowledge all of the issues described above in terms of making the correct diagnosis. It is critical to tell the parents that you understand their child has a problem. Once you acknowledge that the problem exists, tell the parents you are not sure how the problem should be labeled or diagnosed. Also tell them that you will do everything you can to make sure that the child gets helpful interventions and services, even as you continue to help them search for the best diagnostic label. That may mean that for a time parents have to live with a less clear diagnosis, such as unspecified developmental delay or an unspecified disruptive behavior disorder. These types of diagnoses often disturb parents because they imply there is nothing really wrong and there is no specific treatment. Professionals should again point out here that something *is* wrong and that many of the interventions will help any child with similar difficulties without preventing a clearer understanding of the source of their child's problems.

I follow this general rule: If a child meets the criteria for ASD, make that diagnosis. If he or she clearly meets the criteria for another diagnosis, then make that diagnosis. If the diagnosis is not clear, then refer the family to another professional for an opinion.

What to Say to Parents

- *All of the labels can be very confusing.* Parents want a name for the problem they and their child face. Having a name helps in all the ways described above. However, many times when parents receive the name or label it does not seem to help at all and at times can even cause more confusion. I believe that it is important to acknowledge that confusion and to tell the parents that you will continue to work with them. Perhaps over time the confusion will clear. It is also important to tell them that, despite the confusion, they can take steps to make things better, and you are going to help them discover and take those actions. Hence the real problem with a confusing or ambiguous label: it creates greater uncertainty which can lead to greater fear.

- *Autism is defined as problems with social engagement, difficulties with language use, and fixations often associated with repetitive behaviors accompanied by rigidity.* This triad of difficulties that are present in all individuals with ASD cannot be overstressed. Helping parents to grasp these problems as the defining elements of the disorder will help them understand their child and give them the power to explain very succinctly what is "wrong" with their child.

- *Labels are important.* While labels can be confusing and they do not always give parents the peace that they seek, having a label is important for many reasons. Labels do give parents a way of talking to one another, family, friends, and, perhaps most importantly, professionals about their child. A label can be a cornerstone for organizing interventions. It helps to motivate and plan. A label or labels help to access services from agencies and professionals.

- *Labels are not everything and do not define the future.* While labels do provide a certain amount of assistance and even power, they do not define the child or set the future in stone. While many parents will be motivated by a label and ready to take on the challenges, others will become overwhelmed and perhaps even immobilized. They may feel hopeless.

Professionals working with the family should tell them that labels can be overwhelming. Help the family to see the label as a tool for helping the family and the child grow. The label may validate parents' sense of serious problems and their fears that things won't be as they seemed. Things may be even worse than the parents imagined. Even so, you can assure them there is a way forward and you are there to help them on that journey.

How to Answer Questions Parents Might Ask

- *What is the real diagnosis?* Sometimes the label is the "real" diagnosis and sometimes it is not. Sometimes the label is simply descriptive. It is important to tell the parents that sometimes there is no clear diagnosis, but the current label is important in order for them to get help and improve the situation. Our understanding of the difficulties associated with ASD, its causes, and problems is still very new. Actually this is equally true for much of psychiatry in general. Although our understanding of the brain is growing it is still quite deficient, and time may give us a clearer idea of the exact problem facing a particular child.

- *Why are there all these other labels?* All of the other labels are there to fully describe the set of problems a particular child has. Some children only have one label, but most children with a complicated neurodevelopmental disorder like ASD will have more than one label. This helps to identify and clarify all of the issues a child faces; when looking for services and interventions, it helps professionals ensure that all the child's needs are met.

- *Why can't anyone tell us what is really wrong?* Sometimes professionals can't tell exactly what is wrong. Implicit, but unasked is another question: "If we knew what was really wrong, couldn't we fix it?" Explain to parents what you do know, and be equally honest in talking about what you don't know. For complicated disorders of the brain such as ASD there may be a lot of different things that are wrong, but they all ultimately manifest in symptoms that are consistent with the ASD diagnosis.

- *Did we do anything to cause this?* The answer to this question is almost always, "No, absolutely not." While there may be a mother who abused substances or alcohol during pregnancy, even then there may be no clear evidence that those actions caused the problem. Ask the parents about any fear that they may have caused the problem, and help them to explore that fear. It may be absolutely clear that whatever they fear, it did not cause the problems their child is experiencing. It is imperative to reiterate that, regardless of the cause, the most important thing to do now is to get the assistance needed to make things better.

Description of Labels and Diagnoses

To give you a better understanding of the labels applied to children with ASD, the rest of this chapter is devoted to describing the diagnoses used for children with these disorders. I have included a table listing the types of ASD and their diagnostic criteria (see Table 2.1). I then describe each of the types of ASD and discuss how to talk to parents about these diagnoses.

Types of Autism Spectrum Disorder

Autism spectrum disorder means the same thing as pervasive developmental disorder—they both describe a family of related disorders with symptoms that vary along a continuum of similarities. These labels are sometimes used interchangeably by professionals, but there is a growing acceptance that ASD is the preferred term—it makes the most sense to the greatest number of people. Parents and advocacy groups have used the term *autism spectrum disorders* over the past several years to name diverse children with the core symptoms of these disorders: social problems, language problems, and restrictive interests.

Pervasive developmental disorders is the term used in the *DSM-IV* classification system, created and published by the American Psychiatric Association, to list the types of autism spectrum disorders. These are autistic disorder, Asperger's disorder, Rett's disorder, childhood disintegrative disorder, and pervasive developmental disorder, not otherwise specified (NOS).

Autistic Disorder

Autistic disorder is the same as infantile autism or Kannerian autism (Kanner, 1943). At the time, Kanner described these children as demonstrating a "combination of extreme autism [sic—meaning aloof-

Table 2.1 Types of autism spectrum disorders/pervasive developmental disorders—(Autism spectrum disorder and pervasive developmental disorder mean the same thing.)

Autistic Disorder	Impairment in social interactions
	• Problems with nonverbal social interactions such as eye gaze, facial expression, gestures and/or body posture
	• Problems with peer relationships and an inability to form peer relationships appropriate to his/her age
	• Problems with shared pleasure or enjoyment and a failure to seek such interaction with other people (for example, not pointing out interesting objects or not bringing a toy or object to an adult to share in the interest
	• Problems with normal give-and-take of social interactions such as taking turns or expressing emotions when socially appropriate
	Impairment in communication
	• Delayed development or failure to develop spoken language not compensated for by an attempt to communicate through gestures or other methods
	• If speech is present, an inability to initiate, sustain or appropriately close a conversation
	• If speech is present, language may be odd with repetitive phrases or odd or idiosyncratic speech patterns
	• If speech is present, problems with make-believe and imagination
	Fixations often associated with repetitive behaviors accompanied by rigidity
	• Preoccupation with a particular interest or pattern of behavior that is abnormal in intensity or focus
	• Persists in rigid patterns of behavior or rituals that are nonfunctional
	• Repetitive body movements or behaviors such as hand-flapping, hand-wringing, finger-flicking, bouncing, rocking or others
	• A preoccupation with parts of objects

Asperger's Disorder

Impairments in social interaction
- Problems with nonverbal social interactions such as eye gaze, facial expression, gestures and/or body posture
- Problems with peer relationships and an inability to form peer relationships appropriate to his/her age
- Problems with shared pleasure or enjoyment and a failure to seek such interaction with other people. (For example not pointing out interesting objects or not bringing a toy or object to an adult to share in the interest.)
- Problems with normal give-and-take of social interactions like taking turns or expressing emotions when socially appropriate

Impairments in communication
- May have inability to initiate, sustain or close a conversation appropriately
- Often an impairment in intonation and the stress on syllables or words that makes the speech sound odd
- Spoken interactions often resemble a lecture or sound "professorial"

Fixations often associated with repetitive behaviors accompanied by rigidity
- Preoccupation with a particular interest or behavior pattern that is abnormal in intensity or focus
- Persists in rigid patterns of behavior or rituals that are nonfunctional
- Repetitive body movements or behaviors such as hand-flapping, hand-wringing, finger-flicking, bouncing, rocking or others
- A preoccupation with the parts of objects

Two primary differences between Autistic Disorder and Asperger's Disorder are
- There is no intellectual disability or delay in cognitive development
- Language, while odd, is not delayed; child is conversational by age 3

(continued)

27

Table 2.1 Continued

Rett's Disorder	Virtually always affects girls • Normal prenatal and perinatal development • Normal cognitive and motor development for infants up to 5 months • Normal head circumference at birth After a period of normal development • Deceleration in head growth between 5 and 48 months • Loss of previously acquired useful hand skills with the development of nonpurposeful hand movement such as hand-wringing • Loss of a desire for social engagement or interaction • Walking and coordinated movements impaired • Expressive and receptive language severely impaired • Slow, sluggish movements and thinking
Childhood Disintegrative Disorder	Normal development for the first 2 years of life. At some point between age 2 and age 10 child loses previously acquired skills: • Expressive or receptive language • Skills for social interaction and social adaptability • Bowel and bladder control • Play skills • Motor skills Develops impairments in social interaction • Problems with nonverbal social interactions such as eye gaze, facial expression, gestures and/or body posture • Problems with peer relationships and an inability to form peer relationships appropriate to his/her age

28

- Problems with shared pleasure or enjoyment and a failure to seek such interaction with other people, (for example not pointing out interesting objects or not bringing a toy or object to an adult to share in the interest.)
- Problems with normal give-and-take of social interactions such as taking turns or expressing emotions when socially appropriate

Impairment in communication
- Delayed or failure to develop spoken language not compensated for by an attempt to communicate through gestures or other methods
- If speech is present, inability to initiate, sustain or appropriately close a conversation
- If speech is present, language may be odd with use of repetitive phrases or odd or idiosyncratic speech patterns
- If speech is present there are problems with make-believe and imagination

Fixations often associated with repetitive behaviors accompanied by rigidity
- Preoccupation with a particular interest or behavior pattern that is abnormal in intensity or focus
- Persists in rigid patterns of behavior or rituals that are non-functional
- Repetitive body movements or behaviors such as hand-flapping, hand-wringing, finger-flicking, bouncing, rocking or others
- A preoccupation with the parts of objects

Pervasive Developmental Disorder— Not otherwise specified

This label is used when the child or adult clearly has problems with social engagement, difficulties with language use, and fixations often associated with repetitive behaviors accompanied by rigidity but does not clearly fit one of the categories listed above.

Source: American Psychiatric Association. (1994). *Diagnostic and Statistical Manual of Mental Disorders* (4th ed.). Table modeled after "Counseling Points™ Enhancing patient care and providing caregiver support." Volume 1, Number 1, Chairperson: Robert L. Findling, MD, Faculty Robert L. Hendren, DO and David J. Posey, MD, MS, February 2007, (page 5)

ness], obsessiveness, stereotypy, and echolalia" (Kanner, (1943, p. 248). Children with autistic disorder are generally not engaged with the world or are only engaged as little as necessary to satisfy their needs and desires. They may sometimes show engagement or even attachment to parents or other primary caretakers. They may even engage with siblings or peers they see frequently, but then again they may not. It is this aloofness or an apparent desire to be left alone that most defines these children—hence the word *autism*.

Autism is the essence of the disorder, but there is a wide range of presentation. Some children may be quite high functioning and have normal intelligence, but also have significant social and behavioral disabilities. Other children may be very seriously impaired. They may be completely noncommunicative and withdrawn into their own world. They may or may not have very significant intellectual impairment.

Children and adults diagnosed with autistic disorder will also demonstrate most of the symptoms described above in Table 2.1. In terms of communication, many people with autistic disorder do not speak, or they communicate in a very odd way with repetitive phrases or a combination of meaningful requests, questions, and statements intermingled with echolalia (repeating what has just been said or something heard earlier, often precisely). The way they combine words and sentences may make no sense to someone who does not know them well. They often misuse words and grammar. They often will speak of themselves in the third person, saying, "He really likes the Mr. Moose. Yes, Timmy really likes it. Yes, he does. Mama gets it for Timmy. Yes, she will." This is a typical communication of a child I have cared for who was fixated on a moose doll.

Other fixations are often associated with repetitive behaviors accompanied by rigidity. Sometimes these fixations may be almost socially acceptable, such as videogames or cartoons, but the intensity and focus will be abnormal. Other fixations and repetitive behavior may be much less socially acceptable, such as playing with spittle or feces. There may be a fixation with jumping, screaming, or hand-flapping;

fixations on water and water play or with spinning objects are common. Many times these fixations will also include particular movements or self-stimulatory behaviors such as flapping at fans or other spinning objects or repeated head-banging or rocking.

What to Say to Parents

- *Children with autistic disorder can have mild or very severe symptoms.* Parents compare their child to other children. They come to acknowledge that their child has a problem after recognizing that he or she is not doing what other children of the same age are doing. After they receive a diagnosis of an ASD they will look at other children with the diagnosis and sometimes ask, "My child is not like that child, so how can he or she have autism spectrum disorder?" It is important to stress the very wide range of severity. Reiterate the three categories of problems experienced by someone with ASD: problems with social engagement, difficulties with language use, and fixations often associated with repetitive behaviors/rigidity.

- *Intervention for problems with communication is important.* One of the most important and crucial interventions for children with ASD, but especially for children with autistic disorder, is early speech and language intervention. Refer parents to programs or speech and language therapists who will work with them to develop their child's communication and language skills. While all of the other interventions are important because they help decrease problematic behavior and increase interaction, speech and communication deficits most often prevent these children from interacting socially, moderating their fixations and rigidity, and developing other important life skills.

- *It can be very difficult to tolerate many of the behaviors.* Professionals working with these families need to understand and to acknowledge to parents that it's difficult to live with many of the child's behaviors. This is especially true for those with autistic disorder, because of their intense aloofness, lack of language, and inability or lack of desire to understand that certain behaviors are displeasing to parents. For some parents and caretakers this inability to understand or lack of desire to address these problems can be infuriating, especially if the behavior is as socially inappropriate as playing with spittle or feces, head-banging, or screaming. Reassure parents that behavioral interventions can address these problems. Help parents find these resources while reminding them that these behaviors are part of the disorder. Sometimes, though, your most valuable help is given by simply acknowledging how tough it is to tolerate the behaviors.

Questions Parents May Ask

- *What caused the disorder?* Most of the time we do not know what caused the autistic disorder. There has been a lot of speculation about exposure to toxins, especially mercury, once used as a preservative in some childhood vaccines. Other theories point to vitamin deficiencies or food sensitivities as causes. We know that certain genetic or neurological disorders listed above are often associated with the disorder, but it is unclear what leads to the association. No one really knows what causes ASD; probably a lot of different factors lead to the problems associated with the disorder. Scientists are diligently working to sort out the causes. (See Appendix A for websites with information on research into causes and treatments.)

  When parents ask this question, I talk with them about their hope for a cure. It's easy to believe that if we can find out exactly what is wrong—what causes the problem—we can fix it. That might someday be true. I also caution parents about individuals and organizations that claim to know the cause and offer a cure. I have watched many families spend a lot of time and money on treatments that purport to "cure autism." I have yet to see any cases where this was true. Usually these cures are based on simplistic explanations for a very complex disorder, and the treatments themselves are simplistic in their approach. But they usually take a lot of time and cost a lot of money. The treatments that have been shown to make improvements in the disorder take enormous resources as well, but they usually revolve around intense engagement with the child with the ASD. Most often they concentrate on increasing communication and social engagement.

- *What is the prognosis?* The prognosis for autistic disorder is not great for the most part. Some children make amazing gains and there have been reports of children being "cured" with early interventions; and with early intervention, most children certainly improve. Efforts should be concentrated on increasing communication and social interaction. Many other factors affect prognosis, including coexisting diagnoses or other underlying neurological or genetic disorders.

  It is important to explore with the parents their fears about the future and to work with them to face those fears as practically as possible. It can be overwhelming for a parent to know their child's prognosis for improvement is fair to good, but the odds on a cure are a long shot. I try to help the parents look at the future in manageable "bits"—looking ahead to the next few months or the next school year. At the same time, I help them to begin to plan at least financially for the child's adulthood. I point out that with typical children parents usually just focus on the here and now, but they also are probably planning for college. This is the same idea. There's a reason 12-step programs have "one day at a time" as a tenet. It can be a difficult balancing act, but it does help to make the tasks ahead less daunting.

- *How many people are there with autistic disorder?* While the prevalence of ASD is estimated at 1:150 by the Centers for Disease Control and Prevention, the prevalence of autistic disorder is about 13:10,000 (Fombonne, 2005).

- *What can we do to help?* The most important intervention is getting assistance with communication and language development. Resources vary, but in most communities speech and language therapy is available through the school system. The family can also help by simply engaging the child at every opportunity and encouraging communication, both nonverbal and verbal, if present. Spending as much time as possible with their child, encouraging and coaxing interaction and communication can make a big difference in the child's ability to communicate and live with other people in his or her environment. Encourage other family members and caretakers to do the same. Finding places where the child can be involved with typically developing children can also be very helpful, especially if people there will facilitate interaction and communication between your child and the typically developing children.

Asperger's Disorder

Asperger's disorder was originally described by Hans Asperger in 1944. He described a group of young men with marked social problems and restricted interests who possessed relatively good cognitive and language skills. Today individuals diagnosed with Asperger's are mostly male; they seem to develop good language skills early on, although their language is often odd as described above. They have problems with being very literal, and many times they lack the normal variation of tone. They tend to talk "at" someone much more than "with" someone, usually about topics related to their restricted interests. They are often said to be professorial in their speech and presentation of information. These children and adults have average to above average intellectual abilities.

Socially they struggle significantly and are generally at a loss about how to make friends. Unlike children with autistic disorder, children and adolescents with Asperger's often want to make social connections with others but do not know how to engage. They say and do inappropriate, odd things that alienate other children. Their consuming fixations and interests often lead them to deliver excruciatingly detailed lectures, whether on plumbing, butterflies, brides, particular historical events, or even popular culture. These lectures and their lack of ability to carry on a two-way conversation keep other children away. Understandably, children who blurt out completely inappropriate comments or ask inappropriate questions like, "Why are you bald?" or "Have you always been that fat?" are less than endearing to their peers or to many adults.

The professional and advocacy community continue to discuss the difference between Asperger's and "high-functioning autism" (i.e., people with autistic disorder and average or above-average intelligence scores). A primary difference relates to the person's facility with language. A person diagnosed with Asperger's will be much more fluent and facile with language than a person with high-functioning autistic disorder. This difference will usually be apparent in interactions with the individuals. Also, very often people with Asperger's will have high verbal intelligence quotients and lower performance intelligence quotients. Individuals with high-functioning autistic disorder will often have just the reverse. Diagnostically, individuals with Asperger's are conversational by the age of 3 years with no significant delays. By definition, individuals with high-functioning autistic disorder will have significant language development delays.

Generally people with high-functioning autistic disorder show no interest in close relationships with anyone, while people with Asperger's seem to crave that interaction, but cannot sustain it. This leads to more depression and a sense of social isolation in individuals with Asperger's, especially as adolescents and young adults. People with Asperger's approach other people in a way that is fundamentally different than the typical approach.

What to Say to Parents
- *Get help with social skills development as early as possible.* Just as getting help with language and communication as soon as possible is helpful for children with ASD who are struggling with developing speech, social skills interventions are very important for children with Asperger's disorder. In many areas professionals have specific groups and programs for children with social skills problems, and these would be appropriate for children with Asperger's. Many schools have counselors and speech and language therapists

who incorporate social skills work and curricula into their programs. Help the parents to find what is available in your community and get them involved with those programs. Parents can also help by acting as social facilitators in social situations. It is important that the children with Asperger's disorder be involved in community groups such as sports, clubs, or other social outlets. The child with Asperger's, however, will probably need a parent, other adult, or a helpful child nearby to help with the social interactions, working as a facilitator to smooth out awkward moments and help connect the child.

- *Children with Asperger's cannot help how odd they are; it is not anybody's fault.* Children with Asperger's can be oddly endearing and engaging with their stilted mannerisms, professorial speech, and literal way of viewing the world. They can also be infuriating in their adherence to rules and their inability to ever see anything from someone else's perspective. It is important to help children with Asperger's to improve their social skills, but remember that their social difficulties are a core feature of their disability; many times they cannot help how oddly they act. Punishing or attempting to argue them out of their oddness is ineffective. Such tactics cause the child to feel bad and it hurts the relationship between the child and his parents or other caretaker if this useless power struggle is engaged in. Parents do appreciate an acknowledgment that living with such social problems and rigidity can be difficult, and that it is not their fault.

- *Adolescence is a particularly difficult time for children with Asperger's disorder.* We will talk more about this later, but tell parents that adolescence is a particularly tough time for these children. Many of them will have problems with increased social isolation and depression. Sometimes Asperger's is not diagnosed until children are older, so it is important to let parents know that their child's adolescence may be even more difficult because of the ambivalence the teenager has about social engagement. If you are working with an adolescent and his or her family be sure to explore what else is going on in the adolescent's life and make referrals for therapy or psychiatric evaluation as indicated by the reported problems. Direct them to educational resources locally and to other avenues like the Internet. Identity formation during adolescence is tough for most adolescents, but it is doubly difficult for adolescents with Asperger's. Education and therapy can make the difference in how healthfully adolescents incorporate a disability into their adult identity.

Questions Parents May Ask

- *Will my child grow out of Asperger's?* The answer is "no"; but with social skills interventions and the development of a healthy adult identity people with Asperger's can lead nearly typical to extraordinary lives. Much of their prognosis depends upon the severity of the disorder, the level of impairment, the intensity of the interventions, and other problems stemming from coexisting conditions.
- *Is my child a genius?* It is a common misconception that people with Asperger's are geniuses. Most people with Asperger's have normal intelligence. In any group some people have very high intellectual ability. These people are rare. People with Asperger's do sometimes know a lot about a particular topic. Although this is extraordinary, it does not mean their overall intelligence is greater than that of the average person.
- *How many people are diagnosed with Asperger's?* There are about 2.6:10,000 individuals with Asperger's, although this number might rise as we become better at identifying individuals with the disorder (Fombonne, 2005).
- *How do I help my child develop friends?* Tell parents that friendships are very important, and the best way for their child to develop friendships is to be involved with other children. They should take every opportunity to engage their child in social activities even if it is uncomfortable for them and their child. They will probably need to be close by, especially early on, to help facilitate the friendships. It is also important to get interventions to improve social

skills; this takes a lot of work and energy, but it is worth it for the child.

Rett's Disorder

Rett's disorder affects girls almost exclusively. It is characterized by normal prenatal and perinatal development, normal motor development, and normal head circumference, according to the *DSM-IV* (American Psychiatric Association, 1994). This normal period is followed by slower head growth between 5 and 48 months, then loss of previously acquired purposeful hand movements. The children subsequently develop nonpurposeful movements of the hands such as hand-wringing and stop social interactions. They have trouble walking or running and moving the trunk of their body. Finally, such children have severe problems with expressive and receptive speech and language development. There is always mental retardation.

What to Say to Parents
- *This can be a very difficult diagnosis to hear.* The prognosis for Rett's disorder is grim, but children do make strides and can learn. It is important to admit, however, that the course of the disease will be long and difficult. The disease progresses in four phases, beginning with early symptoms, followed by rapid deterioration, a prolonged plateau phase, and finally a late motor deterioration phase that can last for several years. This late motor deterioration usually includes loss of the ability to walk, with subsequent wheelchair dependence. Progressive muscle wasting, accompanied by spasticity or scoliosis, also generally occurs.
- *You did not cause the Rett's disorder.* The disorder is most likely caused by a mutation in the MECP2 gene that contains instructions for a specific protein. It is not clear how this ultimately leads to all of the difficulties associated with Rett's but we do know that there is probably a genetic basis for the disorder.

Questions Parents May Ask

- *What should we do?* There is no cure, but interventions for language, occupational therapy, and physical therapy are all important to lessen the effects of the disorder.
- *How many people are diagnosed with Rett's?* About 1:10,000 to 15,000 girls are diagnosed with Rett's disorder (NIH, April 17, 2007)

Childhood Disintegrative Disorder

Childhood disintegrative disorder, described in *DSM-IV,* begins with regression after at least two full years of normal development (American Psychiatric Association, 1994). By age 10 these children lose their skills in expressive or receptive language, socializing, bowel or bladder control, play, and movement. Their dysfunction includes difficulties with social interactions, communication abnormalities, and repetitive behaviors accompanied by rigidity.

What to Say to Parents

- *We do not know why this happened.* There is no known cause for this rare disorder. It strikes out of nowhere; children who have previously developed normally deteriorate over the course of several months.
- *This is devastating.* Parents who have watched their previously normal child deteriorate before their eyes are devastated. Their children have already developed personalities. They are talking and engaging with the world as autonomous individuals. These are children on their way to a typical childhood. These children gave no prior sign they were different or had a serious disorder—parents had no warning. Parents often say or believe that there should be something you can do, something that will stop the decline. Unfortunately all you can do is watch as the decline occurs, intervening to be as supportive as possible, and then start over to work on redeveloping as many skills as possible, although very few will ever reacquire the ability to even speak. There is no cure.

Questions Parents May Ask

- *What should we do?* There is no cure, but the interventions for childhood disintegrative disorder should mirror those of a child with autistic disorder because the ultimate symptoms presentation is so similar. Help parents find the same interventions for speech and language, occupational therapy, and physical therapy that you would for a child with autistic disorder.

- *How many people are diagnosed with childhood disintegrative disorder?* About 2:100,000 people are diagnosed with this disorder (Fombonne, 2005).

Pervasive Developmental Disorder, Not Otherwise Specified

Pervasive developmental disorder, not otherwise specified (PDD, NOS) is a label given to these children or adults when they do not meet the diagnostic criteria for one of the specific pervasive developmental disorders/autism spectrum disorder. The label could also be "Autism Spectrum Disorder that does not fit a particular type of Autism Spectrum Disorder," but that is not the "official" label in the *DSM-IV*. The "not otherwise specified" describes those children and adults who have some symptoms of autism and seem to belong on the spectrum. These individuals somehow don't quite meet the criteria for one of the specific diagnoses because of the age of onset or they show too few symptoms as established in the *DSM-IV*.

What to Say to Parents

- *Your child does have ASD.* You need to be clear with the family that the child does have ASD. Because PDD, NOS does not seem related to ASD, when most people hear the term, professionals need to reinforce with parents that it *is* indeed part of the spectrum of disorders and has the same problems with social engagement, difficulties with language use, and fixations often associated with repetitive behaviors accompanied by rigidity.

- *This does not mean that your child's problem is less serious than that of other children diagnosed with a specific ASD.* Individuals with PDD, NOS can have problems that are equally as severe as those of anyone diagnosed with ASD. Some payor sources may argue otherwise. Parents and payor sources need to realize there can be very significant problems with development and behavior, and their child is entitled to the same services and will need many of the same interventions as other children with specific diagnoses.

Questions Parents May Ask

- *Does my child have autism?* Yes, in the broad use of that term, meaning ASD. The individual diagnosed with PDD, NOS does have ASD, but not a more specifically named disorder such as autistic disorder, Asperger's, Rett's, or childhood disintegrative disorder.
- *What do we tell other people when they ask what is wrong with the child?* I tell parents it is best to keep it simple, tell people that their child has ASD. I have found that it is generally not helpful to try and explain the difference to most people. Now that more people are aware of autism and ASD, they will have a basic context for understanding the child.
- *How many people are diagnosed with PDD, NOS?* It may help parents to know that most people with ASD actually fall into this category with 2.8:1000 individuals in the diagnostic category (Fombonne, 2005).

How to Help Parents Hear and Understand

Parents will probably be overwhelmed when you sit down with them to talk with them about their child's ASD diagnosis. They may have heard the diagnosis from someone else or you may be delivering it for the first time. Don't expect the full impact of the words to sink in the first or even second time. Encourage the family to ask questions. Ask them to explain what they have heard. Encourage them to take notes. Ask them if they need to go home and think about what has been said. I always offer a second long appointment to discuss questions and concerns that have come up.

I give the parents resources and we talk about Web sites and support groups in the area, including the local Autism Society of America chapter. I give them my e-mail address and ask them to please e-mail me with any questions they have or insights that come to them after they leave the office. I ask them if they would like to bring someone else to the next meeting. Sometimes parents bring grandparents or other relatives. Sometimes they bring friends or other caretakers of the child. I know that when I am talking with the parents they are not always able to fully understand all we are discussing. They are usually tired and exhausted from caring for a special needs child. They are often sleep deprived because of the child's needs and their own worry. They are hearing language and words that they may never have heard before. Their understanding of some of the words and phrases may be different from what you intend. Give the family time to settle into the diagnosis. These meetings with you at the time of getting the diagnosis are life-changing. They will look back on these meetings as one of those moments after which their lives were never the same. Remember how critical you are to their journey with their child.

Our Experience

I have described some aspects of what it was like for me and for our family when we first heard that Frankie was "autistic like." We didn't even get a definitive diagnosis until later and then the diagnosis was PDD, NOS. Even though I knew the diagnostic criteria and nomenclature it still felt like an unsatisfying diagnosis. It was easier just to say he had autism. We were frightened and overwhelmed. We were angry, and weren't even sure with whom to be angry. We were lucky that we had good friends with a son two years older than Frankie who was diagnosed with autistic disorder. They were godsends for us and introduced us as parents to the world of autism support and advocacy. It was a difficult time, but having understanding and caring friends, fellow parents, family, and supportive professionals made all the difference.

CHAPTER THREE

How to Talk about Common Coexisting Diagnoses and Labels

Most children with ASD will also meet criteria for other diagnoses and labels. Children with ASD are at higher risk for other problems. There are also certain syndromes that we listed in the previous chapter that predispose a child to being diagnosed with ASD. In this chapter I describe seven of the most common coexisting conditions that I see in children with ASD. I will then discuss how to talk with parents about these coexisting conditions and explore some of the questions they might have about these additional problems.

The problems I will discuss include mental retardation (also known as intellectual disability), sensory integration dysfunction, attention deficit hyperactivity disorder (ADHD), obsessive compulsive disorder, tic/Tourette's disorder, mood disorders, and anxiety disorders. All of these problems occur at a greater rate in people with ASD than they do in the general population, and they create significant disability for the people who experience them. These problems also create barriers to successful intervention for people with ASD. These disorders and their symptoms have to be addressed clinically in people with ASD as interventions are put into place to address the core problems seen in ASD. For example, if a child with ASD has such significant ADHD that he or she is unable to engage in behavioral strategies prescribed to increase language skills or teach social skills, then in addition to implementing the behavioral strategies, strategies or medication interventions may be necessary to address the ADHD.

Mental Retardation

Mental retardation (MR) is a diagnosis that requires a full scale intelligence quotient (IQ) under 70 or significant global impairment in intellectual skills and significant difficulties with daily living skills. Many people with ASD have coexisting mental retardation. Past estimates described the rate of mental retardation in people with ASD as high as 70%. Thirty percent of children with ASD are believed to be in the mild to moderately mentally retarded range. Another 40% are in the severe to profoundly mentally retarded range (Fombonne, 2005). These statistics are based on past reports that Fombonne reviewed for his article.

Of all the diagnoses associated with ASD, mental retardation is perhaps the most difficult diagnosis for parents to understand and accept. Many times parents accept their child being labeled with ASD, but they cannot accept and do not want to hear that their child is also mentally retarded or intellectually disabled. Nonetheless, if their child meets the criteria for mental retardation based on standardized IQ tests and on their level of adaptive functioning, then the label is an accurate one. I believe parents resist this diagnosis because of the significant, pervasive social stigma associated with mental retardation. Otherwise tolerant or well-meaning people commonly talk about someone or something being "retarded." There are jokes that are made and many forms of entertainment that make fun of people with mental retardation. There is clearly a greater social stigma associated with the diagnosis of mental retardation than of ASD.

Table 3.1 Other related diagnoses and labels

Mental Retardation	Significantly below average intellectual ability with difficulties in daily living skills including at least some of the following: • communication • self-care • home living • interpersonal skills • work • leisure • health • safety • Onset must be before 18 years old. • Multiple causes • Mild Mental Retardation (IQ of 50–70) • Moderate Mental Retardation (IQ of 35–50) • Severe Mental Retardation (IQ of 20–35) • Profound Mental Retardation (IQ below 20)
Sensory Integration Dysfunction	A neurological disorder where the brain does not "process" sensory input from the body in a "normal" or typical fashion, leading to a wide range of symptoms.
ADHD	A neurodevelopmental disorder that leads to persistent difficulty with inattention and/or hyperactivity-impulsivity that is impairing and more severe than usually seen in someone at a comparable level of development.
Obsessive Compulsive Disorder	Frequent, recurring obsessions and/or compulsions that are impairing, take up significant time and may be distressing to the individual.
Tics/Tourette's Disorder	A neurological disorder characterized by sudden, rapid, recurrent, non-rhythmic motor movements, or vocalizations that are irresistible but can be suppressed for a time with great effort.
Mood Disorders	Psychiatric illnesses characterized by disturbance in mood. The mood may be too elevated as in mania or low as with depression. These illnesses include Major Depressive Disorders and Bipolar Disorders.
Anxiety Disorders	Psychiatric problems characterized by intense apprehension and fear.

Source: My clinical practice and American Psychiatric Association. (1994). *Diagnostic and Statistical Manual of Mental Disorders* (4th ed.).

Our Experience

When Frankie was diagnosed with both an ASD and mild mental retardation, extended family members continued to tell people only that "He's autistic," avoiding any discussion of his intellectual disability. They would say, "But he is so clever," or "See how well he does on the computer." We have had to talk frankly to our family and others about the realities of his mental retardation. We say that just because someone has intellectual disabilities, it does not mean that they have no strengths. Children with autism and mental retardation at times may show incredible strengths; the term *mental retardation* recognizes, however, that there are intellectual disabilities.

Were we to ignore Frankie's intellectual disabilities, they would not be addressed, and we would increase the burden of his disability on him. The school might not make the accommodations necessary to address his intellectual disabilities though they were making accommodations for his ASD. I tell friends, family, and parents that we need to stop seeing *retarded* as a dirty word; however, this is probably a losing battle. Recently there has been a greater push to use the term *intellectual disability*, and that may ultimately be the only way to leave the stigma of retardation behind.

I cannot overemphasize how important it is to diagnose mental retardation when it is appropriate and pay attention to children's intellectual disabilities. Every child diagnosed with an ASD needs a comprehensive psychological evaluation that includes a thorough intellectual assessment.

Obviously, ASD overlaps with mental retardation. Be clear about this with families and other professionals. ASD, despite the perception among the general public from movies and books, is not synonymous with the savant syndrome—and even savants can meet the criteria for mental retardation if their IQ is low in other areas and they lack the skills for daily living outlined above. There are individuals with ASD who are savants (people with extraordinary mental capabilities in a specific skill like math or music) but they are rare.

Another common error I see associated with the diagnosis of mental retardation is when professionals do not make that diagnosis, although it is clearly present at the time they make the diagnosis of an ASD. I believe professionals many times avoid discussing mental retardation for the very reasons parents have trouble hearing the diagnosis; namely, because there is a greater stigma associated with the diagnosis and they do not want to further burden the parents. I believe, however, that this ultimately hurts the child, because there is not a clear diagnosis to elucidate the most appropriate interventions. It also reinforces the notion that mental retardation is somehow a much worse diagnosis and people with intellectual disabilities are somehow inferior. This of course is far from true, given the serious disabilities faced by people with ASD and average to above-average intelligence.

Underlying this denial of naming the mental retardation/intellectual disability by parents and professionals is at best a denial of the real issues. At worst it is an unconscious collusion to overvalue intellectual ability in determining a child's worth and worthiness. Parents of these children and professionals who serve them must understand that despite our cultural biases, intelligence alone does not make one person "worth more" or "greater than" another, any more than does the ability to walk, skin color, or which language we use. We have to take care not to send that message to parents. This will likely require us to examine our own prejudices related to intellectual ability and function. I have often heard parents make comments that "at least he has normal intelligence" or "at least she has potential" when describing their child with ASD and average to above-average intelligence. They make these comments despite the reality that the child I see in front of me has serious and sometimes much more serious disabilities than another child with intellectual disability alone or even intellectual disability and ASD.

What to Say to Parents

- *Your child has an intellectual disability/mental retardation.* As I stated above, if a child meets criteria for mental retardation then you need to discuss this diagnosis with the parents. You have to be prepared to listen carefully to their concerns about this label. Oftentimes you need to be ready for anger from the parents for making this diagnosis. Parents often have a visceral response to their child being labeled in this way. I have had parents say to me, "What do you mean he is retarded? He is not retarded. Why would you say that?" I often start the conversation by outlining first the criteria for mental retardation using the words *intellectual disability* and what that means, before saying, "This is the same thing as mental retardation or some people would say that a person with intellectual disabilities has mental retardation." Still it can be very tense and families need to hear that this does not mean that their child is not a great child with lots of potential. It does not mean that their child will have to be placed in a group home or other institution. It does not mean that their child is worth less than another child with average to above-average intelligence. These are all things that the parent may be thinking and you need to ask, "What else is on your mind?"

- *I know hearing these words can be shocking.* Acknowledge that hearing the words *mental retardation* applied to their child can be shocking. I will tell parents that I know how shocking because I have heard those same words applied to my son. For those of you who have not had that experience imagine what it might be like to hear those words or that label applied to your child. Often I think that "he's retarded" is one of the worst fears a parent harbors about their child. I know for me, even though I knew the minute I heard it that it was true, there was still part of me that did not want to believe it was true and I would have done anything to get the pediatrician to take back the words and say she'd made a mistake. Let parents talk about those feelings. Offer to bring them back to discuss their questions so they have time to digest the information.

- *Your child has potential.* Parents need to hear that their child has lots of potential to grow and to learn. Just because a child has an intellectual disability or mental retardation it does not mean that he or she will not be able to learn many things and experience a full and enjoyable life. Not only do I tell parents that their child can learn and find joy in life but I remind them of the gifts that their children have already brought to them and how those gifts will be shared by all the people their child encounters during his or her life.

Questions Parents May Ask

- *What does this mean for our child?* You might say to a parent, "That is the biggest fear isn't it?" This way you acknowledge that the really big question associated with a diagnosis of mental retardation is, What is my child's life going to look like? What does this mean for our lives? In my clinical experience, for some reason even more than with a diagnosis of ASD, a diagnosis of mental retardation brings up these questions from parents. The simplest answer is that you are not sure and the younger the child the less sure you may be in your answer. I tell families that it means that their child will need specialized teaching and interventions to help them learn. I tell them that he or she will learn at a slower pace and will probably need more one-on-one instruction. I explain that for some instruction their child will be pulled away from students without intellectual disability. I tell them they should fight to keep their child as included with the children without intellectual disabilities as much as they can be and still learn. I also explain that much of "what this label means" for their child is dependent on the degree of intellectual disability and that will be more apparent as the child gets older. If you are seeing an older child with an intellectual disability you might have a better idea about the prognosis. Much of the prognosis for children with ASD and mental retardation also depends on the level of disability their ASD presents. Having worked with children and adults with these problems for the past 30 years I have a clinical base from which to talk about prognosis and the future. You may not. It is important to tell families if you are not sure and to help them find professionals who can help to answer their questions about the future. Although, I always tell parents that no one knows for sure, but this is what I think based on what we know currently and my experience with other children and families.

- *How will we tell our family and friends?* It is often really difficult to tell family members, especially grandparents, that a child has mental retardation. Many times they may not be able to accept that a child has ASD much less an intellectual disability. Many times family and friends will act as if the parents are critical or mean about their child. Tell parents to talk with their family and friends about how their child looks in relation to other children of his or her age; to explore what a typical child of the same age does versus what their child can do. I have found that using that kind of illustration helps people to understand what mental retardation means.

- *Will he or she grow up to have a "normal" life?* An intelligence quotient (IQ) score does to a degree correlate with some real life circumstances. In particular an IQ score generally correlates with how successful a child will be in performing academically in school with the standard curriculum without any assistance or accommodation. But a child with mental retardation can make great strides and be successful to a point with appropriate accommodations. It is important to ask the parents to describe their own concept of what constitutes a "normal" life. Of course in a child with ASD and mental retardation, as stated above, many of the difficulties depend on the extent of each of the disabilities and how they affect the child's level of functioning. Basically, children with ASD and mental retardation will have a lot of difficulties and much of how well they will do in their lives will be determined by the intensity and quality of the interventions they receive. I tell the parents I work with that every moment is a teaching moment. That every experience presents an opportunity for intervention. With that in mind a child can certainly live to his or her greatest potential.

- *What do we tell our child?* This is a very difficult question to answer. It depends too on what the child is able to understand. For some children who are seriously affected this will not be a question that the child will ask and the parents will not have this concern. However, for a child who is more mildly affected it is difficult to hear that he or she is not able to learn as quickly or as well as peers. I tell parents to follow their child's lead in determining what he or she may be ready to hear about the disability and to try and use the language of the child as much as possible. Our son has had a very difficult time accepting that he has problems with learning and that he has a diagnosis of mental retardation. He knows that *retarded* is a "bad word" and it confuses him that someone would put that label on him. What he has learned to do is to talk about his "troubles" and will tell people that he has "troubles with learning." We have picked up on his language and told him that all the words *mental retardation* mean is that he has "troubles with learning" and he has been able to accept that. Recently, a child asked him if he was "retarded" and his answer was, "Yes, I have trouble with talking and learning." As difficult as it was to hear the story, I was very proud of how Frankie answered. I have used that model for talking to parents about how to work with their child around the issue of labels and identity.

Sensory Integration Dysfunction

Sensory integration dysfunction (SID) is a neurological disorder in which the brain does not "process" sensory input from the body in a "normal" or typical fashion, leading to a wide range of symptoms. Many, if not most, children with ASD have problems with SID. Symptoms range from mood problems to difficulties with arousal regulation and severe behavior problems. Included in the description of this dysfunction are not only problems with the "classic" senses of sight, hearing, smell, touch, and taste, but also problems with receiving and sending signals from other neurological systems in the body to the brain. This lack of sensory communication can affect functions such as balance and body movement and internal functions such as digestion and elimination. Below we will explore some of the problems associated with this disorder by looking at some of the senses and systems that are affected.

Sight/Visual

Children with ASDs often seem either overly sensitive to or nearly insensitive to various sensations. Children may be unable to tolerate certain visual stimulation or have too little visual awareness. For example, they cannot deal with bright or flashing lights or they seem oblivious to something right in front of them, staring off blankly.

Sounds/Auditory

One of the most frequent problems in younger children with ASD is auditory sensitivity, or being unable to tolerate loud or unusual sounds. They may fear noises such as a toilet flushing and the loud "echoing" sound it can produce, especially in public toilets. Many parents describe problems with thunder or fireworks. Some children fear being in school or public buildings because the fire alarm might sound or a telephone might ring too loudly.

Other children seem to be off in their own world in relation to sound. They do not respond to noise, even though nothing seems to be physiologically wrong with their hearing. This is one of the first symptoms that prompt a child to be evaluated for developmental problems because parents fear he or she is deaf.

Smell/Olfactory

Many children with an ASD also have an unusual response to smells. They may pick up an object to smell it, often choosing items one wouldn't normally sniff, such as a toy, a pencil, or a piece of paper. Sometimes children complain of "awful" smells when other people have little or no awareness of an odor. Or there are children who seem to have no sense of smell, and foul odors will have little effect on them.

Touch/Tactile

Touch is often a major issue for children with sensory problems and those with ASDs. These problems tend to overlap with difficulties these children experience in processing sensory information from their bodies. They may dislike certain clothes or textures or resist clothes tags or underwear binding. They may refuse to wear underwear at all. Oversensitivity to touch or friction may be the root of problems with writing or doing simple tasks, and even cause delays in crawling or walking. Baths and haircuts can sometimes be difficult or nearly impossible because of the tactile sensitivity. Many children will do anything to avoid what they perceive to be noxious touch. The tantrums can be nearly insurmountable.

Taste

Taste or gustatory problems are also one of the difficulties seen in children with ASD or SID. Sometimes the problem involves both touch and taste. Children either cannot tolerate strong taste or they seem unaware of foul taste at all. They may refuse to eat food unless it's served at a specific temperature. Textures bother some children. Feeding such children becomes very difficult, and a referral to experts in feeding may be important for effective interventions.

Sensing the Body/Proprioception

Most children who are not on the autism spectrum understand that the parts of their body are connected. Constantly, unconsciously, they send and receive neurological signals throughout their body in order to walk, see, touch, sit, or move around people and objects. For many children with ASD, the "loop" of neurological signals is broken in some or many places. They can't feel when they hit their hand or need to go to the bathroom. They may not realize they are thirsty. They may have trouble telling when their mouths or stomachs are full. They may stuff food into their mouths. This behavior leads to problems with overeating, eating too quickly, or gaining weight, as well as constipation and excessive flatulence.

Sometimes their symptoms look like attention deficit hyperactivity disorder (ADHD): the child may be unable to stay in his or her seat or feels compelled to spin or hang upside down. This kind of sensory disorder causes coordination and delay of motor development milestones related to walking, running, riding a bike, and even toilet training. The children just do not have a sense of their body and what it needs.

What to Say to Parents

- *It is common for children with ASD to have sensory problems.* Most children with this diagnosis will have sensory problems. However, it is not true that everyone with sensory problems has ASD. This is a common mistake made by people who are unfamiliar with ASD. Children can have all of the sensory problems described above and not have ASD.
- *Children with sensory problems or SID need an occupational therapy evaluation and treatment.* I believe that all children with ASD should be evaluated very early on by an occupational therapist. Not all occupational therapists are comfortable evaluating and treating a child with sensory problems. The occupational therapist the parents choose should be a therapist who is familiar SID and one who has

experience treating other children with ASD. Not getting early intervention can lead to substantial disabilities and impair a child's ability to respond to the interventions being provided to help with the ASD.

- *Sensory integration dysfunction is not usually responsive to medications.* Many times parents look to me to prescribe a medication to help with the sensory problems experienced by a child with ASD. Sometimes this is because the symptoms may look like the problems with attention, concentration, and arousal regulation that is seen in ADHD, and sometimes the symptoms may look like a problem with anxiety. My experience has been that if these symptoms are caused by problems with SID, they are not going to be particularly responsive to medications and sometimes the medications can even make things worse. I have had some limited success with using antihypertensive medications (normally used to reduce high blood pressure) to reduce the overall arousal level of a child's autonomic (involuntary) nervous system. Reduction in the arousal of this nervous system has sometimes helped calm overly sensitive children but the mainstay of intervention has been occupational therapy.

Questions Parents May Ask

- *Can we do anything to help?* Many times these sensory problems can lead to a lot of disruption in a family's life together. The family may be forced to avoid certain public events or even locations such as a supermarket or department store that are necessary for accomplishing daily chores. Food preparation, bathing, dressing, tooth brushing, haircuts, and much more can all be much more difficult because of these sensory problems. Parents want to know what to do. They have learned that punishment does not work and even seems to make things more difficult. Tell them that concentrated work with an occupational therapist can help. Encourage them to take seriously the interventions the occupational therapist suggests and tell them to implement those interventions at home religiously. Tell them to teach other caretakers the interventions and to push for coordination of interventions between school and private occupational therapy services.

- *Will he or she grow out of it?* Many children with SID do seem to get better as they get older, although many of the sensory problems can persist. I believe that as children get older, those with the intellectual capacity understand situations that are uncomfortable for them better. They may feel very uncomfortable but they are able to moderate their responses.

Attention Deficit Hyperactivity Disorder

Attention deficit hyperactivity disorder (ADHD) is another frequent diagnosis for children with ASD, before or even after their first autism diagnosis. ADHD is a very common childhood psychiatric disorder, which is basically a cluster of symptoms that includes difficulty with concentration, attention, focus, and arousal regulation. Children with ASD often exhibit these symptoms. Many times the symptoms of persistent difficulty with inattention or hyperactivity/impulsivity present in a less consistent fashion in children with ASD, mainly because those children demonstrate widely varying levels of arousal but may still meet the criteria for ADHD most of the time. It makes sense to go ahead and make the diagnosis. Naming the problem many times helps in the effort to obtain treatments for the symptoms with behavioral or psychopharmacological interventions. However, as we will discuss later in this book, use of stimulant medications to treat ADHD in children with ASD can be problematic, because stimulants may exacerbate rather than relieve the symptoms.

What to Say to Parents

- *Diagnosing ADHD in children with ASD can be difficult.* I believe that it is important for parents to understand that while children with ASD may meet the criteria listed in the *DSM-IV* for ADHD that does not mean that their child's problems are caused by the same brain problem that causes ADHD in children who do *not* have ASD. This is important information because it helps parents and others involved in the care of the child to understand that the same behavioral and psychopharmacological interventions used to help children with ADHD but *without* ASD may not be as helpful or helpful at all with children who have ASD and who also meet the criteria for ADHD.

- *There are things we can do to help but the treatments may not be as successful as we would like.* ADHD is such a common and known diagnosis for many children that parents and others taking care of a child diagnosed with ADHD, whatever the other problems, many times have the expectation that a medication is going to "fix" the problem. As I stated above, this is not always or even usually the case with ADHD in children with ASD and in fact sometimes the standard treatments for ADHD can make symptoms worse in children with ASD that also meet criteria for ADHD. My experience has taught me that behavioral interventions are generally more successful and the more engaged and verbal a child is the more able he or she is to attend, concentrate, and help modulate his or her arousal level. The symptoms can still be significant, but progress can be made. Another reason that it is important for parents to understand this difference is that it helps them to advocate for more direct interventions from school personnel since the problems are not necessarily going to be helped with medication intervention.

- *Problems associated with attention, concentration, and arousal regulation commonly lead to complaints from school professionals.* If a child with ASD is not aggressive, self-abusive, or engaged in behaviors that create complaints about hygiene, the next most common complaints from school involve problems with ADHD symptoms. Unfortunately, as I have outlined above the expectation of the school is that the problem should be fixed relatively easily, a myth perpetuated by the success of stimulant medications in many children with ADHD. The parents need to be aware that the schools will probably complain about these symptoms if they are present and it is helpful to have recommendations ready when the school asks what they can do beyond pushing for psychopharmacological intervention. Helpful interventions include but are not limited to: (1) frequent breaks with aerobic activity for about 10 minutes such as running around, jumping on a trampoline, or calisthenics; (2) direct one-on-one support available to help redirect the child; (3) regulating blood sugar levels by increasing the protein in the child's diet and giving protein snacks in between meals; carbohydrate laden school breakfasts and lunches are real problems; and (4) a decrease in the amount of work produced while focusing on the quality of work and whether the child is learning the lesson presented.

How to Answer Questions Parents Might Ask

- *Why don't the medications work?* Sometimes medications do help. There have not been many studies that have looked at the effectiveness of medications with problems associated with attention, concentration, and arousal regulation with children with an ASD diagnosis. The problem is that the medications don't always work and they don't seem to work as often or as well with children with ASD as they do with children who don't have ASD but still meet criteria for ADHD. I tell parents the medications are worth a try but I try to limit their expectations. When the medications don't work I try to help them find solutions for the problem through other interventions. I remind them that ASD is a complicated neurodevelopmental disorder that can involve many different parts of the brain and that it is not always predictable how a brain with such complex difficulties will respond to a particular medication.
- *What if the school won't cooperate?* Many times schools have problems coming up with the resources to do what needs to be done to help a child with ASD and ADHD symptoms succeed. If a school

complains of these difficulties or for some other reason is unwilling to put into place the accommodations that might help a child succeed, I offer to help the parents by talking with the school, writing letters, and if necessary helping them to secure educational advocates or legal services. Most communities have both public and private groups and individuals that will help to get a child with disabilities what he or she needs to be successful in school.

- *Will he or she grow out of the problem?* Many children with ASD do at least grow out of some of the symptoms of hyperarousal or hyperactivity as they grow older. In fact, sometimes the problem becomes one of trying to motivate an increased activity level in adolescents and adults with ASD. Problems with attention and concentration, however, many times persist into adolescence and adulthood. There are times that as the children get older they are more responsive to the stimulant medications; however, at times other medications may help in alleviating symptoms. Often, however, people with ASD continue to require self-strategies and accommodations to help them with these difficulties as they grow older.

Obsessive Compulsive Disorder

Clinically there is a high correlation between ASD and obsessive compulsive disorder (OCD). Many children, adolescents, and adults with ASD experience the obsessions and ritual compulsions associated with this disorder. In the children with Asperger's that I see, a very high percentage experience not only OCD symptoms but also demonstrate symptoms consistent with Tourette's, which is very closely linked genetically with OCD. The main problem with diagnosing OCD in children and adolescents with ASD is the confusion of the disorder's repetitive, stereotyped, perseverative symptoms and true OCD. Simple repetitive play or a fixation on a particular topic or activity is not OCD. Rather, OCD involves thinking over and over about something (obsession) that generally leads to a behavior that is ritualized and usually nonpurposeful in the context (compulsion). An example would be hand washing, even though the hands are clean and the person generally realizes the hands are clean but cannot stop from washing them. Or needing to keep the door closed for no particular reason except the door "needs" to be closed. These are examples of OCD symptoms. Talking at too great a length about a cartoon character or flicking a ribbon over and over again are not OCD symptoms but symptoms of fixation or perseveration that exist in individuals with ASD.

True OCD symptoms in people with ASD are generally responsive to psychopharmacological interventions, at least in part. My experience clinically has been that fixations and perseverations, while many times responsive to behavioral interventions, are not particularly responsive to medications.

What to Say to Parents

- *Your child cannot help the obsessive thinking and compulsive behavior.* Some of the behaviors of children with OCD can be extremely annoying. Parents often find themselves endlessly talking to their children about not doing this or not doing that. They may try to punish the children for their behavior. None of that is particularly helpful, and may actually increase the anxiety that drives the behaviors to begin with, making the behaviors worse or at least their expression more frequent. Most of the time children with no or little intellectual disability recognize that the behaviors are odd or disruptive. The best intervention is a coordinated effort to help with medications and with behavioral strategies that decrease the anxiety and subsequently the behaviors.

- *Fixations and perseverative behaviors are not the same thing as OCD.* All children with ASD will have some degree of repeated behaviors or obsessive interest in a particular topic but not all children with ASD will have OCD. With OCD there is generally a fear or apprehension that underlies the obsessive thinking that then leads to the compulsive act. With the perseverative behaviors or fixations of children with ASD this fear or apprehension does not exist. They are engaging in the behaviors because they want to engage in the behaviors or they are "obsessed" with a topic because they enjoy that topic. There is no underlying anxiety. Obsessive-compulsive disorder is an anxiety disorder. Fixations and perseverations are not driven by anxiety but by desire.

- *Medications can help but behavioral interventions are important as well.* Medications can be quite helpful in calming the anxiety associated with OCD and in helping to decrease the amount of time an individual spends obsessing or engaging in a compulsive behavior. However, especially for higher functioning children, behavioral interventions are important as well to help them learn to manage their anxiety and over time give them some control over redirecting the obsessions or resisting the compulsions.

Questions Parents May Ask

- *How do we make him or her stop?* Medications and behavioral interventions are the best way to help. Simply telling someone with OCD to stop or punishing them for their behaviors does not help and as outlined above may make things much worse.
- *How do we explain his or her behavior to other people?* This is a tough one for parents because they may be embarrassed by the behaviors of their child. Sometimes even the child is embarrassed by the behaviors but cannot stop. My best advice is to tell the truth and say that "he has OCD and autism"; some families or children will try to find strategies to hide the behaviors. Finding these strategies to mask a behavior can be helpful sometimes because they are the beginning of learning to develop some control over the compulsions. The most important thing is to try to be nonjudgmental and nonshaming.
- *Will he or she grow out of it?* Like most anxiety problems, difficulties with OCD wax and wane over the course of time. The severity

of the problems can sometimes be associated with other life situations or stressors. Most people with this diagnosis, however, including people also diagnosed with ASD, will experience problems with the obsessive thoughts and compulsive behaviors off and on for most of their lives.

Tic/Tourette's Disorder

Many children with ASD will also experience some form of tic disorder. A tic is described by the *DSM-IV* as a neurological disorder characterized by sudden, rapid, recurrent, nonrhythmic motor movements, or vocalizations that are irresistible but can be suppressed for a time with great effort. As I stated above, there seems to be an especially high prevalence of Tic/Tourette's in individuals with Asperger's. There is no satisfying explanation for why there is such a high correlation between these disorders.

Problems with Tics/Tourette's do lead to increased problems in individuals with ASD. Many people, including many educators, are not very aware of the difficulties that Tic/Tourette's can cause for a child or adolescent and this situation often leads to misunderstandings about particular behaviors. Many times repetitive throat clearing, tapping, sniffing, or humming among other symptoms will be symptoms of Tic/Tourette's that are very disruptive in the classroom or other settings. Children and adolescents are often reprimanded to stop the behaviors and sometimes they are able to do so, but stifling the urges leads to increased anxiety and decreased performance. I explain it to parents and teachers this way, "Imagine you have an itch and you really need to scratch it. Now I know you can resist scratching that itch. I also want you to read this text and then tell me what it says but don't scratch." Generally, they get the idea of how much pressure children with Tic/Tourette's experience in order to keep their symptoms under control.

Medications can be helpful with these symptoms, but many times the medications have very serious side effects that may make their use undesirable. Also, medications that are used to help increase attention and concentration often make the Tic/Tourette's symptoms much worse.

What to Say to Parents

- *Your child cannot stop the motor or vocal tics.* That is not exactly true, but for all practical purposes it is the case that a child with tics cannot stop. The constant movements (blinking, shrugging, tapping, pointing, etc.) that people with tics experience can be annoying to people around them, especially to parents who simply want their child to "Stop moving!" However, as I outlined above, controlling the motor tics and the vocal tics is extremely difficult and takes incredible psychic energy. Our son is diagnosed with Tourette's in addition to ASD and he constantly clears his throat. We know now that he is experiencing a tic, but it can still be very difficult to tolerate. Now if we say something to him, however, he will simply say, "I cannot help it. It is my Tourette's." Helping parents and children understand that the problem is essentially beyond individual will or control is very helpful and keeps arguments and power struggles to a minimum. It also helps to preserve the child's self-esteem.
- *Work with your child to develop strategies for coping with the tics.* Like OCD, with effort and some behavioral strategies children can learn to manage their tics. Encourage parents to find a behavioral therapist who can work with them and their child to minimize the impact of the tics. Help them to give their child information so that they can understand why they are having the tics and so that they can explain it to others if they ask. If the child is cognitively capable of participating in developing these strategies they can go a long way to helping decrease the overall burden of disability associated with having tics in addition to the ASD.
- *Advocate for your child at school.* School can be very difficult for

the child with ASD. When you add disruptive, annoying motor or vocal tics to that mix school can be a misery. If teachers and other students understand the problem, that can go a long way to making things easier at school. Encourage parents to let people at school know the problem. Many cities may actually have a Tourette's Association that will come into the school and help with information and accommodations. Help parents find those resources if they are available in your area.

- *It sometimes helps for another child or adult with Tourette's to talk with your child.* One of the most helpful things you can do for a higher functioning child with ASD and Tourette's is to have him or her meet someone else with Tics/Tourette's. The individual can be a child or an adult and they may or may not also have ASD, but it helps to have contact with someone else who really understands the problems associated with tics. Such meetings can also be helpful for other problems like OCD, but I have found that for Tics/Tourette's meeting someone else with the problem has been particularly helpful. This can usually be accomplished through local support organizations, but a meeting can also take place online through information and support websites. Encourage parents to consider a meeting, always of course keeping safety as a primary concern.

Questions Parents May Ask

- *How do we make him or her stop?* Tell parents: "You can't make the child's tics stop, but with help he/she might be able to exert some control over the tics." Tell parents to be supportive and non-shaming. Remind them that punishment will not work.
- *How do we explain his or her behavior to other people?* Again, as with OCD, I think honesty works best and many times it makes things much easier for the child. Looks of annoyance or disgust can often change to encouragement or understanding if people understand why someone is exhibiting a certain behavior.
- *Will he or she grow out of it?* Tics, like obsessions and compulsions,

wax and wane over time. Tics sometimes can virtually disappear, but they may surface again at some future point.

• *Are there medications that can help?* There are medications that can help, but some of the medications that are used have potentially very serious side effects. Parents need to get all of the information about medications before starting to use them. You play an important role as a professional in their life by helping them to sort out how debilitating the tics are and whether when considering the cost–benefit analysis it makes sense to use medication.

Mood Disorder

It is not uncommon for children with ASD to also be diagnosed with a mood disorder. This is especially true in individuals with less severe symptoms overall. Adolescents with Asperger's are especially at high risk, and any individual with a family history of a mood disorder will also be at risk. Major depression and bipolar disorder are both mood disorders that can be seen at high rates in individuals with ASD. Sometimes making the diagnosis of these mood disorders can be difficult in people with ASD because the symptoms may not look the same as they do in people with more typical development.

With a major depression there is generally a change in the behavior of the individual that includes an increased withdrawal from things that would generally engage him or her. This is difficult sometimes to pick up from a person with ASD because of their usual withdrawal from social interactions; people who know them well would be able to see the change though. There is often a change in diet, usually a decrease in appetite and weight loss. There is a change in sleeping patterns—either increased nighttime awakening or sometimes much increased sleep. Many times there is increased irritability and a decrease in frustration tolerance and perhaps even increased symptoms of agitation or anxiety. Any of these symptoms should be considered possible signs of depression. People with higher functioning ASD may be able to describe chronic feelings of sadness, ruminations about death, or even suicidal ideations, but not all individuals with ASD will have that capacity. Careful attention to possible symptoms of major depression can help with making a diagnosis and getting appropriate treatment.

Bipolar disorder can be especially difficult to tease out at times from the behavioral difficulties and aggression exhibited by many people with ASD. Bipolar disorder is much more than just a shift or change in mood, even a drastic change. In fact we all have shifts in mood that are sometimes not clearly understandable to the people around us but that does not mean we have a diagnosis of bipolar disorder. Because the behavior of individuals with ASD can sometimes be inscrutable, many of their rages and angry outbursts will seem inexplicable and people will wonder whether it is bipolar disorder—usually it is not. In order to make a diagnosis of bipolar disorder there has to be a state of mania. In people with ASD, mania can be characterized by extreme agitation and irritability that lasts for an extended period of time, sometimes for days. In addition to the agitation and irritability, there is lack of a need for sleep or a significantly reduced need for sleep. If the individual is verbal there may be grandiose statements that are unusual for the person. There may be grandiose behaviors like trying to "fly" when that has not happened before, or acting like a particular cartoon or other fictional character when that is not usual behavior. There may also be increased sexual awareness or activity with increased masturbation or attempts to touch other people sexually. There may also be a significant increase in language or babbling in individuals with language. Usually there is also, but not always, a family history of bipolar disorder. Just as with major depressive disorder, it is very important to look for these symptoms in people with ASD, although in the case of mania they are often difficult to miss, and to intervene with appropriate treatment as soon as possible. Especially with frank mania there is sometimes the need for psychiatric hospitalization.

The take-home message is that mood disorders are more prevalent in individuals with ASD. They may present differently from the way they present in others with typical development. When you do think symptoms are present it is important to get the appropriate assessment and treatment.

What to Say to Parents

- *Even nonverbal children with ASD and mental retardation can suffer from a major depression.* People are sometimes surprised that lower functioning individuals can suffer depression. It is important to remind parents that major depression is an illness just like pneumonia or some other acute illness and there are signs and symptoms that allow a trained professional to make that diagnosis. Making the diagnosis can be more difficult in individuals with disabilities but that does not mean that major depression is not the problem.
- *Treatment can help.* Major depression and bipolar disorder can both be very responsive to medication interventions. There can be side effects and these would need to be discussed with the family by whoever prescribed the medication. Medications are not always as helpful as we would like; however, it is still important to pursue treatment to help alleviate the difficulties that come with both of these disorders.
- *Not all "mood swings" indicate bipolar disorder.* It is important for parents and for professionals to remember that just because there is a change in mood, even frequent changes in mood, it does not mean that someone has bipolar disorder. Remind them of the symptoms that are outlined above in someone experiencing the mania associated with bipolar disorder.
- *Every child with severe tantrums and aggression does not have bipolar disorder.* It is important to remind parents of this point as well. Severe tantrums and aggressive behavior can certainly be symptoms of bipolar disorder but the diagnosis is made on more than just these symptoms. Tell parents that these are very concerning symptoms and you will help them address them by helping to find treatment.

Questions Parents May Ask

- *How do you know he or she is depressed?* Individuals with ASD may not say they are depressed or talk about being sad in the same way that someone might who does *not* have ASD. If people with ASD are verbal they may make these statements, but even then they may be unaware of how they are feeling or not be able to label the feeling. Watching for the symptoms I outlined above is helpful in making an educated guess about a depression. I tell parents that I really do not know for sure sometimes that a child, adolescent, or adult with ASD is depressed, but that it is important to consider and at times to even proceed with treatment based on that guess, especially if the person is suffering.

- *Does he or she need psychotherapy?* Some individuals with ASD can certainly benefit from psychotherapy, which can be helpful in giving them strategies for how to cope with their depression and to help them feel better. The psychotherapy would need to be tailored for the individual. I always recommend finding a therapist who has had experience with this population. Nonverbal or lower functioning individuals might not be able to participate in psychotherapy but increased engagement and support would be very important during a recovery from depression.

- *Will he or she get better?* People with mood disorders almost always get better; however, they need significant support and treatment during their illness. People who have had a mood disorder once are always at much higher risk for experiencing problems again. In the case of bipolar disorder, this relapse is virtually inevitable, and it is essential that individuals with bipolar disorder stay on their medication and continue in treatment.

Anxiety Disorder

Anxiety disorder is one of the most common problems I see in individuals with ASD. There are several types of anxiety disorder, but most people with ASD who have anxiety fail to meet criteria for a specific anxiety disorder. The anxiety I see is significant and debilitating. It impairs children, adolescents, and even adults from being able to engage in life as fully as they might. Anxiety basically involves overwhelming fear or apprehension that usually has physical manifestations such as increased heart and breathing rate, sweating, tremulousness, and a sensation of needing to flee from a setting or situation. These sensations and difficulties often lead to inappropriate and sometimes even aggressive behavior in people with ASD. Many tantrums are the result of anxiety. Treatment can help make the individual with anxiety much more comfortable. Successful treatment can also lead to a much fuller life. Untreated anxiety, especially with resulting aggression, often leads to isolation and significantly decreased options for the person with ASD.

What to Say to Parents

- *There is help.* Both medication treatments and behavioral interventions can help with anxiety problems. This is true even in lower functioning individuals. Decreasing the level of anxiety can sometimes lead to a significantly improved quality of life. Encourage parents to find help. Work with them to find treating professionals who can help them and their child.
- *You may need help with your anxiety too.* Many times a child's anxiety is compounded by the anxiety his or her parents experience. As difficult as it may be to address, sometimes it is very important to talk supportively with parents about their own anxiety and offer to help them find help as well. They may be anxious even about seeking the help, but many times if seeking help for themselves can be framed as doing something good for their child they will be more willing and able to pursue that help.
- *Forcing situations rarely makes things better.* Sometimes parents may have the impression that forcing situations where the child is anxious will help them to overcome their anxiety. I call it the sink or swim approach to anxiety. I have never seen such an approach work and usually it leads to increased anxiety that is then even more

difficult to address with medications or behavioral interventions. Acknowledge parents' frustrations with the anxiety and encourage them to do the work necessary to improve the problem by working with professionals who can help.

Questions Parents May Ask

- *Do you always have to use medications?* I tell parents that they do not have to use medications to help with anxiety, but many times the medications can make all the difference in how an individual responds to the other treatments we might put into place. Especially in individuals with ASD, medications can be very helpful as an adjunct to breaking the cycle of anxiety so that the individual can begin to get better. In younger children, because anxiety waxes and wanes over time, it can be okay to forgo medications for a time. Behavioral, and if appropriate, cognitive treatments can be helpful. However, if the anxiety is debilitating it is a good idea to consider a pharmacological intervention.
- *Will the anxiety ever go away?* Anxiety waxes and wanes over time depending on what else is happening in someone's life, but the anxiety can have a life of its own. Parents often do not feel that things are ever going to get better. I let them know that with treatment and time things almost always improve if we work to make it happen.

Above I have outlined some of the disorders associated with a diagnosis of ASD. Most parents of children with ASD will not only face the problems associated with the disorder, they will also face other disorders, some of which we have discussed in this chapter. All of the disorders and labels can sometimes be very confusing and parents may not understand the differences between them. All of the labels can sometimes run together. As the professional working with families your job is to help them keep clear what problems their child has and what steps they need to take to make those problems better. This can be a difficult task for you as well. It is important to remind parents to ask questions and ask for help. They may want to take notes or have someone come with them to help them understand the problems being presented.

You may need to ask questions of other professionals and ask for help too. Children with ASD often have very complicated sets of problems and it takes a lot of work to be clear about what is wrong and to help parents get the help they need. You may need to consult colleagues from different specialties. You may need to read more about the disorders and problems that present. Remember it is okay to say "I don't know, but I will try to find out."

As we go forward, I will discuss how to talk to parents in greater detail about what they can do about specific problems they may encounter with their child. I will also discuss medication interventions in more detail in chapter 11. Helping parents meet the challenge of their child's complicated and sometimes multiple disabilities, is a daunting task. However, by guiding parents through these complexities and lending your assistance you can begin to make a difference in creating the best possible future for the parents and their child.

Our Experience

In facing all of the challenges that are outlined above, I encourage parents to listen to the experts but also to follow their child's lead. Many of the diagnoses and labels above are frightening and seem to offer little hope for the future. I have faced those fears myself. Frankie's diagnoses have included pervasive developmental disorder, not otherwise specified, mild mental retardation, sensory integration dysfunction, attention deficit hyperactivity disorder, and Tourette's disorder. I have learned over time my biggest mistakes in raising Frankie came when I underestimated him or didn't follow his lead. Even now when I refuse to give in to my own fear, and I "allow him the freedom to fail" (as a very wise friend once advised), he continues to surprise me with what he can accomplish and the world he creates for himself.

PART 2

BEHAVIORAL ISSUES

CHAPTER FOUR

How to Talk about Communication

After parents meet with you for the first time and hear about their child's diagnosis and prognosis, they want to know what to do next. As Emily Perl Kingsley describes in her essay about being a parent of a disabled child, "Welcome to Holland," I often have the feeling that I have been placed in a foreign country where I almost speak the language but not quite, and where I recognize the customs, but they are not my customs.

Even though I have worked with children with disabilities since I was 18 years old, I *still* have that feeling. I cannot begin to imagine what parents without experience with this landscape of doctors, teachers, therapists, special schools and programs, and competing treatment approaches must feel. Rarely can family and friends teach them to navigate this strange land. Friends with typical children can be wonderfully supportive, but seldom "get it." Pediatricians and teachers who are used to dealing with typical children can be, but often are not, helpful. Many times they innocently cause more problems.

After the initial diagnosis, most parents bring a list of concerns to their primary professional. They want suggestions or options: "What to do next?" It is important to listen carefully to their list, and then try to help them prioritize the concerns. It's nearly impossible to work on all of the issues at the same time, especially not intensely. Even if parents and therapists could work to address all the issues, consider the avalanche of changes that would present to the child. You have to choose which issues, skills, or situations are the most pressing given the age of the child, developmental potential, family stressors, school concerns, or other factors. Work on those first. Later you will shift your focus to other issues, but always as part of a strategy that makes sense for this particular family and its situation.

After you have helped set priorities, you can begin to discuss the possible interventions. What follows is a practical, but not comprehensive, approach to those interventions. Here are some broad outlines to problems that parents generally raise as primary concerns. Also, an important aspect of your professional role is to help the family recognize other issues that they may not realize are as important as you feel they are. With this guidance you help families set priorities that will lessen problems in the future.

Arguably the major issue for children with autism and on the autism spectrum is communication disorders. It's imperative from the very beginning to rigorously and deliberately address the development of language and other forms of communication. Problems with communication are a core disability, and of all the disabilities a child may have, this is the one that most often holds back further development and progress. Communication problems exacerbate all the other issues, and delay the possibility of addressing social difficulties and the restrictive, repetitive interests and behaviors.

For so many of the children I see, if they could only master some communication or improve their communication skills, even a little, the opportunities in their world would expand incredibly. Generally, the greater the capacity of a child to communicate by age 5, the more optimistic is the prognosis for that child in terms of self-care and eventual engagement with a world beyond the primary caretakers.

Obviously, early intervention is essential. Even when they fail to notice the social delays, most parents recognize very early on if their child does not engage and communicate appropriately. I assume that the earlier the intervention, the better the outcome, and the better the communication ability; but this is a difficult hypothesis to test. As a parent and a professional I push for early intervention. If we know at age 12 to 18 months that a child is not beginning to say words or make eye contact, a speech and language professional should evaluate the child. It is not enough to have "any" speech and language professional but specifically one who knows about interventions with young children and is experienced in treating children on the autism spectrum. Even if the child is speaking but there is something odd or unusual about it, especially in the aspect of rigidity and repetitive behaviors (with or without sensory integration questions), I advise treatment by a speech and language professional.

Part of my approach is related to "How could it hurt?" Other than the cost burden on the family, speech and language intervention cannot harm a child. I have heard professionals advise against using sign language or assistive technologies early on because this will "delay speech development." Frankly, my clinical experience has shown just the opposite. In fact, the sooner a communication system is working, regardless of the mechanism for communication, the sooner the child starts speaking and using verbal language.

Most insurance companies and state Medicaid programs provide for speech and language treatment. Most often children with other developmental issues will also qualify with the state for early intervention services directed at children with developmental disabilities. These serve the child until age 3; then the school system usually picks up some of the intervention costs. Children also can qualify for Medicaid waiver programs in most states, but the criteria for qualification vary. Some states and school systems provide more than others. Besides battling the symptoms of ASD, the other front in the battle to maintain growth and development in communication involves procuring appropriate and adequate services. The mantra for professionals working with such children and their parents needs to be "the more comprehensive and quality programs and interventions put in place early on, the fewer and less expensive interventions the child will require later." Despite the apparent policy of most insurance companies, governments, and school systems, the early years are not the time to be stingy. To deny payment for resources in these early years is to be pennywise and pound foolish.

As a child enters school there is often a tendency to limit speech and language services. Often, the amount of time a particular service provider in the school system can work with a child is limited. Sometimes there is only one speech and language therapist to see many children. Nonetheless, if the child has speech and language delays or other communication abnormalities such as those seen in Asperger's or higher functioning autism, then you need to push for daily speech therapy and speech programming in the classroom. The classroom programming needs to involve peers and teachers so they are also working on improving the affected child's speech and communication.

Legally, the school cannot say that they are limiting the speech programming because of inadequate staff or resources. If a child needs the services to receive an adequate educational experience, then the school must provide the services. If the school is unable to provide those services within the school system, they are obligated to pay for them to be provided by external sources, or to pay for the child to be served in an alternative educational setting.

To avoid more financial obligations, school system personnel may argue that the child has adequate speech and language support. If school personnel offer this response, and you as the professional or the parents disagree, you can request that an outside, third-party evaluator make the determination. Then you can assist the parents in engaging an advocate or even an attorney to work with the school to create a reasonable resolution. In the next chapter I will discuss schools and school–parent relationships in greater detail.

Nearly all children diagnosed with an ASD will require communication interventions throughout their early school years and often into the higher grades. Children who have little in the way of communication skills should not be abandoned; continue to try to develop some form of communication. Assistive technology augmented with behavioral interventions such as applied behavioral analysis or other developmental intervention models can mean the difference between being a part of the world or alienated from it. For children with higher communication skills, efforts must be made to constantly improve their ability to communicate effectively so that abnormalities in speech are minimized and their understanding of language subtleties and abstractions is enhanced as much as possible.

The better these higher functioning children become with language, the richer and more involved their relationships with other people. Programs explore "processing disorders" and language-based learning can serve these higher functioning children. Some of these programs are certainly worthwhile, and children will sometimes respond very well to them. However, the programs are often expensive and very time-intensive. Usually speech and language professionals offer many of these programs, although sometimes they will be offered in the school.

The decision to try these interventions must be weighed against the costs in time and money. Each family has to decide what is affordable and the child's willingness to cooperate in the intervention. These intensive speech and language interventions can be very helpful; some children make remarkable progress in a short time. Unfortunately, like so many interventions related to ASD, there is not a wealth of research that recommends one intervention over another. Given the significant variety in symptoms even in higher functioning children, few professionals feel they can responsibly recommend one program over another. These decisions are complicated more by the entrepreneurial or evangelical nature of many of these programs, raising doubts about the truthfulness of claims.

What to Say to Parents

- *Communication intervention has to be a priority.* From my experience as a parent and as a clinician, there is no more important developmental task. Problems with communication lead to problems with behavior, problems with cognition, problems with social relatedness, and, frankly, even the ability to have a satisfying emotional life. Work on communication has to start from the very beginning. Tell parents that they first need to focus on helping the child to improve his or her communication. This will help them focus their priorities and give them permission to set aside some of the other interventions that they are considering. Parents of children with an ASD are often confused by multiple providers pushing various interventions, both conventional and nonconventional. The first interventions to pursue are those that show promise for increasing communication abilities and language use. The interventions should be intended not simply to increase the number of words a child uses, but to help the child to communicate emotionally and to participate in the give-and-take of nonverbal and verbal communication.

- *Communication and language are different.* While most of us use language as a primary form of communication, we use much more than words to communicate. Communication involves exchanges of facial, emotional, fictional, or other information, and ASD impairs a child's ability to communicate in these ways. Some children with an ASD have language and some do not; all have impaired abilities in communication. Help parents see the difference and focus on their child communicating nonverbally as well as learning and using words. Their child may communicate through facial expressions, gestures, touch, and other means.

- *Follow your child's lead.* Parents should follow their child's lead and be alert for opportunities to communicate presented by the child. As parents and adults we may miss many of the opportunities children present to us. A child playing with a toy, even in an odd way, is an opportunity to engage a child in the give-and-take of communication, even without words. The child can be invited to engage someone in play, and the parents can provide the language for that interaction until the child is able to do so. Even without the use of words, communication is taking place. See every moment as a teaching moment.

- *Fight for as much and as intense a plan of interventions as you can.* Encourage parents to be dogged advocates for language/communication interventions for their children. Tell them to work as hard as possible to get as much speech and language intervention in school as can be given. Encourage them to continue private speech and language intervention. Help them find language programs that can help with intensive training. Tell them to be vigilant about opportunities to treat any road blocks to language assistance; for example, encourage them to work to reduce anxiety with therapeutic or even medication intervention. I even encourage parents to try alternative complementary interventions to help with language/communication development, but only if the interventions are not actually or potentially harmful and the cost of time, money, or other resources is reasonable. Such treatments might include hyperbaric oxygen therapy, accupressure/accupuncture or vitamin therapies.

- *Addressing communication issues will be lifelong.* Convey to the parents that working on communication skills will be a lifelong process for anyone with an ASD. Even in children with Asperger's who have a great facility with language, their ability to communicate and use language appropriately in social and emotional situations is impaired. Every child with an ASD, from the severely impaired child who is unable to use words, to the child with Asperger's with great verbal command, will need communication/language intervention and assistance with social and emotional communication throughout their lives. This is a core deficit in any child with these disorders.

Questions Parents May Ask

- *What about speech therapy? When should he or she start?* Speech therapy should start as soon as a speech therapist will take the child, as early as 2 years old and certainly by age 3. Even before a child begins to work with a speech and language therapist, parents and others can increase communication development. It is important to keep in mind that communication development starts at birth. It is never too early to start work on communication.

- *Why does my child need more speech therapy if we understand him or her?* A child with an ASD continues to need speech therapy because speech is about more than just saying words or being able to articulate appropriately. Speech therapy addresses the problems with communication described above as so vital. Addressing the language and communication disabilities is essential, and parents need to be prepared to insist that schools and other professionals must provide continued assistance with communication.

- *Can medications help?* No medications have been shown consistently to increase speech for individuals with an ASD. Some medications may lower barriers to language and communication problems; for example, medications for anxiety can increase language and communication ability because anxiety is decreased. No medications seem to address the core problem with communication. Some have speculated that serotonin medications (we will discuss them in chapter 11) might make a difference or medications sometimes used to treat Alzheimer's disease and other dementias might be helpful, but the research has failed to show a significant effect. Several complementary alternative treatments as those mentioned above have claimed improvement in language and communication but there has been no definite scientific verification of efficacy. However, when rigorous scientific research criteria have been applied to assess their use and benefit, these treatments have not been shown to have a significant effect.

- *What about other treatments for communication problems?* Beyond traditional speech and language therapy, there are other treatments for communication problems. Social skills groups and social skills training increase communication ability. I believe it is a great help with communication for children with an ASD to be around typical children with typical language development. Inclusive school programming and social engagements are very important. Typical siblings can also be very helpful. Some specific treatment regimens for ASDs put a great deal of emphasis on communication development. These will be discussed later, and they include applied behavioral analysis and DIR Developmental, Individual-Difference, Relationship-Based/Floortime (DIR), and Treatment and Education of Autistic and Related Communication Handicapped Children (TEACCH). As with medications, there have been suggestions that some alternative medical interventions might be helpful with increasing communication. These interventions have included hyperbaric oxygen therapy treatment and toxic metal chelation therapies, among others. Neither has yet been accepted by the medical establishment, and there is no vigorous scientific research that supports their use in children with an ASD.

Our Experience

Our own struggle with language interventions for our son Frankie has been extremely frustrating and confusing at times. Even after receiving so much early intervention for speech, behaviors, and socialization, his two main disabilities are his cognitive struggles and problems with communication. He has been in speech and language intervention from 18 months old, and at age 11 we continue to work with speech and language pathologists and communication specialists to help him develop more functional communication.

Frankie does relatively well, and he will even say when asked less than tactfully "What is wrong with you?" that he has "troubles with my talking." We have debated over and over again whether to pull him from public school and place him in an intensive language intervention program. For now it seems more important for him to stay with friends who have been with him since kindergarten. They have given him a base of peer support that is truly amazing.

I have also noticed that we may not push him to communicate because we have learned to understand what he tries to say. Even now we are unable to rely on Frankie to tell us what "really went on" if there is a problem at school. He is not able yet to defend himself from false accusations or to explain himself in complicated social settings. He does his best but it is often inadequate.

Early intervention by professionals specializing in communication disorders with these children is absolutely necessary. We must do what we can as professionals to direct families to the best services available in our communities. Part of your role is to identify those resources and help parents make those connections as early and as intensively as possible.

CHAPTER FIVE

How to Talk about Social Skills

When most parents first hear the term *social skills*, they struggle for a moment trying to figure out what it means. It is somewhat obvious, but these are words we seldom hear in everyday conversation. People do not often say, "Oh he or she lacks social skills." They simply comment on how odd, unusual, or weird someone's behavior is. We take for granted that people are social. We think people know how to interact with one another. We look for everyone to make eye contact and say "Hello." We generally expect people to know how to make the trivial conversations that allow strangers to talk to each other and work out everyday tasks and business.

If someone can't do this, we often think them rude or withdrawn. We can hardly understand why some people would be unable to do what comes so naturally to us. Yet that is exactly the problem in children, adolescents, and adults with ASD.

These children have to learn the simplest skills of social interaction that come so easily to people without the disorder. For reasons we do not completely understand, the part of the brain that makes these skills and interactions so easy and fluid for most people is not as well developed in people with ASD. Although there is a very wide range of social skills problems in these individuals all of them *have* social skills problems.

Even from infancy, many children later diagnosed with ASD exhibit abnormal social interactions. They make no eye contact or engage less readily than other infants. They resist being cuddled or held. They show little desire for attention from adults and do not show a special interest in their primary caretaker. There is little joint attention (no following of gaze or pointing). Often they do not feed well either. Mothers who have breast fed other infants notice a difference in nursing the baby later diagnosed with an ASD.

As the child grows, reciprocal attention does not develop as it does with more typically developing children. Play is more stilted, repetitive, and subsequently less engaging. The young toddler shows no interest in other children. As he or she grows the child will not join in others' play or allow other children to join him or her. The child may dislike being held by anyone, but certainly will not tolerate strangers. Most children diagnosed with ASDs will not make eye contact unless absolutely forced to do so, and even then the contact is brief and fleeting.

For these children, play lacks the imaginative and fantasy components of most children. They do not bring in things from the outside world or social structure into their play. The child with an ASD is turned inward and cannot connect with the outside world. The word *autism* is derived from this inward engagement and inability to be part of everyday social interactions.

Many children with higher functioning ASDs are first identified in preschool and kindergarten. Many families sense that their children are different, but not until the child is interacting daily with many other more typically developing children is the extent of the difference clear. Preschool and kindergarten teachers are very important in early detection of children with ASDs. Many times their ability to help identify and discuss a child's social problems leads to the early interventions critical in helping a child later with school and development.

These problems with social skills are closely tied to other core deficits in ASD. Many problems with social skills can be addressed while working on language problems. Interventions for repetitive behaviors and restricted interests improve social skills regardless of the child's level of function. Children severely affected as well as higher functioning children can all benefit socially from interventions for the core symptoms. The key to addressing social skills problems is to start working on them as early as possible.

Interventions used for dealing with behavioral problems and other symptoms of ASD can be effective with social skills problems, too. Many communities have specialized preschools for children with social problems starting as young as 18 months. Some school systems have good programs available that start with 3-year-olds. There are also individualized or facilities-based programs in some communities that follow a model of applied behavioral analysis (ABA) discrete trial interventions, Development, Individual-Difference, Relationship-Based (DIR-Floortime) Therapy, or Treatment and Education of Autistic and Related Communication Handicapped Children (TEACCH), among others. Any of these can be helpful. Help parents find a model that works for them and their family, and then try to help them be consistent with the model they have chosen.

What to Say to Parents

- *Autism means "turned inward"; lack of social skills is the essence of the disorder.* From the beginning, most children diagnosed with an ASD have a problem connecting with people. Infants avoid physical touch or eye contact. They fail to respond consistently to their names or to the voices of caregivers. As they grow older they do not look at people or seem to want contact with other children or even sometimes with family members. While the degree of disability varies, this social difficulty is a core symptom of ASD. When parents understand that the term *autism* comes from this aspect, it can help them to accept and explain their child's disability to someone else.

- *Children with ASD have to learn social skills that come naturally for most of us.* Parents and others sometimes have a difficult time understanding why their child does not want to interact with them. It may feel like rejection. For most people, it feels very unnatural when someone has no desire to be engaged and cannot participate in the many small behaviors that comprise a social interaction. They cannot grasp the problem as a disability. Some parents tell me they feel the child does it on purpose. Others think the child is rude. In truth, for children with ASD, there seems to be none of the natural feeling of comfort and satisfaction with interpersonal interactions that draws typical individuals to socialize with others. In fact for many children it is not simply a lack of positive internal reinforcement. Social interaction for some children is exceeding difficult and is experienced as being painful. Children with an ASD learn to engage socially not because it feels good, but because they are told they need to or have to. They may feel satisfaction at accomplishing these tasks, but the reward will generally come from an external source. It will always feel uncomfortable and probably seem awkward to others, even when they are relatively accomplished at the social interactions expected of them.
- *Try to be a social facilitator for your child.* Parents should be encouraged to act as social facilitators for their child. Parents of typical children usually let their children navigate and negotiate childhood society relatively undisturbed and unbothered. For children with an ASD the ability to be in the society of other children and succeed is quite limited. These children need help from an adult, generally a parent or other adult, but sometimes a sibling, to be the facilitator. Helping adults or siblings can hang out with the child; help with introductions, explain when necessary that there are some difficulties. The adult observes as unobtrusively as possible, ready to intervene to help with the social interactions if necessary. Parents should balance their intervention between being too intrusive or protective and being available to make the social interaction successful.
- *There are three major programs of intervention (ABA, DIR/Floor-*

time, and TEEACH). These three interventions are the most accepted communication, social, and educational interventions for children with ASD. Parents need to be reminded that these programs have succeeded in helping children with ASD to overcome their ASD-derived symptoms. While we would love to have more research on these interventions, and each has its detractors, they all have benefits and disadvantages to consider. Not all areas of the country offer them, but if they are available in your community they are worth exploring to help with the communication, social, and educational difficulties children face. They may be available privately through in-home or office based interventions, or they are sometimes offered in private or even public schools. In varying degrees, all these programs address the need for increased, appropriate social interaction.

- *Every moment is a teaching moment.* This point cannot be overemphasized with parents of children with ASD. Though it is probably true for all children, for children with ASD, every event, every encounter offers an opportunity for the child to learn about social engagement and how to be more successful in these interactions. Ask parents to consider how often each day they must interact with someone socially, and it will help them to appreciate not only how debilitating it is to be socially handicapped, but also how each day brings opportunities to learn something new or reinforce an emerging or newly established skill.

Questions Parents May Ask

- *What do you mean by social skills?* These are skills people develop to interact and communicate with others. Social skills are divided into verbal and nonverbal skills. To have satisfactory verbal social skills the child should be able to have a smooth verbal delivery with understandable speech. He or she should be able to vary the tone of voice and to ask open-ended questions. Children should be able to listen to and respond to speech from others. Nonverbally, a child

Table 5.1 Explanation of common interventions

Intervention	Description
ABA (Applied Behavioral Analysis)	Applied Behavioral Analysis is a systematic study and measure of observable behavior and then manipulating the environment to modify behavior. The environmental modifications are designed to increase more socially appropriate and adaptive behaviors. Key aspects of ABA are: • Observation for what behaviors look like and their frequency. What leads to the behavior and what are the consequences positive and/or negative for the behavior? • Breaking down desired skills into steps • Teaching the steps through repeated presentation of discrete trials • Data on performance is tracked to show changes over time
DIR (Developmental, Individual-Difference, Relationship-Based)/ Floortime	Floortime is based on the premise that children learn skills from relationships with significant others in their lives. It is child directed and based on interactive experiences in a low stimulus environment ranging from two to five hours a day. There is a stress on early intervention. The longer a child is left to engage in his/her own world the more difficult engagement with the "outside" world becomes. Integration with typical peers is also important.
TEACCH (Treatment and Education of Autistic and Related Communication Handicapped Children)	The principles and concepts guiding the TEACCH system have been summarized as: "–Improved adaptation: through the two strategies of improving skills by means of education and of modifying the environment to accommodate deficits. –Parent collaboration: parents work with professionals as co-therapists for their children so that techniques can be continued at home. –Assessment for individualized treatment: unique educational programs are designed for all individuals on the basis of regular assessments of abilities.

Table 5.1 Continued

Intervention	Description
	–Structured teaching: it has been found that children with autism benefit more from a structured educational environment than from free approaches.
	–Skill enhancement: assessment identifies emerging skills and work then focuses upon these. (This approach is also applied to staff and parent training.)
	–Cognitive and behavior therapy: educational procedures are guided by theories of cognition and behavior suggesting that difficult behavior may result from underlying problems in perception and understanding.
	–Generalist training: professionals in the TEACCH system are trained as generalists who understand the whole child, and do not specialize as psychologists, speech therapists etc."

Source: Approaches to autism: An annotated list.
(The National Autistic Society, 1993 revised 2003)

should be able to actively listen in a relaxed manner, making direct eye contact. He or she should be able to use gestures correctly. Facial expressions, such as smiling and nodding appropriately while listening and trying to use the other person's name in conversation are good examples of simple social skills. More advanced social skills include the ability to diplomatically handle a disagreement or to feign interest in someone else's conversation. In individuals with ASD these skills are generally significantly impaired, if present at all.

- *What is "social skills training"? What does that mean?* Social skills training is literally the training that is designed to teach these skills to people with ASD. Unlike typical children, they have not developed the usual socialization most children learn as they grow; they need specialized training. At the core of this disorder is an inability to respond typically to the usual ways in which people around them socialize and interact. A social skills curriculum has been created to teach them how to do these things that happen naturally for most of us. ABA, DIR/Floortime, and TEEACH have strong social skills components. There are other curricula that simply teach social skills rather than a comprehensive program for children with an ASD. All of these curricula can be helpful. Parents and caretakers also can develop their own ways to help children develop these social skills.

- *Why is he or she so aloof or rude?* These children aren't being rude, they are aloof because they simply do not have the interest in other people or their activities. They don't gain pleasure from such interactions or connections, so they have no motivation to become involved in them. Labeling the children as rude implies that they are intentionally trying to create a particular reaction from others, and I do not think they have the social awareness or skills to be rude. If they understood enough about the "rules" for social behavior to choose to be rude, it would be a step in the right direction.

- *Should we punish him or her?* Punishing a child who is unable to engage socially is not helpful and would probably lead to further confusion about appropriate social interaction. Positive reinforcement is essential for building their desire to engage in social skills because the internal reward most of us experience is not there. Many children must overcome an internal aversion to and fear of social interactions.

- *Should he or she be in a special school?* Interaction with typical developing peers is essential for developing appropriate social skills. Some inclusion and integration of children with ASD with typical peers is a must. Special schools can be very helpful in providing intense structure and a more concentrated learning environment, but unless they provide some interaction with typically developing peers, then they are missing one of the most important social skills and communication educational tools available. This is true regardless of the level of disability.

Our Experience

To me the key is to start as early as you can and provide as many opportunities as you can for engagement. With Frankie we started him in an integrated preschool program at a specialized preschool at 18 months. We were very fortunate that in our community there was a school where typically developing children were enrolled with children who had special needs. This pairing of typical and special needs children was a godsend for Frankie, and from the start his social interaction increased and he began to engage with other children, however minimally, where he had not done so before.

We also made many efforts to keep Frankie engaged with other children and adults. We arranged for play opportunities. We joined a small church where there were other children with developmental disabilities who were included together with the typically developing children. When he was a bit older we joined sports groups. He has been and continues to be involved in therapeutic social skills groups in the community and at school.

We have constantly worked with him at home to make eye contact, to encourage him to engage with us. We would play for hours with him and try to get him to respond in socially appropriate ways. A friend of ours visiting from out of town when Frankie was about 3 years old was somewhat overwhelmed. He asked, "Does every moment have to be a teaching moment?" I thought about it for a second and then responded, "Well yes, I guess it does." Even today, every moment is a teaching moment for Frankie about so many things, but our primary focus continues to be social engagement. I have seen with Frankie and so many of the other children that I work with, that the problem is not necessarily not wanting to be engaged but not being able to be socially involved. They do not have the skills or the pleasure that most of us bring to social interactions. As Frankie develops more skills and feels more comfortable, he wants to be more engaged. That desire, however, has brought its own problems. Now we are dealing with his growing awareness that he is not like other children and does not have the same level of social or intellectual competence, and that is bringing new struggles. We will discuss those issues later in the chapter on schools and school placement.

CHAPTER SIX

How to Talk about Repetitive Behaviors, Restrictive Interests, and Rigidity

Some of the most difficult behaviors to understand, accept, and even tolerate in children with ASDs are their repetitive, some would say "obsessive," and restricted activities and interests. While children diagnosed across the spectrum of ASDs show great variety of expression of this core symptom, they have similarities in this symptom that are recognizable to those who work with such children.

In children with more severe symptoms and cognitive impairment the behavior may consist of flicking a string or ribbon or spitting or twirling. It might be lining up items in a certain way or insisting on absolute sameness in the furnishings and even knickknacks in the home. In higher functioning children the behavior can be flapping of hands or odd facial expressions, but also the fixations on topics such as dinosaurs, trains, electronic games, trading cards, or certain charac-

ters or videos that consume the child's time and conversation. I work
with one girl who is essentially nonverbal and makes little if any social
contact with anyone outside her family. Her usual repetitive behavior
is to continually fling a long ribbon as she jumps and twirls around
the room, always with her eyes on the ribbon. The first question I
ask parents, and myself, when observing such behaviors is, "How impairing is the behavior?" In this particular case, where is the impairment? Then I consider, "What pleasure or satisfaction does it give the
child?" and, "Am I reasonably certain that changing the behavior
would be possible in a way that would not further impair her or over-
tax the family system?"

For this girl, the behavior, though benign compared to self-injury,
is quite impairing, and she does it almost constantly. This undermines
her ability to learn other skills, especially improving her communication, but it does seem to bring her great joy. She is very happy when-
ever she does it. Additionally, neither her family nor her teachers seem
to be particularly interested in changing or eliminating it. We have
worked minimally to reduce the behavior, but with limited success.
The girl is now a teenager, and the likelihood of success in stopping
the behavior now is less than if she were younger. The behavior could
be eliminated, but it would take intensive intervention; none of the
day-to-day caregivers working with her are prepared to invest that
effort. So for now, I am limited to trying to constrain some of her
hyperactivity with medication interventions that are a limited success
at best and have the potential to cause her physical harm on a long-
term basis.

In the best of situations we would use some medications to support
an intense behavioral intervention to engage the girl in more interactions with others. This effort would ultimately help her be more self-
sufficient, and I believe, be generally more satisfied—although the joy
she experiences from her repetitive behavior is apparent.

Other behaviors displayed by children with more severe ASDs can
include spitting or even fecal smearing. These behaviors always require intervention due to the health and social problems, and as you

might expect, parents and teachers have no argument about or lack of interest in changing these behaviors, regardless of the joy the child experiences.

Children with higher functioning ASDs present more of a dilemma over certain restricted interests or behaviors. If the behavior or interest involves a potentially dangerous activity, it is clearer. When it is clearly socially unacceptable, efforts can be made to change, eliminate, or restrict the behavior or interest. One high-functioning child is fixated on wooden survey stakes, and he will literally jump from the car to snatch one up for his collection. Another child is fixated on Hitler's Germany and romanticizes the period in a positive way. Obviously the first is quite odd and involves some physical danger. The other interest is unlikely to be viewed positively in most social settings.

With each of these children, behavioral interventions (i.e. positive behavioral strategies using reinforcement for appropriate new behaviors and negative consequences for the behaviors to be stopped) are appropriate. Social group intervention can be helpful, and many times peers in the neighborhood or at school will help to extinguish the behavior. "That's gross," or "You're weird," can be spontaneous negative reinforcement for the child. Sometimes in professionally facilitated social groups peers can also provide positive and negative reinforcement as appropriate. Consequently, the parents should be consistent with their behavioral interventions and clearly communicate that the behaviors are not "okay." It is helpful for the parents to have professional help in developing these behavioral interventions, and most areas have psychologists or other behavior therapists who can help.

The child's rigidity or inability to change or tolerate change in his or her surroundings is almost always a symptom of ASDs. Rigidity and repetitive restrictive interests and behaviors in these children are closely related to the problems with rigidity. I believe they are part of the same neurological malfunction. Certainly, there is a lot of rigidity in the repetitive behaviors, to the point where they are very often ritualistic. These rituals differ little from the behaviors, such as always having to go the same way home or to school. Restrictive interests, of course, can lead to rigidity, with the child being unable to talk about anything except the interest, or insisting that things be done a very specific way, such as playing a particular game or examining a particular event or item. The rigidity involved in these repetitive behaviors and restrictive interests, when violated, often leads to tantrums.

What to Say to Parents

- *Repetitive and rigid behaviors can be some of the most annoying and difficult behaviors to tolerate in a child with an ASD.* Other than problems with severe aggression, the most frequent complaint I hear from parents is about their child's repetitive/rigid acts. These behaviors can be very frustrating and make daily life difficult for families. The behaviors can also decrease the time and attention available for learning. They can lead to tantrums or aggressive behavior if the child is stopped or thwarted in any way from pursuing a behavioral interest. It is important to acknowledge for the parents that these behaviors are difficult to tolerate. They are often constant reminders that a child who looks "normal" on the outside has serious problems. The behaviors are frustrating, sometimes dangerous, disruptive, and in public can be embarrassing. Let parents know you have some understanding of their feelings.

- *Fixations can also be a godsend and might lead to a special vocation or joy for a child with an ASD.* While some behaviors can be annoying and overwhelming as discussed above, there are others that may provide something useful for the patient. A patient who has a fixation on animals might be able to work with or around animals when he or she gets older. Children consumed by the computer can get jobs that require working on the computer all day. I know of children who enjoy spinning and repetitive rocking that have loved jobs like working in a laundry folding clothes or shredding paper. Other children have special joys associated with their fixations that help them to be more engaged with the world. Sports like basketball or a game such as chess are examples of potentially positive fixations. All of these fixations or behaviors tied to fixations can be trying and overwhelming, so help parents to look at the behaviors and fixations in a way that might envision some positive outcomes. Not all odd/rigid perseverative behaviors have a positive side, in fact most do not, but help parents to at least look for some potential.

- *These behaviors can lead to tantrums.* When parents, teachers, and others constantly give in to the child's fixations or repetitive behaviors, the behaviors persist and grow to an unhealthy extent. There is a difficult and tough balance in weighing whether to be indulgent to a degree versus acting on the need to make a change. I consider whether the repetitive behavior or fixation brings joy without disruption or destructive or damaging consequences. Damaging consequences can include the amount of time spent in the activity, putting the child or others at risk, or consuming so much time the child is unable to engage in more appropriate social or learning activities. Thwarting these behaviors and interests almost always provokes a tantrum from the child. If the behavior has generally been indulged over time (for example, having to look at all of a building's plumbing each time he or she enters the building), those times when the child cannot do this (for example, when visiting a hospital, airport, or other restricted environment) will likely lead to a tantrum. Helping a child have some control over repetitive behaviors and fixations is a very important task for the child's team of caregivers.

- *To restrict or eliminate a behavior, everyone has to be on the same page.* Behavioral interventions can be amazingly effective in controlling and eliminating problem behaviors, while medications, for the most part, are not. Many times parents and teachers believe there "must be" a medication that will help, but sadly, this is seldom true. Some professionals insist these behaviors and problems are obsessive compulsive disorder (OCD) and diagnose them as such.

Nonetheless, OCD is seldom the case. OCD is usually responsive to medication intervention. For more detail, please refer to the previous chapter. These rigid perseverative behaviors are core features of ASD, and they are less responsive to medications, although serotonin medications can make some difference (see chapter 11). I think people want a medication to "fix" these behaviors because the behavioral treatments that are quite effective in helping require quite a bit of work. Everyone working with a child—teachers, after school programs, therapists, parents and extended family, even babysitters—must be consistent in their response to the child's behavior. This takes an enormous amount of energy, effort, and commitment to help a child gain some control of his or her behaviors and fixations but it is possible when everyone works together.

Questions Parents May Ask

- *Should we indulge him or her?* The simple answer is, "No, you really shouldn't." But there are exceptions. You need to talk with parents about the balance between a repetitive behavior that brings joy without disruption or destructive or damaging consequences and a fixation that clearly puts a child or others at risk or consumes the child leaving less time for more appropriate social or learning activities. This can be really tough for parents. So often they are so happy that their usually aloof child actually enjoys something that they feel conflicted about controlling it. Or sometimes they are so overwhelmed by the everyday care for a child with disabilities that they allow the behavior in order to gain some down time for themselves. The drawback, of course, is that the indulgence can lead to an entrenched behavior that becomes increasing problematic.
- *How do we stop the behavior?* For lower functioning children behavioral interventions are the best way to stop a repetitive behavior or fixation. For higher functioning children a combination of the following interventions work well: behavioral interventions, in-

creased social engagement, and more socially appropriate distractions which can encourage new behaviors and interests. Social engagement will work with lower functioning children, too, but it's sometimes necessary to first use behavioral interventions to decrease or extinguish the problematic behaviors. Medication can help decrease anxiety so the children can tolerate the interventions, but I have seen little success with medication on its own decreasing or stopping the repetitive behaviors.

- *What should I say to other people about his or her behavior?* These behaviors are sometimes tough to explain. Without question, many of the behaviors are odd, and the children are very driven by the fixation that leads to the behavior. People without experience of ASD will be surprised by the behaviors and their intensity. Explaining the child has an ASD or simply saying, "He's autistic," is sometimes the best you can do. I tell parents to admit that it looks odd or unusual but, "He is autistic, and people with autism have a problem getting stuck on things." This usually works for us and other parents. As more people know about ASD, it should become easier to explain, but it will always be difficult. So many children with ASD look typical, and people expect them to behave typically, too.

Our Experience

With Frankie we have been through several of these kinds of behaviors and some have required firm, rapid, and significant interventions and others have been modified to serve a potentially useful purpose; others, while unacceptable, have been tolerated longer and more gradually addressed. He has grown out of some of these more odd behaviors as children do. When he was younger, he had behaviors that were quite unusual such as only eating things that were red. This behavior we ignored for a while and, with the introduction of foods that appealed to him that were not red, it eventually dropped out.

His fixation on trains was good in some situations and not in others. It did give him something to talk about with other children. If there were trains to share he would engage other children in play. However, it was difficult when he wouldn't sleep without a particular train, and we had to establish a behavioral intervention for that problem. Of course, that was after several weeks of us changing our behavior by always attempting to meet his demand for his restricted interest item (i.e., the train). We quickly learned that attempting to completely comply with his interest was a disaster for our family and not good for him.

He was also fixated on snakes, and that seemed okay until he caught a snake in the yard and brought it into the house. We quickly substituted another interest. More recently he has developed fixations on chess and electronic games. These fixations have given him interests that seem to engage other kids and they do not require as much verbal skill in order to communicate. That has been helpful for him socially.

Over time we have also worked on other repetitive behaviors and restricted interests and have even engaged peers and teachers to help. All of these interventions have been made in an effort to make him more successful socially. An example of these behaviors is smelling papers and other odd objects. We have told Frankie that this is not what other children normally do and would be considered strange or weird, so now he will prompt himself when he feels the urge by saying to himself or one of us "that would be weird" and refraining from the behavior. Another example is repeating a phrase over and over again. He has several friends that prompt him to say something once and then say, "Let it go Frankie."

For many children with ASD, including Frankie, the addition of a psychopharmacologic intervention is also helpful to take away some of the anxiety and perseveration that seem to plague them. Selective serotonin reuptake inhibitors (SSRIs) can be useful for treating these symptoms and at times blood pressure medications and even neuroleptic medications can work. Interestingly enough, sometimes the first psychopharmacologic intervention that is made for these problems is the addition of a stimulant medication. In my experience, I have actually found that these medications exacerbate the problem rather than assist in decreasing the intensity (see chapter 11). So for these behaviors and interests, care has to be taken to sort out whether it is a problem or not. If it is a problem, decide how significant a problem, and then determine the extent of the intervention. Remember always that our first and foremost obligation is to do no harm.

CHAPTER SEVEN

How to Talk about Tantrums and Aggressive Behavior

Tantrums are problem behaviors closely related to restrictive interests, repetitive behaviors, and rigidity. As much as or more than other behaviors associated with ASD, tantrums create the most distress for parents and other primary caretakers. Tantrums are also a primary cause of social isolation of children with ASD and their families.

Tantrums may appear to "come out of the blue," and in children with significant cognitive disability it can be difficult to know the trigger. However, there is always a reason. Many tantrums result from the child's inability to tolerate a change that violates his or her sense of "how things should be." Somehow it conflicts with the rigidity discussed above. Other times the major trigger seems to be fear associated with "sensory issues." Tantrums can be triggered by pain that may not be obvious. Anxiety or frustration about something the child doesn't understand also can trigger tantrums.

Part of the difficulty with the tantrums observed in these children is that without the usual social understanding, tantrums often occur more often, are more intense, and last longer than in a typical child.

This lack of social awareness can increase the likelihood that the tantrum will occur at almost any time and anywhere, because the child is not restrained by the usual social concerns that may hold other children in check.

When first consulted about a tantrum issue, listen carefully to the parents and what they say about the child's behavior and their own. Be sure to help them rule out any health problem (beyond the ASD) that might cause the problem. In younger children and children with more severe cognitive disabilities, tantrums and aggression—especially an acute change or increase in severity of behaviors—can signal physical discomfort or pain. Many times I have found this to be true with my patients. Treating the underlying problem usually decreases or eliminates the behavior.

Many times parents unknowingly sustain tantrum behavior, especially when the tantrum serves to help a child avoid a particular situation. For example, letting a child leave a task undone that she does not want to complete, or letting a child withdraw from a situation he finds uncomfortable, can encourage the behavior. Other times parents or others caring for a child will inadvertently create a situation that reinforces tantrums because it is related to attention-seeking. For example, the child throws a toy just to get the parent's attention. The parent responds. The child gets the desired attention, and the behavior continues.

In these situations the assistance of a trained behavior specialist can help sort out what leads to and sustains the tantrums. The specialist can then develop a plan to help decrease and ultimately eliminate the behavior. Tantrums that cause the child to be aggressive toward himself or other people present major problems. Aggression such as biting, head-banging, hitting, spitting, and other attacks undermines a child's access to care and treatment. It also isolates the child and the family.

Unfortunately, tantrum behavior that is not identified early, analyzed, and stopped often leads to aggressive tantrums. As a professional you must state clearly that tantrums cannot be tolerated and interventions need to occur early. The family needs to be dedicated to implementing the program to stop the tantrums so that more aggressive behaviors do not develop.

A combination of applied behavioral interventions, coupled with supporting the parents and increasing the child's communication and social awareness through one or more developmental interventions, has the best chance of decreasing and stopping tantrum behavior. If these interventions alone do not work, then look again for any physiologic reason for the behavior. If you find no physiologic cause, then psychopharmacologic interventions are warranted.

Everyone, from the parents to the prescribing physician, must be absolutely clear that medication is simply an aid. The medication can help the behavioral interventions succeed and alleviate some of the child's distress. This allows the child a chance to respond to the interventions. The medication is never the main treatment. Thinking that the medication itself is "the" treatment sets up a situation where the aggression may resurface with more significant force and consequences. In my view, the medication is like a cast that holds the injured body part in place until the healing can take place from within. In this metaphor the behavioral therapy works to mend the behavior so the child can again function effectively. The medication is there to assist the behavioral intervention change the child's behavior. Once the change is complete the medication should be discontinued, if possible.

Using all of these interventions in combination if necessary can generally address even the most severe of tantrums. However, the longer a severe behavior persists or the more the child's environment reinforces the behavior, the more difficult and dangerous the behavior can become and the more difficult it may become to treat. Aggressive uncontrollable behavior, in my experience, is the leading cause of some children and adults with ASD having to live in institutional settings. By letting parents know this, you may help them understand the consequences of "just living with" this behavior. Tantrums in a 5-year-old may be manageable; tantrums in a 25-year-old are usually not. Early intensive intervention is essential to the life of the child and the family. In the long run, such intervention costs much less to society than lifelong institutionalization.

What to Say to Parents

- *Tantrums, especially tantrums with aggression (either self-directed or at others) may be the most distressing problem in children and adults with ASD.* Most aggression seen in ASD is associated with tantrums. Some aggression seemingly comes out of the blue, but most aggression is the direct escalation of a tantrum. As with all children, tantrums start early. By age 2 (sometimes even younger) children with ASD can scream, grab, throw, fall to the floor, kick, hit, and bite when angry. All children are more likely to throw tantrums when they lack the verbal skills to make their wishes or frustrations known. Before age 2 most children lack the social inhibition that reduces tantrums as they grow older. For children and some adolescents and adults with ASD, this lack of social inhibition is the very problem that makes tantrums more likely to persist as they grow older. Early intervention with appropriate behavioral therapy stops the tantrums so that they do not persist into later childhood and adulthood. The longer the history of a tantrum and aggressive behavior, the more difficult it is to stop. Acknowledge to parents that these are among the most distressing aspects of some children's experience with the disability. Strongly encourage them to get help to control the tantrums and aggressive behaviors as quickly as possible. I also acknowledge to parents that children with an ASD are tough to discipline, and the usual parenting skills that parents bring to dealing with behaviors are often ineffective. The interventions that are helpful are sometimes counterintuitive. They likely will need help.
- *Tantrums and aggression are the main reasons why people with ASD are socially isolated. Do not tolerate it.* Get help. It is imperative to tell parents that problems with tantrums or aggressive behav-

ior isolate people with ASD and their families. I work with many families whose child's behavior has made them prisoners in their own home. Some of the children are now adults, and for years the parents have been unable to have other social experiences. Children with ASD who have tantrums or are aggressive must be restricted in their options for school settings. After schooling is complete, there are no appropriate day programs equipped to handle tantrums or aggression. Many residential facilities will not take people with histories of aggression and tantrums. Many of the treatment facilities treating aggression and tantrums in children with ASD stop treating patients when they reach 21 years old. Parents need to be encouraged to seek treatment early and as often as necessary to keep the child's behavior at a controllable level to permit the child and the family to remain a part of the social fabric.

- *There is always a cause for the tantrum; it just might not be obvious.* So many times parents, teachers, and other caregivers tell me that the tantrums just "come out of the blue." Over the course of many years, I very rarely have seen a situation where a child seems to have a tantrum or outburst of aggression that comes from nowhere. Even in those situations where there is a cause for the behavior (an antecedent), it's just not obvious. Trained behavioral specialists and others more neutral about the day-to-day interactions with the child can often pinpoint the antecedent when the parents or caregivers cannot. There are times when the antecedents are hidden, and the trigger is internal. Physical illness or pain very commonly triggers tantrums and aggression in lower functioning individuals with ASDs. When the child's behavior suddenly changes with no clear medical problem, and trained behavioral specialists see no trigger, get a complete physical evaluation, preferably by a medical practitioner who knows the child well. A good medical practitioner can ensure that there are no underlying medical problems driving the behavior. Sometimes even medical practitioners are unable to rule out the causes such as a headache or abdominal pain in some very low functioning individuals. They may choose to try pain medications to gauge the effect on the behaviors. It is also important to note that some aggressive and tantrum behaviors can persist once they have become established, even though the pain or underlying medical problem has been treated. Be sure to continue behavioral interventions with a behavioral specialist even if an underlying problem has been discovered.)

- *You may unwittingly be sustaining the behavior. Be open to solutions that may not make intuitive sense.* Parents, teachers, and others seldom realize the role they play in creating an atmosphere where children's inappropriate behavior is encouraged. In fact parents, teachers, and other caregivers usually will tell you all the ways that they discourage the behaviors. They will admit that their tactics do not work, and they believe "nothing will work." When parents tell me—and they do all the time—that they have tried "everything," it really means, they have tried everything they know to do. When the child's behaviors are analyzed by an experienced behavioral therapist it usually becomes clear that one of the caregivers is sustaining the behavior. Many times the cause is the attention given to the behavior, the response of the caregivers during or after a tantrum, or something equally simple. Scenarios differ, but a trained behavioral therapist can help parents spot the problems and create a plan to decrease the tantrums and aggressive behavior. The treatment can sometimes take several hours a day over several weeks, but it is worth it, given the consequences of uncontrolled tantrums and aggressive behavior for the child, the family, and those around them. The treatment may also include doing things that seem to make little sense—ignoring behaviors such as spitting, "talking back," foul language, or kicking the floor. Giving attention to these behaviors may be rewarding the child for using them. Unless you are a behavioral specialist, you cannot adequately sort out the complexities of many of these behaviors and what sustains them. Help the parents find a good behavioral therapist trained in techniques to decrease the tantrums and aggressive behavior and who will be available to keep working with the family and school if they need to return.

Questions Parents May Ask

- *What is causing the tantrums/aggression?* Sometimes it is obvious what triggers tantrums or aggressive behavior. Most of the time it's when a child is told "no"—meaning they cannot have something they want, or they cannot do something they want to do, or they must stop doing something they are doing. Without language skills to express their distress, children with ASD may be more easily frustrated or they may be less able to tolerate changes in their environment because of their rigidity and need for sameness. But other things can cause tantrums and aggressive behavior so it is critical to work with a behavior specialist when children exhibit tantrums and aggressive behavior. Sometimes the underlying cause may be increased anxiety, mood, psychosis, or extreme irritability that psychiatric medications may relieve. Other times physical problems or illness contribute to the aggression and tantrums, and these need to be addressed medically. Nevertheless, a consultation with a professional for a behavioral assessment of the child can determine the best course of action related to interactions with the child to prevent tantrums and aggression from occurring and respond to them if they occur again.
- *Why does he or she target me?* Parents often ask this when they are understandably overwhelmed as the target of their child's aggression. Parents usually are the targets because the children are using aggression and tantrums to have control over their environment, and the children see their parents as having control over them. Children may consider parents the safest targets of tantrums and aggression because their reactions are predictable. Because of their aversion to social interactions, these children see parents as

more attractive targets. To change this dynamic, parents and care-givers must be part of the behavioral assessments and interventions, eventually becoming trained as a behavioral interventionist for their child.

- *How can he or she hurt himself like that?* Because most children with ASD have significant sensory problems, often they seem to experience less pain than their parents or others would experience. Sometimes they are more sensitive to physical pain. It is extremely distressing for parents to see their child hurt him- or herself. It is important that professionals acknowledge to parents how difficult this is and to work with them to find a solution. The most useful help for self-injurious behavior is behavioral interventions with a trained behavioral therapist. Medications can sometimes provide some assistance, and I will discuss treatments with medication in a later chapter.

- *Does spanking work?* Corporal punishments or spankings don't work with children with ASD, in my experience. It may briefly stop or decrease the tantrums or aggression, but relief is short-lived. Soon the child is having as many if not more problems with aggres-sion and tantrums.

- *What is the best approach?* The very best approach to decreasing tantrums and aggressive behavior is to use applied behavioral analy-sis with the right behavioral interventions prescribed by the thera-pist who analyzed the behavior. When referring a family to a thera-pist, look for therapists who are certified. The most respected certification is board certified behavior analyst (BCBA) awarded by the Behavior Analyst Certification Board, Inc. (the standards can be found at http://www.BCBA.com). Over the years, in dealing with many behavior problems in children with ASD and other develop-mental disabilities, I have been amazed at the power of these inter-ventions. These interventions truly help children with ASD and their families. Their effectiveness is demonstrated by years of rigor-ous scientific research on reducing and eliminating these disruptive, life-stifling behaviors. Long-term strategies of treatment should go beyond behavioral therapy to work on decreasing the core symptoms of the ASD that exacerbates the behaviors. Interventions that develop communication and decrease rigidity and repetitive behaviors should continue. All these interventions work hand in hand to create an environment free from tantrums and aggression.

- *Do medications help?* In chapter 11 I will fully explore the use of medications. I tell parents that medications can be helpful, but they are not the sole answer to problems with tantrums and aggressive behavior. Medications can complement the behavior therapy. Even if medications are treating an underlying psychiatric or physical problem that may be exacerbating the behavior, appropriate behavior treatments must still be put into place. It is so tempting to imagine that a medicine will make all the difference, and the solution to these devastating behaviors would be that easy. Unfortunately, even if it helps the situation for a short time, medication ultimately will not solve the problem.

Our Experience

The tantrums started early for Frankie. His earliest tantrums were associated with frustrations and not that atypical of other children except that there was an intensity and persistence to the tantrums that I did not usually see in other children. As he grew older the tantrums were consistent with his core ASD symptoms. For example, he could not tolerate taking a bath or having his head or hair touched or washed. Trying to cut his hair was impossible. Any of these could often lead to tantrum episodes that were so severe that he seemed to literally be in fear of dying. Bathtubs terrified him. We were able to use positive reinforcement and engagement with distractions to gradually overcome the bathing problems, but it was not until he was 5 years old that he was able to tolerate a haircut and that was mostly due to our finally finding the right barber who had the patience.

As he grew, the tantrums that led to the introduction of medication were related to a specific fear and rigidity. At about 3 years old he could not tolerate crossing thresholds. He would not come into a room or leave a room or get into the car or out of the car without screaming and crying. He was never aggressive as some children are, but he was in significant distress, and his distress and behavior led to increasing restraints on the family's behavior. Finally, he was placed on a selective serotonin reuptake inhibitor (SSRI), and his behavior improved significantly. His tantrums decreased to the point where we could put into place behavioral interventions that eventually led to an elimination of his tantrums.

CHAPTER EIGHT

How to Talk about Sleep

Other than tantrums and rigid behaviors, sleep difficulties in children with ASD rank as the next most frustrating array of problems parents usually face. I see parents very distressed about their child's communication disability, social oddness, tantrums, and other developmental concerns, but parents are oftentimes simply worn out from the lack of sleep. Their marriage, work, and relationships with family members and those outside the family all suffer. It is almost impossible to be pleasant when you are exhausted all the time. The child with an ASD may suffer, too, but many times he or she seems unaffected by little sleep. If the child is affected, he or she may have more tantrums or irritability, piling more stress on the family.

Unfortunately, we know little about what causes sleep problems in these children. I have found through my clinical work and my experience with Frankie that idiosyncratic ASD behaviors can fuel sleep problems, in addition to any physiological brain differences that may reduce the need for sleep in these children.

For most of my patients a combination of behavioral interventions and "herbal" or pharmacologic sleep aids make a big difference in a child being able to go to sleep and remain asleep. Basic sleep routines

and "hygiene" are essential, as they are in many aspects of living with
a child with an ASD.

Planning and scheduling are essential for bedtime. The most important approach for bedtime is to establish a routine and stick with it
(see "Our Experience" below). Wind children down before bed. For
our family this means that after dinner, the children do not use devices
such as televisions or computers. It makes some intuitive sense to me
that when one stares directly into a lighted screen, whether television
or computer, when it's time to sleep, one's brain is less likely to understand that it is night and time for sleep. I believe this is especially
true for children diagnosed with ASD because of their problems with
certain neurotransmitters essential for sleep. For my family and the
families with whom I have worked, an evening respite from television
and computers has been productive. In addition to the wind-down
time, establish a set time for bed.

I do frequently refer children to a sleep clinic to make sure there
are no other sleep problems that might require treatment, such as
obstructive sleep apnea. In this disorder, the patient's airway becomes
blocked during sleep. An involuntary "startle response" wakes the patient and restarts breathing. Also, more often these days, sleep clinics
have a strong psychological component, enabling them to address all
the issues in one place. It is important to talk with a physician experienced in treating sleep problems in developmentally disabled children. This professional can advise you about the potential "herbal"
and other pharmacologic interventions for a particular child. However, it is wise to look beyond pharmacologic remedies to solve the
problem long term. Lifestyle and behavioral changes on the part of
the parents and the child are essential to success.

What to Say to Parents

- *Most parents of children with ASD report sleep problems in their
  child.* This has been true in my clinical practice. A very common
  complaint is that a child can't fall asleep or he or she consistently

wakes up and can't fall back to sleep. Some people suggest that children with ASD have no more sleep difficulties than other children, but that their parents are simply more concerned about their child's sleep. I do not believe this. In any event, sleep is an issue for most families with a child with an ASD. Letting parents know that other families experience these difficulties is usually comforting.

- *You must have sleep. Work out a way that you can sleep as much as possible.* In my practice, parents are often exhausted by lack of sleep. They sometimes are up every night for parts of the night or do not get to sleep at all. Many times they will bring their child to bed with them out of desperation, but even then the child stays awake and the parent still is unable to rest. After a while this becomes the norm, and parents can't remember what it feels like to be rested and have energy. When their child has other acute or urgent issues, sleep difficulties can be ignored. It's an invisible problem. Parents may feel they just have to keep going. In truth, many of the behavioral interventions, social skills building, and communication skills development rely heavily on attentive interaction, facilitation, and teaching moments with the parents and caregivers. Unless they have adequate rest, parents simply cannot have the patience and energy levels to do this. Their fatigue, tension, and irritability will likely bring forth less than desirable behavior in their child. I work with parents to find a solution to the sleep problems. I also tell them that they must work out a way to get sleep. If there is another adult in the house, I have the adults take shifts staying up or getting up with the child. Some parents have hired babysitters for the night. Perhaps one room can be set up to be safe for the child where he or she can be awake in the evening, depending of course on the child's level of functioning and the need for monitoring. Each child requires a different level of safety, but talking with parents about what such a room might be like is helpful. They may reject it out of hand as a possibility, but it is worth mentioning. Some parents have installed hall alarms to signal when their child gets up or leaves the room. Baby monitors in the room can be helpful if the child will not destroy them. Because of the wide range of functioning in children with ASD, one solution never fits all. But as a professional working with the family, try to explore as many options as you can for the parents to get some sleep. If they are unable to get regular sleep, they will be unable to care for their child with ASD and they will also be unable to do all of the other jobs that need to be done to take care of a family.

- *Lack of sleep affects the behavior of your child.* Lack of sleep affects the parents, but it also affects the child with an ASD, even though at times the child seems to not need sleep. When sleep disturbances in children with ASD can be reduced or eliminated then many other behavior problems seem to improve. Children have more attention and focus. They have fewer tantrums or temper flare-ups and frustrations. Their ability to respond to teaching improves. It is important to help parents find solutions to the sleep difficulties they report.

Questions Parents May Ask

- *What makes him or her wake up?* Most people wake during the night. But typical children and adults are aware of cues such as darkness and quiet that tell them they should still be asleep, so they generally fall back asleep. Children with ASD often lack this social sense. Consequently they get up and expect everyone else to get up with them. After being awake several hours, they become tired, wanting to go back to sleep about the time everyone including them should get out of bed. I also think that some children with ASDs get up in the evening to engage in their preferred behaviors, often related to their fixations. Some suggest that an impairment of the brain's ability to respond to or produce melatonin may be the root of the sleep problems in ASDs, but there is no research that supports this theory. (Melatonin is a hormone produced by the pineal gland at the base of the brain that is responsible for drowsiness and regulating our diurnal cycle.)

- *Why doesn't he or she seem tired?* Some children with ASD do not seem to be disturbed by their lack of sleep. Although these children may not seem tired or drowsy during the day, that is not always an indication that they do not need sleep. Children with ASDs simply may not show the effects of their lack of sleep as clearly as typical children do. This is probably related to their difference in social interaction and awareness.

- *What can we do?* Most sleep disturbances in children with ASDs can be addressed with behavioral interventions. There are behavioral specialists who specialize in helping with sleep problems. Many times the behavioral therapist will have families make videotapes of the bedtime routine and the bedroom to see what delays the child's sleep onset and what happens if the child wakes during the night. Analyzing these tapes gives the behavior therapist very useful information in helping parents to devise strategies to help with sleep. There should be an established routine (e.g., first a bath, then pajamas, then getting into bed with no overhead lighting, a story time, followed by quiet interaction with the parent for a limited time, and then lights out, with the parent leaving the bedroom). A noisemaker or fan can be turned on to drown out noise. If sleep disturbances are severe or persist, evaluation by a pediatric sleep specialist (usually a pediatric pulmonologist or pediatric neurologist) is in order. The specialist may order an overnight sleep study in a sleep laboratory to determine the problems with the child's sleep. I always talk with parents about all of these possibilities as we discuss sleep issues and then refer them to the appropriate evaluation and treatment professionals.

- *Is there a medication we can give? Is it dangerous to give a "sleeping pill?"* Medications can be helpful with sleep problems in these children. Many people use an over-the-counter version of the hormone melatonin to help with sleep. In my own practice, I have found that melatonin is helpful. Unfortunately there are not many long-term studies that give a clear picture of long-term side effects or difficulty with using this remedy. Parents often ask if there is a problem with its use, and I am honest in telling them that I do not know. But I have used it safely with children for the last 10 years without significant adverse effects. There are other herbal sleep aids, such as chamomile, that appear to be reasonably safe. I do discourage parents from using stronger herbs, such as valerian root, because of potential side effects, such as liver toxicities. Prescription medications can be used to help with sleep, and many physicians prescribe diphenhydramine or clonidine. But these medications can have side effects as well. Unfortunately there is no simple answer to parents' questions about the safety of these sleep aids—no one knows for sure. Any time a supplement is added there is potential risk for harm. If more potent prescription "sleeping pills" are necessary for a child with an ASD to sleep, then absolutely refer the family to a sleep specialist.

Our Experience

Sleep difficulty has certainly been a problem that I am intimately aware of in my own family. I doubt that Frankie ever consistently slept through the night until he was about 7 years old, and since then, he continues to have nights where he does not sleep. Thankfully, he sleeps through the night much more often. However, we still have an alarm in our bedroom hallway to alert us if he gets up in the evening because he does not always return to his bed.

Part of Frankie's problem as an infant seemed to be his inability to self soothe and return to sleep. As he got older, his lack of awareness of the social cues to return to sleep and remain in bed led him to wake up and do whatever he wanted. For a time his waking at night was also fueled by his fixation with the weather and wanting to know the weather for the next day. He would get up at 3 a.m. or 4 a.m. to find the newspaper outside and check the weather forecast. Of course, this involved leaving the house and going outside in the middle of the night. Understandably, we were very upset when we found out, and we placed a deadbolt on the door. Children with ASD can be so extremely clever and creative that, as in our family's case, it has taken two parents with postgraduate degrees and a trained special-needs nanny to stay ahead of Frankie's ability to outfox us.

A bedtime routine is essential to a good night's sleep. In our house bedtime is 8:00 p.m. At 7:15 p.m. the boys brush their teeth and put on pajamas. At 7:30 p.m. we play a card game or board game for about 20 minutes, or just sit and cuddle and talk. At 7:50 p.m. the boys get into bed and we read a story for 10 minutes. Then we turn the lights out. This has worked well to get Frankie to sleep.

In working to keep Frankie asleep over time, herbal remedies have helped. Behavior strategies have helped, too, including rewards for staying in bed, as well as consequences for getting up and staying up without telling us. Devices that restrict movement (such as the motion detector mentioned above) or restricted access (such as deadbolts and locks on cabinets that have his favorite foods or the television remote controls) have helped too.

Sleep is a very important issue for many of the families you will work with. Remember to ask about sleep. Ask how it affects the child, but also ask about the whole family. You will be amazed at the information you can gather by just asking where and how people in the family sleep. Helping families get interventions for sleep problems can make a big difference in the quality of every family member's life.

CHAPTER NINE
―――――――――

How to Talk about Toilet Training

Lack of toilet training can prevent many children with ASD from being accepted to therapy programs and cause ongoing difficulties for family and caregivers. Many of these children are trained by age 3 or shortly thereafter, but a large number of them, especially lower functioning children, are not.

Conditions such as sensory issues can create a problem with the child knowing that he or she has to urinate or defecate. Sometimes a child understands one urge but not the other. They may fear toilets or toilets flushing. Some children develop specific fecal withholding. At times gastrointestinal abnormalities or food sensitivities may create problems. Communication problems may stem from language delay. Any or all of these can complicate or delay toilet training.

Nonetheless the older the child, the more toilet training becomes an issue. Even though children, teenagers, and adults are still able to get services, being toilet trained dramatically expands their horizons. Every encouragement and support should be given to families to toilet train a child as soon as he or she is ready. Families should keep trying to have the child as toilet trained as possible, even if it is incomplete.

When a particular child struggles with toilet training, it generally takes a concentrated effort and the commitment of everyone involved to succeed. We are lucky in our community to have several behavioral clinics and programs willing to work with parents to create a program. But parents can set up a program themselves by reading books on toilet training available to the public. There are even books written specifically for parents of children with developmental disabilities. The principles of positive reinforcement outlined in these books are universally accepted as effective ways to toilet train any child. Parents of children with disabilities often find it helpful to have a professional walk them through setting up a training program. If there is a behavioral specialist available in your area, he or she can assist in setting up a successful program for parents.

What to Say to Parents

- *You can toilet train your child.* Parents need to hear that their child can be toilet trained and they can be part of that success. They may need help from a professional to get it done but they can do it. It is also important to tell parents that it is not unusual for children with ASD to have a difficult time with being toilet trained. The sensory problems create difficulty because the child may not sense that he or she has to go to the bathroom. The child may be oversensitive to the bathroom or to the sounds of the toilet. The child may even fear the sensation of sitting on a toilet that flushes. As with other appropriate social behaviors, children with ASDs may not see the reason why to even use the toilet, or their rigid adherence to a schedule may simply not allow for them to stop and use the bathroom. The child may not be verbal. All of these are obstacles to being toilet trained but utilizing behavioral interventions any child with ASD can be toilet trained. It may take several weeks or even months, but it is possible. I have seen profoundly affected nonverbal, wheelchair bound individuals with ASD who were toilet trained, and I firmly believe that short of serious physical problems with the bowel or bladder, every child can become able to control his or her bladder and bowels.

- *Not being toilet trained affects placement.* Not that parents need much more motivation to toilet train their child beyond having to change diapers, but if they do they should know that not being toilet trained significantly limits placement and the older a child is the harder it becomes to find an appropriate placement. Even if a child with ASD has intellectual capabilities to be in an inclusive setting and as I have stated before I think this is very important, there will not be any chance of placement with typical children who are toilet trained if he or she is not. Teachers will not tolerate it and it will impair social interaction. If a child gets to adolescence or adulthood without being toilet trained the restrictions on placement are even greater and lead to very restrictive placements in what are essentially adult daycare-type settings.

- *It takes a lot of support to toilet train your child.* Tell parents to take the time and get the support they need to toilet train. Encourage them to call upon relatives, friends, and the school to work with them to get this accomplished. As I stated above, sometimes it is important to call in a behavioral specialist to help design a positively reinforced behavior plan to get the training accomplished. At first it takes almost minute by minute vigilance. It may take from several days to even a couple of weeks for most children. There are children who will need more specialized treatment and it may takes months of implementing a plan to get a child trained, but it is possible and parents need to know that there are behavioral therapists who are willing to work with them to get a child toilet trained. Therapists who work with developmentally disabled children realize the impact that not being toilet trained has on an individual's life.

- *Positive reinforcement does work.* Many parents of children with ASD will have tried the standard toilet training methods that all parents use to toilet train their toddlers. For some of these children this will work well, but for many it will not. For the parents who have been unsuccessful the idea of using "positive reinforcement" to get their child to toilet appropriately will be a joke. They will tell you right up front that "positive reinforcement does not work." They are right in that the positive reinforcement they were using obviously didn't work. That is the tricky part: many times children with ASD do not respond to the expected positive reinforcement, and sometimes the aversion to being toilet trained is so great it takes a very powerful and frequent positive reinforcement to make it work. I refer parents to trained behavioral therapists. There are generally board certified behavioral therapists somewhere within driving distance of most places in this country. These behavioral therapists have techniques for assessing what a better reinforcement might be and then in determining the appropriate schedule for that reinforcement. They can also help the parents to break down the task of learning to toilet train to all of its components, and thereby help the parents to start small and in reasonably handled chunks to get the child to the point where he or she can be effectively trained. It takes time and hard work but it can be done.

Questions Parents May Ask

- *What do we do since he or she is nonverbal?* Even nonverbal individuals can be toilet trained. First, while some children with ASD are nonverbal they may have other means of communicating, and these can be used to let someone know they need to be toileted. Second, even children who do not communicate can be put on a schedule of toileting that allows for them to be toileted without using diapers. These kinds of toileting schedules require training and reinforcement as well, but they are also very effective.
- *He or she is not responding to positive reinforcement, what should we do?* Find a board certified behavior therapist to help. There are almost always board certified behavior therapists within

driving distance of most families. Many schools have board certified behavior therapists on staff who may be willing to help devise a plan. The Autism Society of America has helpful resources online, and there are many books on toilet training individuals with special needs. I also encourage parents to talk with other parents and teachers who have been through the process before (see appendices A & B for helpful information).

- *Are there people who can help?* Behavior therapists, other parents, teachers, teacher's aides, and even family members can be a big help. I encourage parents to ask for help from as many sources as they can. However, I tell them that they need one plan and everyone needs to be consistent and persistent with that plan. The behavior therapist is the chief and everyone else follows the therapist's directions. If parents can work this out they can have success. There are times when it might require intensive day treatment or very rarely a very short stay away from home to accomplish toilet training, and those options are available in some locations.

Our Experience

Toilet training Frankie was a challenge. We were determined to have Frankie trained before he turned 4 years old, and we just barely missed that goal. He was completely trained at 4 years and 1 month. We only accomplished this with much effort on our part and with several other assistants. Children diagnosed with ASD present a special set of problems. For us the problems were related to language first and foremost. We decided to wait until Frankie could communicate with us about his need to use the bathroom and until he could understand what we were trying to say. Although you can also train children without language or who have very limited or no communication skills, it is more difficult.

Second, Frankie had sensory sensitivities to overcome. Frankie was terrified of toilets. He was especially afraid of public toilets, but no toilet was seen as friendly. He seemed to be terrified of the closed-in space of bathrooms and cubicles. He resisted taking off his pants and sitting on a toilet seat. He seemed to dislike the feel of it on his skin. Most of all, he did not, and would not, tolerate the sound of a toilet flush. To this day he holds a finger in one ear as he presses his other ear into his shoulder while he flushes a toilet. If the toilet happens to be self-flushing, he literally runs from the cubicle or urinal before it flushes. Obviously, this is something that looks odd socially, especially when he is leaving half-clothed. With this description it is easy to see why toilet training was so hard for Frankie. As strange as it may sound, our story is similar to stories I hear all the time from my patients' families.

For many children the key to successful toilet training is looking and waiting for the signs they are ready, although this is not true for all children. We literally waited years for the right time to start. But we tried to lay a good foundation by working to desensitize him to bathrooms, toilets, and flushing from the time he was about 2½ years old. Every time we were out, especially if we were in a quieter public space, we would take Frankie into the public toilets and just let him look in the door. As he became more comfortable we would take him into the bathrooms to look around. He would eventually start to play with water faucets and become more comfortable. Of course, if anyone came in, he would immediately run out. With similar steps to help him get used to the toilet itself, he was able to use a public bathroom after he was more fully trained.

As we were training him, we developed a sense of the times he needed to use the bathroom and we worked diligently to keep his diaper dry and clean. We used other children as models in his integrated/inclusion preschool. When he was finally able to work with us so we could be reasonably expect him to toilet independently, we set a date and took the time off work to do the training in coordination with home and school. My mother-in-law even came for the week to help out.

We toilet trained Frankie around the clock for a solid week with a second week of intermittent positive reinforcement. At the end of that time he was essentially trained and has been ever since. The training was the usual training with the exception that we used a very rigid schedule of taking him to the toilet, and we gradually expanded the time intervals. We vigorously reinforced any voiding or defecation, and we always paired and reinforced going to the toilet with a sign for "potty" or a verbal cue from him. For the most part, he is now independent in all of his toileting. This has opened up doors for him socially and educationally that would have been closed to him otherwise. We were lucky to have the complete cooperation and assistance of the school while we were going through this process. I think the key was the concerted, intense effort we put into the project.

CHAPTER TEN

How to Talk about Food and Eating

Food and eating present a number of problems for families and children with ASD. Quite a few of the problems with food and feeding can be traced to other issues such as rigidity, restrictive interests, sensory problems, and even arousal regulation problems. Children with ASDs can overeat or not eat enough. I have seen children diagnosed with failure to thrive, a condition where the child cannot or will not eat enough to sustain health. I have also worked with children who were seriously obese from overeating.

All healthy children need appropriate physical activity and this is especially true for children with ASDs. Some of these children are so hyperactive it's a struggle for them to get enough nutrition to fuel their extreme calorie expenditure. For most children the activity level varies a lot, at times they are extraordinarily hyperactive and then very docile or almost lethargic.

Too many people diagnosed with ASDs are significantly overweight, creating problems for the individual and the family. For a teenager, being significantly overweight limits social involvement and creates one more hurdle between the teenager and social engagement. If the child is lower functioning or has significant communication problems, being heavy and large can intimidate other students and teachers. Being overweight can limit placement options for a child. Many times medications prescribed to help with behavioral and mood regulation problems increase appetite and carbohydrate cravings. Unless food intake and activity levels are closely managed, this can lead to a child being overweight.

Some parents, teachers, or caretakers, driven by a desire to engage or to placate these children, use food in an inappropriate way that leads to obesity. When Frankie started the third grade he began gaining weight rapidly. We were puzzled. We eventually discovered that the "lunch room ladies" were giving him more food because he was "so cute." Already heavy for his frame, he was eating two or three extra portions a day.

Sometimes when people lack ways to connect with special needs children they offer them food and treats. This hampers a child with an ASD. Many special needs classrooms are filled with food, and food is used as a reward, and frankly, at times, as a sedative for the children. I have worked with parents who literally watch their children get obese, feeding them large amounts of one or two inappropriate foods because, "She won't eat anything else." Parents have trouble understanding the need to limit portions, even if the child eats only chicken nuggets, bread, or chocolate milk. If the calories are from an unhealthy source, more calories do not mean better nutrition.

I often refer children to behaviorally oriented "feeding/eating" programs. With a child who limits food intake to a life-threatening extent or with a child who overeats, applied behavioral interventions make a big difference. When working with a family make note of the child's eating behavior, weight, and activity level, as well as the activities the family has developed for the child. These are all essential components to helping the child and the family have a better and more fulfilling life.

What to Say to Parents

- *It is not uncommon for children with ASD to have problems with eating and food.* Many children with ASD start out as picky eaters. Sometimes the pickiness has to do with sensory problems. The child dislikes the food's texture or temperature. The child overstuff his or her mouth because of sensory problems. Sometimes the problem relates to rigidity—children may only want to eat one kind of food. For about a year, our son would eat only red food. All of these difficulties can lead to problems around food and eating.

- *Professionals can help families with feeding and food problems.* The best help associated with food problems and eating comes from a behavioral approach to feeding problems. A board certified behavior therapist can assist a family to develop a plan that will make mealtimes more pleasant and vary the child's diet. The sooner these issues are addressed, the better it is going to be for the child with the ASD and the family long term.

- *Do not let your child develop obesity.* While a few children with ASD don't eat enough, this is uncommon. Although most parents worry more about children eating too little, the most common problem is actually children eating too much and the subsequent obesity. Many parents of children with ASD give their child far too many calories because the child will eat only certain foods or types of foods. Parents try to compensate for the lack of nutritional variety by feeding the child more of the preferred foods. By age 9 or 10, the child is obese. This is not only a serious health problem, but a significant social and educational problem as well. Obese children with ASD are less likely to be around typical children in school and less likely to receive the same personal attention from teachers and others as a child with healthy weight. My own discussions with teachers and teacher's aides lead me to believe that school staff are fearful of larger children with ASD and tend to interact less with them. Because these children are unable to communicate that they are not a threat to anyone, they can be difficult for others to "read" socially, and people become wary of them as they get older. Experience, education, and getting to know the child help to dispel adults' fear of the unfamiliar. This is harder to overcome if the child is obese. I stress to parents that they can protect their child from obesity with early intervention and diligence about food and eating issues.

- *Do not overfeed the child with food he or she likes in an effort to increase nutrition. This only increases calories.* It is important to stress this to parents. Tell them, "Just because he or she likes it, do not feed lots of it." Parents and others may feel guilty or feel "sorry" for a child with an ASD. They may feed these children more of foods they like because the foods "make them happy." For children who are more difficult to interact with, food becomes a way others connect with them. I discourage all efforts to use food as a positive reinforcement for behavior or as anything other than what it is— fuel for the child's necessary energy. All children should enjoy food, but food should not be given merely for enjoyment. Obesity is too serious a consequence for these children who already have significant disabilities.

Questions Parents May Ask

- *Should we give supplements?* There is certainly no problem giving supplements to a child with an ASD. Some practitioners use nutritional supplements as part of their treatment regimen; it may or may not be helpful. The scientific literature does not offer clear guidance about the use of supplements. But certainly, for a child who avoids some kinds of foods or restricts his or her diet in some way, supplements can be helpful.
- *What is a healthy weight for our child? How many calories should my child consume each day?* When parents have these concerns I show them charts of Body Mass Index scales based on age, weight, and height. If they have serious concerns, refer them to a registered

dietitian. While anyone can call themselves a nutritionist, a registered dietitian has passed specific education requirements to advise clients on the science of nutrition.

- *What about special diets?* Questions about special diets, especially gluten-free or casein-free, are very common from parents of children with ASDs. The gastrointestinal system and the brain are connected—many brain chemicals that affect brain function are also found in the gastrointestinal tract. Cells in both systems form simultaneously from the same cell lines as embryos develop. This prompts many theories about this interaction and its role in the pathology of some ASD subtypes. For now, clear evidence on the diets' effectiveness has yet to be found, but some families believe they are helpful. I caution families to do what they can do. These diets can be very demanding and difficult to follow rigorously. I also caution parents about financial costs and costs in family time and energy. For children who eat little anyway, further restricting their food choices may lead to less nutrition and more opposition from the child.

Our Experience

Frankie has trouble with overeating. Since he was an infant, he has seemed unable to tell when he is full. Even now we need to remind him not to "stuff" his mouth with food and to "slow down" while eating. I hear similar complaints from other parents. I believe sensory problems are partially the cause, and this points to the need for occupational and speech therapy as discussed above.

We monitor Frankie's diet carefully. Like many other children with ASD, in addition to eating too much, he also craves carbohydrates. Even today he will get up in the night, if we've forgotten to turn on the hall alarm, and eat a whole loaf of bread or several rolls. He will go through six "sweet" yogurts or a whole box of cereal, so we limit the kinds of food we keep in the house.

Frankie also tends to be less active, and we work hard to keep him active so his weight does not become a major problem. Increasing his activity level also helps to keep him socially engaged and to regulate his arousal level more effectively. As mentioned above, we have placed him in inclusion sports. Of course this has often meant that we had to volunteer to be assistant coaches for the teams, and this has kept us more active, too.

Our family keeps active outdoors by hiking, biking, and swimming year round. As Frankie has gotten older and less able to participate fully in more competitive team sports, we have placed him in a karate program. In addition to helping him stay fit and active, karate teaches skills and techniques that have been great for continued mastery of his gross motor system. The concentration, discipline, and specific exercises that he learns in karate have been very valuable as well. He also continues to participate in an adaptive physical education program. Every morning we run a mile with him, and he has participated in Special Olympics. It takes a lot of effort to develop these activities, but we feel that given Frankie's problems with eating and food cravings, increasing his activity level and making it fun is essential for his health. The exercise also helps with his mood, his self-esteem, frustration tolerance, and general stress level. Keeping him active forces the rest of us to exercise and that is beneficial for the whole family.

Health professionals should encourage parents to make the necessary effort to ensure healthy eating patterns and activity for their children. Help them to see that appropriate eating and activity are important for the long-term success of a child with an ASD. Talk with them about doing their part to eat in a healthy way and stay active both for themselves and their child.

PART 3

MEDICAL, SOCIAL, AND PSYCHOLOGICAL ISSUES

CHAPTER ELEVEN

How to Talk about Medical and Other Biological Treatments

As a practitioner working in the field of ASD, or even as a professional just seeing one family with a diagnosed child, it is important to be conversant with medical and other biological treatments for ASD. Generally speaking, there are no specific medical treatments for ASD. The diagnostic category is so broad, the problems so varied, and the probable etiologies so numerous, that no one treatment or even group of treatments will be generally applicable to all children.

However, there are treatments to address particular symptoms that a specific child demonstrates. We talked earlier about certain symptoms responding to behavioral interventions and speech, occupational, and physical therapies. So-called traditional medications prescribed by medical doctors can be helpful with symptoms. Complementary and alternative medications prescribed sometimes by medical doctors and sometimes by other practitioners can also help.

I am more comfortable with standard medical treatments for symptoms of ASD. However, my medical training and clinical experience over many years has reinforced my belief that both traditional and alternative treatments can be valuable adjuncts to relieve symptoms in these disorders. No treatments are curative. Standard medical treatments often carry risks of significant side effects. Alternative treatments may also have side effects, although they are generally no worse than the side effects of standard treatments, and sometimes they are less noxious.

Many families are referred to me for help after the child has already been diagnosed with an ASD. I am sometimes asked to confirm the diagnosis, but most times I am asked to help with symptoms or to evaluate the possibility of comorbid psychiatric disorders, such as attention deficit hyperactivity disorder (ADHD), bipolar disorder, depressive disorders, obsessive-compulsive disorders, Tourette's disorder, or others. With all of these disorders, however, just as with ASDs, the medical treatments I prescribe offer only symptomatic relief. Unfortunately there are few, if any, cures in psychiatry.

Many children are so hyperactive and inattentive they are unable to learn. Or they may be aggressive or self-injurious, so they are at risk of serious harm, either to themselves or others. Sometimes the family has tried formal behavioral interventions, sometimes not. Many times they have tried alternative treatments and have not found these helpful in decreasing symptoms.

My role is to listen to the family and to help them clarify and prioritize the symptoms. I try to understand exactly what is going on and what further exploration is needed. I make appropriate diagnoses and enumerate the symptoms. With the family's help, I suggest treatment possibilities to help decrease those symptoms.

Underlying everything I do, however, is the safety of the child. I always tell parents that the risk posed by the child's symptoms has to be greater than the risks posed by the possible medical or other biological treatment. I also expect any intervention to have robust benefits. If the side effects are overwhelming or if there are no substantial benefits, I recommend discontinuing treatment. I also work very closely with the family, and if possible the child, to make all treatment decisions.

What to Say to Parents

- *There is no cure for ASD.* I have made this statement before but I believe that it is worth reiterating when talking with families about medical and other biological treatments. More than a few parents believe that if their child has a diagnosis there should be a medication to fix it. Some of the complementary alternative treatments will claim to offer a "cure." I believe that it is important for parents to consider these treatments with their eyes open to possible problems and to have a clear understanding that while the treatments may help to eliminate symptoms, none of them can cure the disorder. Complementary and alternative treatments can include vitamin supplements, medications, antibiotics, antifungals, diet strategies, chelation/mercury detoxification, and non-biologic treatments for communication or sensory problems.

- *Medical and other biological interventions can help sometimes.* The fact that medical and other biological interventions will not *cure* ASD does not mean that the treatments don't help. Many of the treatments can effectively decrease symptoms and really improve the quality of life for the child with an ASD and the family. Professionals must weigh the benefits against the risks to decide whether to recommend a particular treatment to the parents.

- *Just because you start a treatment, you don't have to keep using it.* For some reason parents will often not begin a particular treatment because they are afraid that it won't work. They don't seem to fully understand that if a treatment doesn't help, or especially if it is hurting in any way, they can just stop it. There is no reason to continue with ineffective treatments. I think parents find it very empowering to hear, "Why don't you just stop?" They sometime feel guilty or compelled by obedience to a particular professional, to continue a treatment they feel is not helpful. They need to hear, "You can stop."

- *Using medical and other biological treatments does not mean you are a bad parent.* Many parents feel they have failed if they have to use medical and other biological treatments, especially if they are using medications. They think using medications means they cannot handle or discipline their child appropriately. Other people tell them they are "drugging their children." They even hear such nonsense from the media. Every family has to make its own decisions. I tell parents that it is never a sign of weakness to ask for help, and it is never bad parenting to accept help that is offered. On the contrary, asking for and accepting help shows how much they value their child's well-being. What better measure is there of being a good parent?

Questions Parents May Ask

- *If I want to consider using medical and other biological treatments, who should I see?* Parents should only see reputable practitioners licensed by the state. I also tell them to talk with people experienced with both the practitioners and the treatment. They should talk not only with people the practitioner recommends but they should also go online to local listservs or ask in local support groups about other parents' experience. Parents should always talk with their child's physicians and other treatment professionals before making a decision about treatment. They should have all their questions answered honestly and completely.
- *What if the treatment has side effects?* Parents need to understand that any medical and other biological treatment will likely have side effects. The parents and the practitioner have to weigh the side effects against whatever benefits the child experiences. If the side effects are too great or the benefits too small, then it is appropriate to discontinue the treatment.
- *If the child starts on medication will he or she always have to take medication?* Some medications may require long-term use for the benefit to continue. Most children will not take most medications for the rest of their lives. As situations change, treatment options broaden, and children's brains and bodies mature, so their

need for medication often changes. But some people do stay on a particular treatment for many years, especially if it is effective and the side effects are minimal.

Our Experience

We struggled with the question of whether to use medication to help Frankie with some of his symptoms. We finally turned to a medical doctor for help when it was clear that Frankie seemed to be miserable much of the time. His rigidity became so significant that transitions were impossible. His tantrums immobilized him any time we tried to move from one activity to another. He would cry hysterically if he was forced through an unfamiliar threshold or if he had to ride in an elevator. Day after day his tantrums and anxiety grew worse and more sustained. Although we were working with applied behavioral analyst (ABA) therapists, even these interventions did not seem to alleviate his overall level of distress.

We finally agreed to try a low dose of a selective serotonin medication, and within a couple of weeks he was much improved. He could go to preschool again and benefit from the ABA therapy. He seemed to suffer no significant side effects, and so far we have continued the medication. Over the years we have tried several times to decrease his dose or to wean him off of the medication altogether, but each time his anxiety and fear response return.

Frankie has been on the medication for seven years, and we have yet to see any serious side effects. But I remain vigilant and I worry that there may be something that just is not evident at this point. I do know, however, that without the medication Frankie is unable to function in a way that allows him the day-to-day freedom and joy he now experiences.

Mainstream Medical and Other Biological Treatments

Over the past few years increasing amounts of research have focused on understanding and treating ASD, but relatively limited research has explored medical and other biological treatments to alleviate symptoms. Some studies are planned or in progress. For the most part, few studies have been completed, and the number of children involved in each study has been small. The completed research studies have drawbacks in terms of application because of the diversity of population and etiologies of ASD. I will explain what has been helpful in my practice and what concerns me about the treatments. I also will discuss the different medical treatments based on the most common symptom clusters I am asked to treat with medications.

I find it frustrating that quite a few people—teachers, school psychologists, behavior specialists, other therapists, and even parents—assume that just because one can name a symptom or give a diagnosis, a medication will fix it. Unbelievably, many parents will bring me a note from a teacher or therapist saying the child needs a specific medication because of a specific problem. They assume that any "named" problem has a medication to make the problem go away or at least mitigate it. Many parents, teachers, and therapists become frustrated because they believe that if the child just had "the right" medication everything would be "fixed."

Unfortunately, there is rarely "the right" medication. Practitioners, parents, therapists, and families need to accept what benefit the medication provides and find other ways to address residual symptoms. I view medications as being a brace, or crutch, for symptoms. The medication does not fix the problem, but it brings the child some relief until specific behavior interventions can be devised. These behavior interventions relieve symptoms until the child's brain matures and the symptoms disappear or, at least, are less problematic.

Problems with Hyperactivity and Arousal Regulation

A common set of problems I see in children diagnosed with ASD is hyperactivity, arousal regulation, and inattention. These are very common symptoms in children with any brain disorders, as well as ASDs. When talking to parents about hyperactivity, arousal regulation, and inattention in a child with an ASD, it is important to convey to parents that these are just symptoms, which may or may not represent a diagnosis of attention deficit hyperactivity disorder (ADHD). When discussing possible medication, I believe it is most important to focus on the symptoms to be alleviated rather than the "true" diagnosis. A medication may alleviate these symptoms but no medication will fix or cure the problem—they generally cannot treat or correct the underlying dysfunction that is causing the symptom. So what can I offer as a medical doctor when I see a child with these symptoms? There are several options, but ultimately there is no guarantee any of them will work. It is complicated isn't it?

When I first see a child who presents with attention and arousal regulation problems and a diagnosis of an ASD, I try to make sure there are no clearly treatable conditions that could be causing the symptoms. For example, hyperthyroidism, mild iron deficient anemia, glucose regulation problems, or sleep apnea, among others, could cause or exacerbate the symptoms. I gather as much information as I can from those who spend time with the child each day. I want to have their input before and after we start any treatment. Then, based on the age of the child, I weigh the potential side effects, and considering the other symptoms that the child shows, I will prescribe a medication trial.

Any time I decide to use medications for any symptoms, I start a trial only after we have support in place for the parents through a therapist or family network. I also require some behavioral and environmental interventions in the home. These include no smoking in the family, very limited or no television, consistent bedtime and wake-up routines, an hour of outdoor activity each day, a diet high in protein and low in simple carbohydrates, as well as gathering the family for at least one meal together each day. I ask these behavior and lifestyle changes of families, regardless of the psychiatric diagnosis of the child. I have found over the years that these changes can be especially important in children with arousal regulation symptoms and other behavioral problems.

Regarding hyperactivity, arousal regulation, and inattention, what kind of medications do we try? In children below age 5 with ASD I will usually start treatment with a type of blood pressure medication called an alpha-adrenergic agonist. Basically, this is a class of medications that help to decrease the overall arousal level and sensitivity of the child's central and peripheral nervous system. It has the added benefit of increasing the brain function that maintains attention. My clinical experience has shown me that these medications are less likely to cause problems for these young children, and they are more likely to at least partially alleviate symptoms. They are generally safe, if monitored closely, and there is no evidence of serious long-term side effects. They make some children too drowsy, and other children's blood pressure drops so low that they cannot tolerate the medications. With these medications and many others, sometimes the child experiences an abnormal or even paradoxical reaction and has significant problems.

Other medications prescribed for these symptoms are stimulant medications. Ritalin and Adderall are commonly prescribed stimulant medications. They represent the two major categories of stimulant medication—methylphenidate and amphetamine salts. Ritalin is a methylphenidate product and Adderall is an amphetamine salt product. All of the stimulant medications now used for treatment of hyperactivity, arousal regulation, and inattention are methylphenidate, amphetamine salts, or a derivative of one of these compounds. These medications can be very effective in treating problems with arousal regulation as well as attention and concentration in children with ASD. However, they are not as effective in children with ASD as with children diagnosed with only ADHD. In typical ADHD these medications are effective in substantially reducing symptoms. In children with these problems and ASD they have been less effective in my practice. I have also found that in some children diagnosed with ASD these stimulant medications lead to problems with irritability and even greater hyperactivity.

Stimulant medications have side effects of decreased appetite and sleep disturbance. Both of these can be of significant concern to parents with a child diagnosed with an ASD. Many of these children already have problems with eating and sleeping. Another drawback is that stimulant medications only last a few hours, even when effective. The longest-acting formulations only work 12 hours and usually not that long. So these medications may be somewhat helpful in children with ASD, but there are serious considerations related to the age of the child and the other symptoms that he or she exhibits.

Some other medications can help with symptoms of hyperactivity, arousal regulation, and inattention, such as Strattera, a nonstimulant medication for treatment of problems associated with ADHD. Several antidepressant medications are sometimes used to treat these symptoms in children with ASD.

Tantrums and Aggressive Behavior

Another common symptom I am asked to treat in children with ASD is tantrums, with or without aggression. Probably more than any other symptoms, tantrums create heart-breaking problems for families. Tantrums often present together with other symptoms, such as arousal regulation, rigidity, restricted interests, and fixations/perseveration (see chapter 7).

Of course, many things that can lead to tantrums in general and tantrums in children with ASD at times seem to come from nowhere. There are, however, always triggers to the behavior. In my practice most children with ASD who exhibit tantrums respond well to behavioral interventions. As discussed earlier, behavioral interventions applied through the clinical intervention of a board certified applied behavioral analyst usually work the best. Many times this intervention alone will be sufficient to diminish symptoms or even extinguish the episodes. In most parts of the country families can locate a psychologist or a certified applied behavior analyst to evaluate and develop a behavioral treatment plan.

However, there are times when medications are needed to help with whatever neurological problem is sustaining the tantrum behaviors. The medications can serve as a brace or crutch to help until other therapies or maturity helps.

The alpha-adrenergic medications discussed above are blood pressure medications that often help with arousal regulation, but they will also help with tantrums. These medications seem to work by stopping the negative physiologic feedback loop that is seen in anger. When a child or anyone gets angry, the heart rate and blood pressure rise, breathing quickens as our bodies respond to the surge of adrenaline or epinephrine that courses through our bodies. These blood pressure medications and their close relatives, the beta-blockers, stop this autonomic surge and "take the steam" out of the anger. My clinical experience has shown me that both of these types of medications often reduce the frequency and the intensity of tantrums by about 50%. This drop is often enough to create room for the behavioral interventions to be helpful and further control the problem. Although these medications are effective, their side effects include sleepiness; and a decrease in blood pressure can also be significant. Of course, sometimes they just don't work. Every child is different and while there are general expectations about a particular medication's effect in a particular instance, physicians are not scientifically sophisticated enough to predict 100% of the time what a medication may or may not do to a particular child. We do not know the specific physiology and anatomy as minutely as we should in any individual to make that determination. We are getting closer with more sophisticated and complex genetic and other diagnostic tools but we are not there yet. That's hard for parents and other nonmedical professionals to understand.

The second group of medications that I consider for especially aggressive tantrums are medications known as neuroleptics. I most commonly prescribe Risperdal. The Food and Drug Administration (FDA) has approved it for treatment of people with autism who exhibit temper tantrums, irritability, aggression toward others, self-injurious behavior, and quickly changing moods. In fact, Risperdal is the only medication that has the nod from the FDA for the treatment of symptoms associated with ASD.

I have found Risperdal (risperidone) to be very effective in controlling problems with aggression and tantrums. Other neuroleptic medications are Zyprexa (olanzepine), Geodon (ziprasidone), Abilify (aripiprazole), Seroquel (quetiapine), Mellaril (thiopidazine), and Haldol (haloperidol), among many more. Be aware if using any of these medications about the serious potential side effects associated with their use. These side effects include significant and sometimes extreme weight gain and several other very serious potential problems. When children with ASD are placed on Risperdal (risperidone) or another of the neuroleptics, especially the so-called atypical neuroleptics (Zyprexa (olazapine), Geodon, Abilify (aripirazole), Seroquel (quetiapine), Risperdal (risperidone), carbohydrate craving can increase tremendously. This craving leads to increased calorie intake. If the caregivers are not especially careful, the increased calorie intake leads to weight gain. Increased problems with blood sugar and lipid/cholesterol regulation associated with Risperdal (risperidone) and this class of medications may or may not be associated with the increased appetite and weight gain. There is some indication that this may not be as true with Geodon (ziprazidone), but I have had patients who seemed to experience significant weight gain with this product as well.

Among the other side effects of this class of drugs, the most worrisome is the genesis of a movement disorder known as tardive dyskinesia, which causes the patient to have persistent, uncontrollable facial or body movements that generally do not go away when the medication is discontinued. The medications can also cause acute muscles spasms called acute dystonic reactions. These dystonic reactions can be very scary, and professionals unfamiliar with possible side effects of neuroleptics often confuse this with seizures or some other problem. All of the neuroleptic medications mentioned above have serious side effects, some more so than others. Some of these medications have additional serious side effects that differ from drug to drug. Very careful and thoughtful consideration must be given when using any of these medications. In my mind, it must be more dangerous for the patient to remain untreated before I can justify prescribing these medications. This risk–benefit analysis has to be done before prescribing, and be continually reviewed as long as the child or adult with ASD takes any of these medications.

Fixations, Rigidity, and Repetitive Behaviors

The medications that seem to help most with fixations and rigid, repetitive behaviors are selective serotonin reuptake inhibitors (SSRIs). These medications are often used to treat depression and obsessive-compulsive disorder. This group includes Prozac (fluoxetine), Zoloft (sertraline), Celexa (Citalopram), Lexapro (escitalopram), Paxil (paroxetine), and Luvox (fluvoxamine), among others. These medications help by decreasing anxiety in children with ASD. At times they also help to decrease rigidity and lessen fixations.

In my practice these medications are somewhat helpful. They tend to have few evident acute side effects and no known long-term side effects. I have used them to help decrease the frequency of tantrums and to try to decrease the day-to-day problems associated with an inability to let things go. However, these medications can cause an agitated or irritable state. Some children describe the sensation of wanting to crawl out of their skin, and they cannot stop pacing and moving. There can also be problems in children who have serious mood disorders where the mood appears manic. They experience irritability and agitation, often with nonstop talking and giddiness that can correspond to a decreased need for sleep. When these problems occur, the medications obviously have to be discontinued.

There are other medications that I have prescribed less often, but do so from time to time. In fact there are many other medications that are used to try to control serious symptoms in children with ASDs. There are times when I will use medications used to treat seizure disorders. I have also used the more powerful benzodiazepines to treat anxiety. On occasion I will prescribe an older antidepressant. It is critical, however, to understand and stress to parents that all medications have significant side effects to be considered when treating a child. None of them has specific application to ASD, and only Risperdal (risperidone) has an FDA-approved use for the disorder.

Many children with ASD are on multiple medications. Sometimes this seems necessary to help with the symptoms, but it is always a very difficult decision to place a child on medications with such significant side effects, especially when the medications are only helpful in controlling symptoms. They do not address the origin or cause of the problems at all. These powerful medications frighten most parents. They generally only ask for this kind of help when they feel there is nothing else to do. It is essential to help parents minimize the kinds and numbers of medications their child takes. The best way to limit this exposure to side effects is to keep parents involved in behavioral and other therapies that address the core disabilities of ASD more directly than do medication.

What to Say to Parents

- *Behavioral medications address symptoms but do not fix the problem.* This statement is a corollary to the statement that there is no cure for ASD. It is essential when behavioral medications are prescribed for a child that parents understand that the medication is simply an attempt to address symptoms that are debilitating to the child. The medications will not, and cannot, cure the underlying difficulties that led to the disability. Some therapies address the core symptoms more specifically than medications (e.g., behavioral therapy or teaching strategies) and make a long-term difference, but medications, for the most part, only work as long as they are taken.
- *Medications have serious side effects, but are sometimes worth the trade-off to make life better for the child and the family.* From

the beginning, I tell families clearly that all medications have side effects. Fortunately most children will not experience most side effects. I try to let parents know that "potential" side effects should not stop them from starting a medication trial unless the potential side effect for a particular child is too great a risk. In that case most practitioners would not prescribe it anyway. Practitioners should help parents weigh the risks and benefits. Sometimes it is best to take a risk, even a big one, if the potential payoff is a significantly better quality of life for the child and the family.

- *Medications should not be used alone, but always with other behavioral/educational therapies that address the core symptoms.* Families need to understand that behavioral medications and other medical and other biological treatments are just a small part of the overall treatment and intervention for problems associated with ASD. The behavioral, speech, occupational, even family therapies, and education are all part of the most effective treatment for these individuals. Medications should never be given simply to constrain a child chemically without other interventions. To do so is a disservice to the child and ultimately will not provide long-term symptom relief.

Questions Parents May Ask

- *Why should I consider using medication to treat my child's symptoms?* If a child's ASD has symptoms so significant that they severely impair the child's quality of life and threaten the stability of the family or the child's ability to live in the least restrictive environment, then medications should be considered. If a child with an ASD can't learn or benefit from behavioral or other therapies because of severe symptoms that interfere, then medications should be considered. If the child has another coexisting psychiatric disorder that might respond to medication then this should be part of the overall treatment plan.
- *Are these medications safe?* Most medications are extremely safe,

but some have more risks than others. I think it is important to help parents become educated about and good advocates for the safety of medications recommended for their child. They should ask if there are safer medications and what other medications might be appropriate. Parents should be encouraged to be informed, asking all of the questions they may have about a particular medication. While looking up medications on the Internet may be overwhelming and information overload, nonetheless it is a great tool for parents. A reasonable practitioner should be willing to answer any questions raised by even the most erroneous or misleading website, responding to parents based on his or her scientific knowledge of the treatment. If the practitioner is unable to do this, then parents should consider a different practitioner. Of course, paying attention only to the information on websites over the counsel of a licensed practitioner is not a reasonable course of action for parents to take. There are risks: For the most part medications are safe, but they do have potential for serious consequences. But so do many things that we believe are ultimately essential and important to our children's growth and development such as swimming, riding a bicycle, riding in a car or, especially, driving a car. It is important to put the medication risks in perspective.

- *How do I know whether to keep using the medications?* Every time parents see the practitioner who prescribes the medication they should discuss whether to continue with the treatment. Every visit includes an evaluation of the treatment along with the benefits and the risks. There should be discussion about the plan in the short and long term. Decisions about whether to continue a treatment should be made with the practitioner who prescribed the treatment. The only caveat to this is if a child appears to be acutely experiencing a harmful or life-threatening side effect and the practitioner does not seem to be responding to the parents. Then it is appropriate to stop the medication in an emergency consultation with another practitioner, perhaps the primary care practitioner.
- *Who should prescribe these medications?* I believe that behavioral

medications and mainstream medical and other biological treatments should only be prescribed by physicians licensed to prescribe and treat or licensed nurse practitioners or physician assistants working with licensed physicians. In most cases I believe that complicated behavioral medications, especially in the face of coexisting psychiatric problems, should be prescribed by a child psychiatrist experienced in treating individuals with ASD.

Our Experience

As I noted above, in our struggles with Frankie we have had to confront our fear of medication. Before we began using medication, he sometimes had several tantrums a day. They often lasted from several minutes to an hour. When the physician we were seeing suggested a selective serotonin reuptake inhibitor (SSRI), I was skeptical. Actually, at first I was absolutely opposed to using the medication, but as we continued to experience more and more problems with the tantrums, despite significant behavioral interventions, I relented. Frankie was started on a low dose of medication. Within just a few weeks his anxiety lessened and subsequently his behavior significantly improved. Despite our concerns about long-term use of the medication, over time he has not exhibited any significant side effects.

In addition to the SSRI, Frankie also takes medication for attention, concentration, and arousal regulation. Frankie has been in some sort of school placement since he was 18 months old. When he started kindergarten it quickly became clear that if he could just focus better and decrease his "fidgeting," he would be much more successful with his social interactions and his learning. Again, after we resisted for some time and tried other options, Frankie was placed on medications for these symptoms and he has found some relief. Granted, the relief is not as significant as we would expect in a typical child with ADHD, but he has responded enough that he is able with modification and assistance to spend time successfully in an integrated classroom setting at school. I continue to worry about Frankie being on the medication, but for now I will continue with these interventions because they appear to be helping him. I do, however, continue to weigh the risks and benefits and consider the analysis of whether the risks of being on the medication are less than the risk of being without it.

Alternative Medical and Other Biological Treatments

Many parents are drawn to complementary and alternative medical and other biological treatments. These treatments may or may not be prescribed by medical practitioners. There is significant debate about whether rigorous research techniques have been applied to test these interventions. Groups of practitioners, including some medical and osteopathic doctors, have formed associations to share information and strategies about alternative treatments. Some of these treatments do not address symptom reduction but claim to be curative in their application. There are multiple theories put forward as to why the symptoms present as they do. Some of these are related to toxin or allergen exposure. Others are related to problems associated with nutritional deficiencies or sensitivities of one form or another. Still other theories offer a hypothesis of errors in metabolism that lead to neurological dysfunction.

The idea seems to be that if you can correct the underlying problem then you can see a change in function. This proposition is reasonable, but the problem arises because there are so many different etiologies that lead to the set of problems we call ASD. Some of these interventions seem to make some difference for some children. However, I have found none that is curative. There are, however, claims of cure by some of the groups that promote these treatments. I have not witnessed any such cures. However, that being said, as long as the treatments are not harmful to the child or outrageously expensive, I generally do not discourage parents from trying different approaches.

I am neither an expert on any of these alternative treatments nor do I prescribe them for my patients. What I know about alternative treatments, I know through reading and from what parents have taught me.

I always try to keep an open mind when families are pursuing alternative treatments. I encourage parents to tell me what they are trying and how they perceive it to be working with their child. I have patients who try everything from gluten- and casein-free diets, mega vitamins, antifungals, and other dietary supplements, chelation of various types, and hyperbaric oxygen treatments. I encourage parents to be honest with me about the different interventions they try because the various alternative interventions can affect whatever I might prescribe to help alleviate symptoms.

I tell parents that they need to be sensible about the treatments. If I believe there are risks from a particular treatment in general or to a child specifically, I let the parents know. If the parents are overextending themselves financially, physically, or emotionally pursuing treatments in hopes of a miraculous cure, I let them know what I honestly think about their chances for success. I try to help them reflect on the risks and benefits in the same way I would do about treatments I prescribe. However, I am always careful to let them know that I am not an expert on the treatments, and ultimately, as long as I do not feel they are putting their child in serious immediate danger, the decision is theirs to make.

A couple of the alternative treatments I do routinely talk about in my practice include the use of melatonin for sleep and chiropractic care or acupuncture. Melatonin has made a big difference for some children with sleep disturbances, and I talk with parents about its success for some of my patients.

Several years ago I worked with a Chinese patient whose father wanted to pursue acupuncture as a way to reduce his son's need for medication to control anxiety and aggression. I reluctantly agreed to work with a practitioner, and to my surprise the boy improved. Over time we were able to take him off of the medication completely. I have since worked with other children who have had similar success.

Their ASD is by no means cured, but their symptoms have decreased. I have found similar reduction in symptoms for my patients working with particular chiropractic practitioners. When looking at acupuncture or chiropractic treatment, I strongly encourage the family to look for a practitioner who has experience working with patients with ASD. The practitioner also needs to be willing to work with me or their other medical practitioners involved in the patient's care. All of the practitioners need to work together and be respectful of what each has to offer. Also I remind parents to be concerned about any promises for dramatic improvement or cure and to be very careful about the risks and costs involved.

I am not able to say why acupuncture or chiropractic interventions work, and I do not know of research that validates these treatments. However, as with everything that I do as a practitioner, I try to follow evidence-based medicine when it can guide me, and at other times I turn to what might work if I can determine it will not cause harm. On the long road to finding answers for children and adults diagnosed with ASD and their families, I am unwilling to rule out any treatment unless it is clearly harmful. Additionally, if a treatment is patently unhelpful, or the people promoting the treatment are trying to exploit the hopes of people who aresuffering, then I warn the parents pursuing that particular treatment.

Secretin is a case in point. After initial indications that it might indeed be a miracle for children diagnosed with ASD, several studies, including Owley et al.'s (2001) indicated that it was no better than placebo in alleviating symptoms. Families spent tens of thousands of dollars pursuing this treatment, and at least in my clinical experience, no one who tried it found significant help.

What to Say to Parents

- *Complementary, alternative medical, and other biological treatments seem to relieve some symptoms.* I have witnessed what seem to be improvements in my patients from these treatments. However, the lack of accepted rigorous scientific research on these treatment protocols is a problem. There are also complementary alternative treatments that are simply not helpful and may be harmful. Families have to be very judicious and informed consumers about these treatments, and they should research them thoroughly as outlined above before proceeding. They should be especially aware of the credentials and reputation of the treatment provider. Advise them to verify those credentials through a state licensing agency.

- *Make sure all your treatment professionals, especially your physicians, know the treatments given your child.* Because of the negative stance of some mainstream treatment professionals against complementary alternative treatment professionals and vica versa, parents are not always completely open with either practitioner. It is absolutely necessary that families be completely honest with their practitioners. Not being honest could lead to serious, even deadly consequences for the child, due to the potential of negative interactions between medications and alternative or herbal treatments. If practitioners are unwilling to work together then the family should find different professionals who can.

- *Avoid treatments with high risks and high costs.* Many complementary alternative treatments are not covered by insurance (Medicaid, other state insurance programs or commercial). Parents should be cautioned against spending savings or borrowing money to pay for treatments for which there has been no rigorous scientific testing. Likewise, treatments that seem to carry inordinate risks—just as with mainstream medical and other biological treatments—are not reasonable options for treatment.

- *If you feel as though you are talking to a salesman you probably are.* I tell parents all the time that if they feel they are being sold a used car they probably are. The key to assessing any treatment is caveat emptor (let the buyer beware) and this is very true when dealing with practitioners and treatments outside the mainstream. People can make extraordinary promises of improvement or even cure if you only pay this much down and so much per month. Parents should be told to be very skeptical.

- *You don't have to pursue every treatment option.* I believe that it is important to give parents the permission to not pursue every treatment that promises to cure or make a big difference in the life of their child with an ASD. Families can spend too much time and far too much money trying to find the "silver bullet." Sometimes parents need to come to a reasonable acceptance of their child's disabilities and appropriate expectations. This does not mean parents should stop trying to improve the quality of life for their child or their family, but it means that sometimes improving the quality of life for the child and family means not pursing the latest, "greatest" treatment.

Questions Parents May Ask

- *Are complementary, alternative medical, and other biological treatments safer than mainstream medical and other biological treatments?* For some reason many people believe herbal or alternative treatments are safer than mainstream medications or medical and other biological treatments. This may or may not be true. Most medications prescribed by a medical practitioner are approved by the U.S. Food and Drug Administration as a pharmaceutical agent, having met generally very rigorous scientific standards for safety. However, only Risperdal has an indication for use with children who has ASDs. So questions about safety are reasonable. Nonpharmaceutical agents prescribed by practitioners using complementary alternative treatments generally do not have FDA approval as a medical treatment, and they may only meet minimal standards for safety. Again, it is very critical for the parents to research the treatments suggested by any practitioner and to ask hard questions about safety and risks.

- *Are complementary, alternative medical, and other biological treatments more effective than mainstream medical and other biological treatments?* They are not generally more effective but there may be some complementary alternative treatments that work well for a particular child who has not responded to mainstream treatments. Because of the wide variability of difficulties and etiologies of ASDs there is absolutely no one-size-fits-all treatment.
- *Can I use mainstream and complementary alternative treatments together?* Parents can use mainstream and complementary alternative medications together, but they should be totally honest with all their practitioners about what they are doing so as to keep their child safe. Practitioners should be willing to work together, and professionals should encourage parents to be open and honest.

At the end of the day, as a parent with a child diagnosed with an ASD, I want know that I did all I could to help my child. I want to know that I pursued all possible reasonable treatments. I want to try and make the best decisions based on the information available to me, knowing that I must weigh risks and benefits. I know the risks include not only physical risks to my child, but emotional and financial risks to him and our family. Some, if not most, of the time weighing all of the options is overwhelming, and there is not a day that goes by when I do not wonder whether I have made the right decision. I do my best in consultation with my spouse and others who love my son, as well as the experts who counsel us. This is all I or any other parent can do. It may lead to many sleepless nights and days of worry, but as a friend of mine once told me "that is what parenting is all about."

CHAPTER TWELVE

How to Talk about Family Stressors

Surviving and thriving as a family these days is tough in the most ideal situations. Raising a child with ASD adds stress that many families do not survive intact. Those families that do stay together face struggles and challenges that may seem never ending and overwhelming.

It is difficult to imagine the continual stress, worry, and fear families experience unless you are close to or the member of the family of a child with ASD. Even so, as a professional working with children and families, by keeping your mind open and listening beyond the actual words expressed, you can do a great deal to help families survive and grow.

When a young child is first diagnosed with ASD, parents' feelings are often extreme. As I tried to illustrate in the first chapter, many of the feelings may be irrational. Under the stress of this diagnosis most parents find their usual emotional defenses inadequate, and they often experience more visceral feelings and behaviors. They may isolate or withdraw. They may deny the problem. They may use work, eating, shopping, caretaking, or more negative compulsive behaviors such as substance abuse, gambling, or sexual behaviors as escapes. There is often chronic, sometimes debilitating sadness and even clinically significant depression. Parents may argue more. They may reject offers of help or become too needy and appear paralyzed. Many experience a devastating crisis of faith that leaves them without a religious support that had previously offered comfort and hope.

Fear of the future often overwhelms parents when they first receive the diagnosis. Most parents faced with raising a child with ASD have no frame of reference. Most did not grow up in a family with a disabled child, and few know anyone intimately who did. Many parents now raising a child with ASD have never known a person with disabilities. Moreover, there is no peer reference because, until recently, most schools separated children with disabilities from mainstream students.

The prospect of living with and raising a child with ASD is a terrifying unknown. Few parents know where to start. Until the diagnosis most families have been at least partially in denial, raising their child like any other child.

With the diagnosis, parents realize their child has special needs which require them to change their parenting approach, but they have no one to tell them how. Most grandparents have little experience to offer. Most ministers are at a loss. Even the family's own primary care physician may not be helpful.

Families usually begin by seeking help from the professional or agency that makes the diagnosis. It is essential they find other parents of children with ASD. The families who thrive are those who reach out for help from other families at the very start. They draw on the tremendous, powerful support of others who have traveled the same or a very similar road. For our family the support of other families struggling with similar issues and concerns was life-saving.

Of course, not all families are overwhelmed at the diagnosis. Some families are so extraordinarily resilient that they experience few of the problems mentioned above. However, in my clinical experience, all the families that are raising a child with ASDs come to some point of crisis where support from professionals, other families, or both is essential.

So what do families need to survive? First, they need information. They may not be ready for all the information that you can give them or all that they could find, but they need basic information. Sometimes this information should come from the professional making the diagnosis. This person, one hopes, has years of experience working with these children, and based on the presentation, can give parents some clues about what to expect, at least in the short term. If not, the professional should refer the family quickly to a professional with this knowledge. While prognosis for children long-term may be difficult, most professionals can inform parents' about what to expect for the next four to five years.

When I am working with families, I usually talk about the next two to three years with pretty good confidence about what needs to be done and what to expect. For the years immediately after that and into adulthood, I try to give worst-case and best-case scenarios so that the parents can at least start to think about what their life might look like in the future. Of course, I always say that no one knows, but I want them to at least have heard the possibilities so that they can file those away to consider as they are able.

After the parents are armed with some information about possible problems with ASDs, I try to get them involved with at least one other family that is experiencing similar difficulties but is further along in raising a special needs child. I try to match the families one to one, or if the parents will attend, I send them to a support group. Many communities have at least one support group for parents of children with disabilities, and many have support groups specifically for families of children diagnosed with ASDs. I also try to get parents to join at least one listserv for families with children diagnosed with ASD. Local or national autism support or information websites often link to these listservs. Even if parents have no computer at home, they at least can set up a free e-mail account with providers such as Google or Yahoo using a computer at the local public library. Then they can monitor the listserv discussions, access important resources, and ask questions if they wish.

What to Say to Parents

- *Nearly every parent of a child with a significant disability feels overwhelmed and confused at first.* It is important to normalize for parents their sense of being overwhelmed. It is probably reasonable to say that the feelings of being overwhelmed and confused will come and go over time. Normalizing this for parents lets you begin to talk with them about the kinds of things that they can do to help take care of themselves. It also gives them permission to not feel as though they should have all of the answers or know what to do.

- *Managing your fears and anxieties will go a long way in helping you cope with and enjoy your life.* Parents need to be encouraged to find ways to help manage their fears and anxieties. Things that I have found helpful for myself and for other parents include: making time for themselves even if it is 30 minutes at the beginning or end of the day; exercising if just for 20 minutes; finding time to meet and talk with a group of friends; finding a good therapist; writing down thoughts and feelings in a journal; talking with other parents of children with ASDs; and making time for vacations without the children. These and other strategies can be helpful to suggest to parents.

- *Build connections to other family, friends, and parents experienced in caring for a child with a disability.* Explain to parents that while they may need intense help and support at first, as they gain experience and confidence they can give support and guidance to others. It is a blessing to have friends who can truly understand their experience of raising a child with ASD or some other disability. More experienced parents can give help to parents with younger children, and as their child grows, those parents in turn have the opportunity to help others. Being part of an understanding and caring community where the parents can take what they need and offer what they have makes a big difference to parents who can then feel that they have some control in a life that often feels significantly out of control.

- *Take care of yourself, then your child, and your family.* As I indicated above, parents need to find time for themselves. It is good, however, to reiterate that this means they should take care of themselves first. I discussed this in an earlier chapter but you cannot repeat it often enough. If parents cannot take care of themselves they will not be able to offer care for the other family members, including the child with ASD.

Questions Parents May Ask

- *Will my child always need this vast amount of time and attention?* This is a tough question because there are some children who will always need very intense care. Others will grow and be more independent, but not quite as independent as their typical peers. Over time parents can learn strategies and develop networks with social agencies, school, and friends that allow for less intense attention and time from them to personally take care of their child.
- *It seems like our whole lives revolve around the needs of my child with an ASD. Does it have to be this way?* The life of the entire family does not have to revolve around the child with an ASD, but the nature of the illness is such that it will always require more energy and effort to shift the focus of the family. Special care will need to be taken to make sure that the child with an ASD is accommodated. This often makes it feel that every event and every decision requires special accommodation, and the truth is that it does. However, that does not mean that other family members' needs and concerns are not also taken into consideration. Just as the family compromises around the needs of others to accommodate the child

with ASD, there should be times when the needs and concerns of the child with ASD are compromised because of the needs of other members of the family. For example, the family may go away on a vacation without the child with ASD, leaving him or her with grandparents. Or, parents may decide to reschedule therapy appointments or not pay for an experimental treatment, so that they might be able to provide music or sports lessons for a talented sibling.

- *Our friends want to help, but they are put off, or their children won't play with our child. We feel so alone. What can we do?* The first message you can give to parents who bring you this question is that talking about the pain and loneliness is the first step toward trying to find a place where they can feel welcome and fit in. Just as with other events in the life of a family, friendships and social supports shift. As a child with ASD grows, friendships shift and parents can maintain relationships with friends who are supportive, to the extent that is possible. But it is also very important to find new friends and develop new relationships with people who can include and embrace the whole family, including the child with ASD. It is also important for them to find children who can be friends with and be a part of the child's life.

- *I go back and forth between despair that things will never get better and great hope that we can find a cure. Do other parents feel this?* Every parent with a child with any disability feels this way. Additionally, they are also always wondering if the cure is out there, but "we just aren't looking in the right place." It is the very rare parent who is so realistic and stable that he or she does not vacillate between irrational hope and unmitigated despair. Having friendships with other parents of children with disabilities helps to normalize this roller coaster and keeps parents feeling less overwhelmed, guilty, and alone.

- *We're scared we don't have the money to give our child the treatment she needs. Is there help?* In most, but not all places there are resources available through state, state sponsored service organizations, and nonprofit groups and foundations. Not all of these resources are available to all families, and some communities and state governments are more generous than others. Trying to find money for treatment is one of the most frustrating tasks parents and professionals working with children with ASD face. Each state has its own set of entitlements, as well as a unique set of rules and requirements about how to access those entitlements. Professionals working with families need to explore the rules of their particular state by contacting the state agencies that deal with children and adults with developmental disabilities. Additionally, they should contact local nonprofit resources, such as the local or state chapter of the Autism Society of America, to determine what other resources are available in their community. That being said, families can spend fortunes on treatments and interventions that ultimately are not helpful. It is important to work closely with families to make sure the money they are spending, whether theirs or from some other source, is appropriately and reasonably spent. Not only does the issue of the money come into play but also the appropriateness of the treatment, the safety and the time and energy necessary to pursue the treatment. In the end families do what they can do, and it is important to help them accept what is and is not possible.

Surviving as a Couple

Ideally, parents (if there are two parents) will both gather information and connect to support systems. However, I know from clinical experience that rarely do both parents take on these tasks. Most times, by necessity, one parent shoulders the task of coordinating all of the information and interventions. This approach often leaves one parent feeling overwhelmed, but the "expert," and the other parent feeling left out and vulnerable to accusations and guilt about being "less dedicated" or "committed" to the child. Even for couples with a strong relationship, this arrangement is difficult. If there are already strains in the relationship, this division of labor for the child with ASD can precipitate a complete breakdown of the marital relationship.

I believe it is essential from the very beginning to work with parents to shore up their relationship and to help them develop strength as a couple. As they go forward as a family raising a child with ASD, they will need that strength and more. Soon after the diagnosis, most parents should meet with a family counselor or social worker to begin to talk about their feelings about the diagnosis, their child, their marriage, and family. A family counselor can help establish a solid base for the family to grow stronger and care for the child with ASD. It is important to try anything to help parents survive as a couple. It is always better to have two parents raise a child with ASD simply because of the heavy demand for caregiving and the physical, financial, and emotional support it requires. I know many wonderful single parents who are doing an excellent job raising a child or children with ASD or other disabilities, but I believe most of them would agree that having two parents would make things much better for them and their child/children.

In family counseling one of the most important issues parents must solve at the beginning is the division of labor to care for their child with ASD. Dividing the myriad of different parenting and management tasks necessary for care is very important. Unless from the beginning a division of labor can be established that allows both parents to feel involved and useful in making a difference for their child, then a distance will grow between them that over time becomes almost impossible to traverse.

Not surprisingly, since the mother usually takes the role of primary caretaker in families without disabilities, this predisposes her to assume this role with a child with ASD. If she has a job or career, she may be unable to keep working. There are a multitude of therapy appointments and meetings. The child with ASD usually cannot endure a typical daycare setting, and many times there are no other options for daycare. Appropriate early intervention programs rarely last the whole day, so parents face transportation and aftercare needs.

During holidays and other days off school, the child with ASD usually cannot tolerate interim daycare settings. A parent or other caregiver familiar and adept with the child's needs will have to care for him or her at these times. If the family is lucky, sometimes extended family members can help with child care. Dual-career couples have long been challenged to juggle work, housekeeping, after-school care, and summer/holiday child care for typical children. Raising a child with ASD is at least double this commitment.

While physically taking care of the child, sacrificing a job or career, and coordinating the intensive interventions, the primary caretaker (usually the mother) becomes the expert. She becomes the expert on the disorder in general and on her child specifically. She keeps and manages all of the important information about treatments, behaviors, other interventions, and resources. This role gives the mother tremendous power and a tremendous burden.

The other parent (usually the father) often feels left out and pushed aside. I have spoken with many fathers who come to feel their only role is to ensure that financial resources are adequate to keep the family going. This becomes doubly difficult when the primary caretaker gives up a job to take care of the child with ASD. Fathers often complain they feel unsupported and isolated because they lack the time to be more involved and they usually know far less than the mother does about what is going on with their child. Moreover, because the mother's emotional energy and time can be monopolized by the child with ASD, there is no emotional room left for the parents to relate as a couple. This dynamic also creates problems for siblings, as will be discussed later in this chapter.

So, the mother is emotionally and physically overwhelmed, and the father is bereft emotionally and physically. Each moves in different directions to care for the family. The job of the couple and family therapist is to divide the tasks of raising their child with ASD so each parent has a direct role in parenting, they work closely as a couple, and the family survives financially. This adjustment in roles takes creativity and demands flexibility and open communication. Parents will likely have to stretch to do tasks which may be uncomfortable at first. Each family creates its own solution. It may mean each parent works part time and then take turns going to meetings or therapy appointments. It is very important to copy both parents on all communications about the child and that decisions about interventions, treatments, and placement are shared.

As important, if not more so, is setting aside time for the parents to be a couple. Individually each parent needs a break, but they also need time just to be with each other. The parents need to be as disciplined about taking this time together as they are about pursuing the most appropriate options for their child. A good therapist can help families accomplish these goals and address underlying problems in the relationship that may threaten to split them. As I noted above, careful attention needs to be paid to these fault lines because the strain of raising a child with ASD can certainly increase pressure on the parents and their relationship to where they are at a snapping point.

What to Say to Parents

- *Couples should take time to plan how to care for their child in a way that keeps them both connected and informed. Be prepared to change the plan as needed.* Finding a way to divide the tasks and facilitate the communication about the major enterprise that is taking care of a child with ASD is essential to keep one parent from feeling overwhelmed and the other from feeling completely excluded. Nothing will destroy a marriage quicker or make life more difficult for the whole family than ignoring this crucial step in caring for a child with ASD.

- *Give yourself and your spouse times off.* Encourage parents to take time individually and together for their own rejuvenation. Even if it is only for a few minutes or a few hours, the time is essential. Here again it is important to establish a network of support that allows parents a respite. Beyond not sharing the responsibilities and communicating about the issues involved in raising a child with an ASD, remaining isolated and having no one to provide respite puts another major stress on a family. Even if there are few economic resources, if there is a sense that one or both parents "never have time off," then there will be serious problems maintaining a healthy balance in the family and between the couple.

- *Don't try to be perfect or selfless. You will burn out.* Remind parents that they will not be able to be perfect parents. Remind them that they cannot be totally selfless or live their life only for their child, children, spouse, or family. First, being the perfect or perfectly selfless parent is impossible, and second, trying will rapidly lead to feelings of guilt and shame that are of no help to anyone, least of all the child with ASD. Remind parents that no one is keeping score and that few, if any, are judging them. If people are judgmental, then those critics need a better pastime—and perhaps a role can be found for them supporting the family or specifically the child with ASD. Help parents to be gentle with themselves and with one another. That is the only way they can survive the very long road of taking care of a child who needs so much.

- *Work to minimize and resolve conflicts in your family as they arise. Being busy is an easy excuse to avoid dealing with issues. Left unaddressed, they will drain you and your partner's energy and joy while adding stress and frustration.* Help parents to make a rule that nothing should be left unsaid before going to bed each evening. Every couple deserves the opportunity to start each day fresh. If there are things that cannot be resolved before bedtime, help couples find a way to set them aside until they can deal with them later with the help of a therapist or another close advisor. Maybe the parents would be amenable to setting up a time to "talk things through." Help them realize that by finding creative ways of talking through issues and communicating effectively they will not only have a more satisfying relationship and a more peaceful family, but it will also be helpful for the child with ASD.

- *Be patient and kind with yourself and one another. This kind of adjustment takes a long time, maybe years. But it can only be lived a day at a time. Find simple things that make you strong and bring true delight and joy.* Talk with families about enjoying the small successes and the peaceful times. While they need to keep an eye on the future, help them to work with each other to avoid becoming overwhelmed with what tomorrow might or might not bring. Help them to live in the day, so whether it is horribly stressful or incredibly joyful and peaceful they have the experience in that day and then move on to the next. Talk with them about taking deep breaths and letting go of all of the things that they cannot control; help them to laugh at the absurdities that are everywhere when raising a child with ASD in a world of "neurotypicals."

Questions Parents May Ask

- *My wife and I seem to be tense and angry. I know I feel afraid a lot—afraid about money, work, and doing the wrong thing for my child. What can I do?* Most parents' and couples' coping mechanisms are overwhelmed by the experience of raising a child with ASD. Raising any child with a disability accentuates all of the natural fault lines and rifts in a relationship. Even the best relationships suffer under the strain, and those built on less than solid ground probably will not last. Couples need help beyond themselves. They need the help of professionals who understand the stresses of families dealing with a chronically ill child, and they need the support of other families living through the stressors they are handling. Tell parents to find help. Let them know it is okay to admit they are overwhelmed and feel helpless in the face of this devastating disorder. It is okay to cry "uncle" and seek relief.
- *We have so much to do to care for our child and make a living. My wife and I don't have any mental or emotional problems, so why do we need family therapy?* Raising a child with ASD and

keeping a family intact is impossible without help and community. Therapy is not the only way to get that support, but therapy is generally a quick way to work through issues in the short run that if left unattended will affect the couple, the family, and the child for a long time to come. Getting therapy is not about being crazy or even mentally ill, it is about being smart enough to know when help is needed and having the sense to get it.

- *I'm a private person. Why should I talk about personal things to complete strangers just because we both have a child with the same disability?* Tell parents they are not going to like every other parent who has a child with ASD. They are not going to make friends with people with whom they have no other common ground. However, I have for years now sat in rooms with families and people very different from me who were talking about their experiences with raising their child with ASD. I almost always learn something new or feel connected in a way that I did not expect. A friend of mine told me one time, "You never know what bozo is carrying the message that you need to hear today. If you don't hang out with the bozos you may just miss your message." While most of the people I encounter each day are not generally "bozos" this has been very good advice and helped me more times than I can count.

- *Since the diagnosis, and my wife quitting her job, it seems like everything is falling apart. How can we start to put it back together?* Parents can work with a therapist or with clergy to try and piece back together a torn relationship and family. Finding ways to share the burden and open communication is the only way to survive. Sometimes just sharing how difficult things are and talking about the enormous burdens is enough to help with the healing. However, sometimes you have to talk with families about whether it makes sense to put everything "back together." Sadly, sometimes the best thing to do is to figure out if the best way to survive as parents caring for a child with ASD is to remain parents but not a couple. Again, working with a social worker or other family therapist is important to help make sure that, regardless of what happens, the family regains some stability. This is essential for the long-term care of the child with ASD and indeed the welfare of any children.

- *I just can't accept my child is like this. My spouse seems to be able to love him as he is. What's wrong with me?* I have had parents talk to me in hushed, guilty whispers about resenting their child and all that he or she demands because of the illness. They will also sometimes talk about being unable to accept the child with ASD because they feel that if they do they will be somehow accepting autism as being "okay." They desperately want everything to be "normal," and as irrational as it is, sometimes they blame the child for not being "normal." As you talk with parents who are courageous enough to share these feelings, help them to understand that the feelings are natural for people placed in situations and circumstances where their typical coping mechanisms, experiences, and expectations of life are overwhelmed. Tell them they are courageous and strong, and there is nothing ever wrong with feeling this way or that. The only wrongs come from not dealing with feelings in a healthy and appropriate fashion. Help them to walk through their complex feelings for their child and for the disorder. Help them to separate their child from the disorder and from the struggles that the disorder creates in the child's life and the family's life. Help the parents talk together about their feelings, if possible, and work with them or find someone to work with them to support each other and handle all the crazy feelings that come up when life is difficult.

Siblings

Siblings of a child diagnosed with ASD also have distinct stressors and issues triggered by this disability. For most siblings their family is their "normal." Most siblings simply accept their brother or sister. Depending on the parents' ability to encourage and create a role for them as being supportive, loving siblings, their engagement with the family and their commitment to their sibling with ASD is generally strong. While they may occasionally compare their own family to one without a child with ASD, they rarely dwell on it.

For siblings to feel connected and important to the family, they need a clear role. This gives them the validation of being important and able to make a difference for the family and their sibling. That role, however, should not be totally directed at the child with ASD nor become that of a surrogate parent. Brothers and sisters need to understand the importance of their love and support for their affected sibling and how their part in the family's social and emotional network helps the sibling with ASD relate to and understand the world. I have seen siblings play an essential role in opening up a world of possibilities for their sibling with ASD.

Unfortunately, I have also seen families where siblings have been kept at a distance from the child with ASD, so that there is no strong relationship. Or siblings have become resentful when they have been burdened with a primary caretaking role for the child with ASD. Even more often, I have seen siblings marginalized in the family, almost left to raise themselves because their parents' time and energy is so absorbed by the brother/sister with ASD.

Having a sibling with ASD potentially brings increased awareness of the world and its diverse people, and it can help a child mature into a loving caring adult; but there are costs. Many times children who have a sibling with ASD realize that the family's financial hardship limits resources because of the costs of raising the special needs child. The siblings might miss important opportunities or events because of problems with their brother/sister. Parents might be unable to volunteer or attend school, sporting, or other activities and events because of the child with ASD. Just as parents make sacrifices, there are tremendous costs to the siblings as well. Most parents do their best to give their other children enough time, money, emotional energy, and patience, but that does not fully mitigate the fact that it takes many more resources to raise a child with ASD than a typical child. Parents often struggle with guilt when they see they are coming up short in time, energy, and patience, not to mention money.

At times there can be significant emotional/behavioral problems in typical siblings as they act out their feelings about having a sibling with ASD. They often benefit from meeting with a family counselor to look at how siblings are included, cared for, and receive parenting. Siblings who are older when the child is diagnosed with ASD should be given information appropriate to their developmental level. Siblings who are younger than the child with ASD should be given information that is developmentally appropriate for them so that they can understand their sibling's diagnosis, abilities, and disabilities as they mature.

In many areas there are support groups for siblings of special needs children and even specific groups for siblings of children with ASD, just as there are support groups for parents. Sometimes there are even special overnight activities or camps for siblings. These activities allow for ongoing support and development of the nonaffected sibling. Ultimately, these supports work to make the family strong, helping all of the children grow to meet their potential. These supports are important, because in families where there is a child with ASD, long-term care for the affected individual will most likely mean that the whole family continues to be involved for many years past childhood.

In many families of adults with moderate to severe ASD, the siblings serve as backup supports to the parents. When the parents die, the typical children often take over as primary guardians or support for their brother or sister. If there are unresolved family problems related to the affected child these later caretaking roles for typical siblings and their affected brother/sister can be much more difficult and fraught with emotions and potential acting out that leads to problems for all the parties involved.

What to Say to Parents

- *Create a role for your other children in the family to ensure they stay connected and understand they are loved and valued.* Help families to work together to keep the whole family and household running as smoothly as possible. Divide responsibilities for all of the needs of the family and give those to each of the members, including the typical siblings and the sibling with ASD. Work with each of the children to find their particular gift or joy and help them to pursue that joy; carve out time just for them. Spend time together as a family as often as possible. Spend at least one meal together each day. Check in with one another every morning and every evening. Laugh together and point out accomplishments and strengths for everyone every day. When necessary point out struggles that each person is experiencing, even the parents as appropriate. Share the joys and the worries, again as is appropriate to the developmental ability of the children. When necessary, help families find a therapist or outside professional to help get things back on the right track. Support them in not being afraid to ask for help.

- *Being present and loving with all of your family is the most valuable gift you can give. Don't let the "to do" list of appointments and therapies rob you of that quality time.* It seems all families these days have an unending "to do" list and this can especially be true for families with a child who has ASD. There are always therapies, tasks, forms, and meetings, and that can overwhelm the family. It is important to work with families to help them triage what is and what is not essential, important, and even worthwhile. Carving out time each day, and days at a time on occasion, to spend together is essential to the health of the family. It provides a forum for connection and a place to discuss good things and troubling things. Time together to enjoy each other provides the backbone for solid relationships when things get really tough.
- *Start writing everything down and ask others to do the same.* Sleep loss and exhaustion wreak havoc on the memory. A whiteboard on the refrigerator and a family calendar used by all can be a lifesaver. Note doctor and therapy appointments, as well as the other children's activities, to make visible the range of family activities and avoid "I forgot!" Teaching family members to write grocery and toiletry items on a "Shopping section" makes it easy for either

partner to know what's needed on a run to the store. To involve extended family, make sure everyone has an e-mail address and copy them on correspondence with schools and therapists, or information you may find on listservs. Keep a running list for yourself that you can update easily throughout the day, noting new items as they crop up. Reduce stress by creating a routine for chores such as filling the car with gas, taking out the trash, paying bills. Write out a schedule for home maintenance, and similar things to prevent them being pushed back week after week, only to ambush you when you least expect it.

Questions Parents May Ask

- *What will this do to my other child or children? I have heard it said that the best thing a family with a child with ASD child can do is to have another child.* The theory is that having a typical child paired with a child who has ASD will provide the typical role model that will help to decrease the autistic symptoms of the affected child. So one can make the argument that typical children are good for the child with ASD, but what about the typical children? Is having a child with ASD good for typical children? Whether having a sibling with ASD is generally a positive experience depends to a great degree on how the family is able to integrate all of the children into a cohesive whole. For children who are part of the family and part of the blessings and troubles of living with someone with ASD, my experience has been that they benefit significantly from being part of that process. They learn to accept people with differences. They learn a lot about themselves and they gain skills that they would not have otherwise developed. So having a sibling with ASD can be a very positive experience, if the parents can structure it effectively.
- *How do we make sure we are being good parents to our other children?* If parents feel they are failing their other children, help

them to find a family therapist to work through the issues that are of concern to them. If family members have concerns, take their worries seriously. If nothing else, family therapy for a brief period will give the parents a chance to learn how to communicate effectively enough with one another to get a sense of what is going on with their other children. Extended family and other families with typical children and children with disabilities can also be a good source to gauge what is and is not all right with the family and the attention and care the typical children are receiving.

- *Does this mean we give up on a college education for our other child?* The answer to this question will obviously depend on a lot of factors, but the short answer is no. Of course the college education might not be what the parents dreamed it would be, but then there are a lot of life's circumstances that might change that dream. Helping parents to plan as early as they can will be an aid in keeping this dream alive for all of the children.

- *My other child says we ignore her. She's threatening to run away, and she was caught shoplifting last week.* Help the parents determine if there is any serious psychiatric disorder present and if the problems are related to acting out emotional hurts and difficulties associated with being part of a family under stress that may or may not be partly related to having a sibling with ASD. Help the family to find a good family therapist and a reasonable individual therapist for the acting out child. In the hands of a good family therapist the acting out can be recognized for what it is and be a true growth experience for the typical child and the whole family.

Extended Family

Sometimes extended family is a godsend, and sometimes the close involvement of extended family can be very problematic for the family raising a child with ASD. Grandparents, aunts, and uncles as well as other relatives can provide much-needed support and backup.

Many times these relatives are the only other adults beyond the parents who understand and accept all the idiosyncrasies the child brings to any situation. Grandparents or other family members can provide much-needed respite for the parents to be alone or for the family to attend an event for another child in the family that would be too stressful for the child with the disorder. Extended family members can help with transporting a very hyperactive, anxious, or aggressive child to therapy or doctor appointments. Extended family can also be a refuge when parents or siblings are emotionally drained or overwhelmed by the difficulties of living with a family member diagnosed with an this disorder.

The extended family that is constantly criticizing or second-guessing what parents are trying to do for their child can be a major stressor. Or even worse, some extended family members will disregard therapeutic interventions that have been carefully established. They undermine the treatment by not following through. A long history of family difficulty and dysfunction usually compounds the problem.

My solution to issues associated with extended family is to always try to include them in developing and implementing interventions as much as they are willing to become involved. I also recommend family therapy for the extended family, especially to work on entrenched issues that predate the birth and diagnosis of a child with ASD. Some families are amenable to these suggestions, and others are not. The point is to arm the parents with as much information as possible about the disorder and the difficulties unique to raising a child it so the extended family can play a helpful role. I also encourage the extended family to learn as much as they can learn about ASDs in general and their particular child's problems specifically.

Most families agree that having support available can be very important to nurturing a healthy family where everyone is growing to his or her potential. Especially in families where there is a single parent raising a child with ASD, an extended support network of family or others can mean all the difference in the long-term prognosis for the child. My clinical experience has shown me that the more support and resources are available in the early years to a child with this disorder, the more independent the child will be and he or she will require fewer resources later in life.

What to Say to Parents

- *Involve your extended family if at all possible.* Parents of a child with ASD often close in on themselves and they may not reach out to other families. They may not even reach out to their own families, and when they do they may be met with denial about the extent of the problem or the difficulty of the tasks involved in raising the child. They may, however, be met with acceptance and an offer to help in whatever way is necessary. Either way it is important to encourage families to engage their extended family in the experience and care of their child. Sometimes this might mean addressing longstanding family difficulties from the past. Other times it might mean dealing with issues that have arisen since adulthood or marriage. Sometimes it might turn out to be an unhealthy or unwise effort, but I encourage families with children with ASD to at least make the effort and to have the discussion. In the long term it will be very important to have all of the resources that they can muster.

Questions Parents May Ask

- *My in-laws think our child with ASD needs more discipline and just acts out for attention. They won't follow the behavioral intervention plan. What can I do?* Help get the extended family engaged in the behavioral plans and therapies that the family is utilizing for their child. Have the child's immediate family invite their extended family to therapy sessions and doctors' appointments to discuss their concerns. Have the families share literature they have been given or even invite extended family members to support groups or on to listservs. All of these tactics can be helpful in show-ing an extended family exactly what kind of problems the child and immediate family is experiencing.

Our Experience

As I wrote earlier, I was very shaken by Frankie's diagnosis. Even though I knew at the time what the diagnosis would be, hearing the words and actually facing the future was crushing. My first response to that diagnosis was to completely withdraw. I wanted to avoid the diagnosis altogether. I felt alone and abandoned. I did not feel my spouse could support me. Since I had the background and training, I felt like the entire job of "making this right" fell to me.

Of course, I was being neurotic and feeling sorry for myself. I was not looking at things objectively, realistically, and certainly not hope-fully, but I understand that I tend to be a worst-case scenario person. As perverse as it may sound, if I can see how absolutely horrible and terrible a situation could be and I figure out a way to survive, then anything better than that is good news. My spouse tends to be more of an optimist and denier, so we generally balance one another and work well in tandem. While I wallow in despair he is moving ahead with what needs to be done in the next moment.

Within a few days of Frankie's diagnosis we began to move forward with our plans to get the interventions that he needed. Luckily, we had been in couples counseling in the past, and we knew the potential pitfalls in our relationship. This did not protect us from having trou-bles, but at least we knew what to do when trouble appeared. We both explicitly and implicitly laid out a plan for how we would address Frankie's problems. We were lucky enough to have the resources to hire a nanny to work with Frankie, which allowed each of us to con-tinue with our careers, ensure adequate resources, and increase op-portunities for him. I deal with health issues, appointments and therapy interventions. My spouse takes care of legal matters. We shared school-related issues and direct care.

We hired our current nanny after the birth of our second child, when Frankie was about 3 years old. We hired a nanny with specific experience and training in working with children with disabilities. She has been an important part of our parenting team. As with all relationships and arrangements, all of us make compromises. However, it has been invaluable having a third adult who knows and loves Frankie working on his behalf. As he has grown older, her role has expanded to keep us informed about happenings at school and to facilitate social relationships for Frankie. She also provides much-needed support for Frankie's brother.

McCrae, Frankie's younger brother, has struggled with having a brother with "troubles," as they both call Frankie's ASD diagnosis. McCrae does not always get the attention he craves or get to do all the things that he wants to do. But for the most part, with three of us adult caregivers working together, we have been able to provide a very full childhood for both of them. By just being a brother, McCrae also has done more to draw out Frankie than any of the therapies we have tried. McCrae, too, is probably more responsible for Frankie's speech being as good as it is because he has provided a constant role model. For several years before Frankie would talk, McCrae was his interpreter.

Even now there are times when McCrae is the only person who really seems to know what Frankie wants or needs. I know this has been, at times, a difficult role for McCrae, but he loves his brother, and being his spokesperson has given him a special bond with Frankie that none of us shares. We have already begun to have discussions with both of them about their lifelong commitment to one another.

We have also established some boundaries between them as well to help each of them be comfortable with his development. We made the decision at the beginning of elementary school to send them to separate schools. We had started them off together, but because of other circumstances we chose separate schools for them after a year. This arrangement has worked out well so far because it has allowed each of them to develop a social network of his own. The element of academic competition that might have arisen if they were in the same school setting is not an issue. They share other social settings, and the balance of some shared and some separate time has been helpful.

As for extended family, we moved to the city where we had extended family when Frankie was 5 years old. Having extended family involved in our lives has been a blessing. We have been lucky that Frankie's grandparents have been accepting and engaging without being intrusive. There have been struggles on occasion, but for the most part these have been easily worked out because we talked with one another and avoided the pitfalls of unclear boundaries. At the end of the day, everyone is clear about who has the final say in decisions related to raising both of the children, and we have all respected those boundaries graciously.

Additionally, we have worked to create an extended family of friends and a religious community for both the boys. While this has been a struggle at times because of the time needed to develop friendships and the problems we have faced because of the lack of understanding that is sometimes part of other people's experience of children with ASD, it has ultimately been important for us as a family and for Frankie in particular to have a community that loves and accepts him.

PART 4

SCHOOL

CHAPTER THIRTEEN

How to Talk about Preschool

When you are the parent of a child with ASD, there are few issues that are the source of more worry and concern than school. Every day I speak with parents who are struggling with choosing a school. Many times there is only one choice, and it does not seem to be a good choice. Parents worry about school almost continuously. Sometimes things will be okay for a time, but something keeps happening to once again bring into stark relief the difficulties associated with finding the best school for our children. As a child grows the issues remain, and every year there are new problems that arise and new issues to consider.

Some families are fortunate. They live in communities with good options. Most families are not as lucky, and either there are not good placements for a child's particular needs, or there may be good placements but there is no funding available. It is heartbreaking to watch families struggle to do what they think is best for their child. One of the most common mistakes professionals working with families can make is to underestimate the terrible weight of decisions about school placement.

I know most parents have some concerns about sending their children into the care of others when they start daycare or school. It is, however, much more difficult to send a special needs child into these situations. For parents of a child with ASD, who has language and social disabilities, it is much more difficult. Parents ask themselves, "What is happening with my child?" "Is he liked by the caretakers?" "How are the other children responding to him?" "Is he able to let people know what he wants and what he needs?" "Is he learning anything?" "Can they teach him?" "Is he happy?" "Is he safe?"

While all parents wonder about their child's success at school, when a parent has a child with ASD these questions never seem to diminish. Rarely is a parent with a special needs child able to trust as fully, as other parents might, that there are positive answers to these questions. Because of the serious language problems of most children with ASD, even as the child gets older, knowing the answers to these questions can be very difficult, if not impossible.

Parents of children with ASD know their child is different, even difficult. Of course, they love their child and even love the quirkiness and differences. With good reason, however, they realize not everyone will have a positive reaction to their child. Children generally are wonderful in the way they are able to engage adults and other children to get the care, attention, and support they need. But children with ASD are fundamentally unable to engage others in this helpful way. This core disability can lead to serious problems in school settings, especially where no one on staff has significant experience or training in working with children like them.

What to Say to Parents

- *Sending any child to school can be scary. Sending your child with ASD to school is especially scary.* Parenting a child with any special needs puts parents in a very vulnerable place. Trusting any child to the care of strangers is tough. Parents whose children cannot tell them what happened during the day, how they were treated, or how they feel about their experience, have a much more difficult time trusting their child's caretakers. Frankly, most of the time they will not completely trust the individuals. As a professional working with children with ASD and their parents you can help them acknowledge that fear and then plan how to make preschool as safe and beneficial as possible for their child. First acknowledge that placing a child outside of the home is difficult for the parents and that you understand this. It is very important to recognize, not minimize this fear.

- *It is hard to make a good decision about school placement. There are many things to consider.* Parents of children with ASD are always second-guessing their decisions about school. I have found that simply stating the obvious, "It is difficult to know if your decision is the right one," helps parents recognize the unease and then come up with strategies to find the best fit for their child. It is helpful to have parents sit down and list what they want for their child in a school placement. Help them to prioritize their desires. This exercise will guide them when they are looking at placement options. If there are only one or a few options, the list can help them understand what they can work on in that placement to make it a better fit for their child. Things that might be important include elements in the school setting that address the core symptoms of ASD; for example, an enriched speech and language program or a social skills curriculum in the classroom.

- *Rarely is there a perfect choice.* After all, there is no perfect choice for any child. Parents are always second-guessing themselves because rarely does a program truly meet all of the needs of a particular child. There is always a nagging sense of guilt for parents that they should be doing something more or different. I have yet to talk to one parent who has not had those feelings at least some of the time. Help parents recognize there is no perfect placement and acknowledge the discomfort of living with that recurring suspicion there should be something else they can do.

Questions Parents May Ask

- *How do I know if he or she is in the right school setting?* Parents ask me this question all of the time. I answer by asking them, "Exactly what are you expecting out of the school placement?" That question helps them identify what is important to them for their child. Then we can talk about whether the current school meets any of those criteria. If not, then we talk about possibilities for change. Sometimes changes can be accomplished within the current setting. Sometimes only a change in the placement will meet the child's needs.

- *How can I know my child is safe?* I encourage parents to be as involved as possible in their child's school. From the very start parents need to spend as much time in and around the school and the classroom as they can. Meet all or as many of the professionals and other parents. This is time-consuming and hard work, but being there and being involved is the best insurance policy for protecting a child. There are a number of ways to promote this level of involvement. Encourage parents to take their child into the classroom each morning and speak with the teacher, and to pick up their child at the end of the day and again briefly check in with the staff. Parents might also volunteer to help with classroom activities, such as reading or parties, or to act as supervisors on field trips. Parents can arrange for play dates with other children after school, on the weekends, and during other breaks. They can also join the parent-teacher organization offered by their local school district. Building relationships with teachers, school professionals, and other parents increases the likelihood your child will be given the utmost patience, goodwill, and understanding. The relationship gives you a chance to continually share with school professionals information that can help them understand and better teach your child. If a school or classroom is unwilling to have that kind of involvement or scrutiny then I help parents look for a different placement and advocate appropriately for more access. Alliances with school administrators and other parents are important to helping make those changes.

Our Experience

I know for me, school has been and continues to be one of the most significant daily concerns I have about Frankie. He entered his first school placement when he was 18 months old. We were fortunate that there was an early intervention program for children with special needs that was part of a local university. Luckily, this program had considerable experience with children who had ASD. Not only was he able to get many of the therapeutic interventions he needed, but the preschool was based on an inclusive model. Typically developing children were in the classroom along with the special needs children. Frankie thrived in this environment and made enormous progress. He was able to stay until he was 3 years old. When he turned 3, we had to look at other placements.

Preschool

For most children with ASD, an appropriate early school placement is essential for the child to get the interventions he needs. I recommend placement by at least 18 months, and in some situations, even earlier if an appropriate setting is available. Early intervention can make a major difference in the prognosis of the disorder. My clinical and personal experience has shown me that with early intervention many of the core symptoms of social difficulties and speech and language problems can be ameliorated.

Some families can provide intensive interventions in the home including applied behavioral analysis (ABA), discrete trial interventions, or development, or individual-difference, relationship-based (DIR-

Floortime) therapy among others. If families have the financial and time resources for these intensive therapies in the home wonderful gains can be made. However, even with these home interventions, I still believe that early peer social interaction is important. Just being around other children is therapeutic in ways beyond what a parent can provide, and some school placements include these interventions.

In some communities early interventions include the Treatment and Education of Autistic and Related Communication Handicapped CHildren (TEACCH) system. Founded in 1966 by Eric Schopler of the University of North Carolina at Chapel Hill, TEACCH provides training and services to help autistic children as part of an integrated school setting.

Once a diagnosis of ASD has been made, even if it is provisional, parents need to look at the options in their community for a preschool. It is helpful for professionals to be ready to offer suggestions and make referrals. In looking for that first placement, it is important to help parents talk with other parents in the community whose children have been in the various placements. Such conversations with other parents will likely continue to be the most valuable resource for placement information throughout a child's life. There is nothing more important in making a decision about school and school placement than knowing other parents' experiences.

I ask parents to look for a setting where teachers are trained and have experience in working with these children. They should look for low staff turnover and a school where staff members make positive comments about children with special needs in general, and children with ASD in particular.

An inclusive setting is one of the most important features I recommend to parents. This means children with special needs and children who are typically developing attend school together. This type of placement is not always available, but when it is, it is a great benefit. Clinically I see the difference in progress for children placed in an inclusive setting versus a restricted setting for children with special needs or children with ASD. I firmly believe that children with ASD need typical children as models. I also believe that it benefits the typical children to be exposed to children with all kinds of special needs so that they will be more comfortable and supportive of efforts at inclusion as they grow.

I believe so strongly that typical peer modeling is important that if parents live in an area without an inclusive preschool, they should work to have their child placed in a regular preschool setting for at least a few hours a week, with whatever support the child needs to be safe, secure, and happy in that environment. Of course the interventions for speech and language, occupational, and other therapies must continue.

Every U.S. state and county has some sort of services for early intervention before age 3 that is federally funded in part. Some states are more generous in program subsidies than others, and some counties certainly have more resources, too. These are issues to be considered when families look at their choices in terms of location.

When a child is 3 years old, the school system in most places becomes the institution responsible for providing placement and early intervention. It depends on the school system and the systems resources whether this transition is a positive one. Ideally, the child can continue in the same placement from 18 months until he enters kindergarten.

What to Say to Parents

- *By 18 months your child should be in a preschool placement.* Parents have to start early to look for appropriate placements for their child with ASD. Although it can be difficult, your job as a professional is to help them overcome the denial, anxiety, or a combination of both that may prevent them from pursuing early intervention placement. They may be overwhelmed, so introduce them to other parents who can guide them through the maze of decisions. You can put them in touch with local public early intervention programs. If it is unclear how to find them, contact your state department of health, and they should be able to point you in the right direction. If the parents are pursuing an intensive intervention program in the home the placement could be for just a few hours a week for socialization with typically developing children. If there is no intensive intervention program in the home, the placement should provide as much as possible in terms of specific interventions for these children.

- *Find a preschool that has experience working with children with ASD.* There are a lot of good preschools. There are good preschools that work with kids with special needs. It is very important, however, that the school has experience in working with these particular children because they do not offer the same kind of reciprocal emotional interaction as other preschool children. This sets them up to be ignored—or even disliked or maltreated. Preschools teaching children with ASD need experience working with these children over time so that they learn the wonders these children can offer when teachers spend time and energy getting to know them. This understanding only comes from experience, so someone at the school must help make the accommodations to the seemingly complete withdrawal presented by children with ASD. Preschools with this experience will be able at least to begin to address the core symptoms. The importance of a school's experience with children with ASD and the strength of their early intervention programming depend on how much intervention and assistance a child gets outside of the school.

- *Talk with other parents.* Encourage parents to talk with other parents. I have discussed this topic several times but it bears repeating. Especially when it comes to schools there is generally no better source of information than other parents, especially those with special needs children. They can advise parents what to expect. They know the weaknesses and strengths of a program. Parents can also give support to one another and be essential in helping to advocate for their child with the administration of any school.

- *Your child should spend at least some portion of his or her preschool experience with typically developing children.* There are many specialty preschool placements that enroll only special needs children or only children with ASD. Such intensive specialty programs can be very beneficial in creating an environment where therapy is very focused on the problems a child experiences. But children with ASD need to be around typically developing children who will show the child with ASD how to talk with peers and how to socialize with other children. Because the typical child learns with children who have ASD early on, there will be greater awareness and acceptance of children with these disorders later in school and in the community.

Questions Parents May Ask

- *Should I provide intensive interventions at home?* This is a really difficult decision for parents. Of course parents are generally very engaged with their children with ASD, and that engagement itself is an intervention. Parents should be encouraged to connect with their child as much as possible and to not be satisfied with allowing their child to spend a lot of time engaged in self-stimulatory behaviors (e.g., hand flapping, twirling, handwringing, and jumping) or noninteractive activities such as television or the computer. The intensive intervention programs parents can set up for their child in the home differ markedly from the usual parent engagement. The intensive home-based intervention programs include ABA therapies, DIR/Floortime interventions, the Son-Rise Program, the Relationship Development Intervention (RDI) program, and others. All of these programs are very intensive. They require a lot of direct personal intervention, and the costs for the programs and their implementation can be quite great (up to several tens of thousands of dollars each year). It is very easy to help parents become informed through the Internet about each of these interventions. All of the programs have benefits, and I believe that children can gain value from any of them. It is important, however, if a family decides to implement one of these intervention programs that they choose one and stick with it. Switching from one program to another is fruitless. The benefits from the programs occur after months or years of work, resulting from the quality and consistency of the intervention. So when a family is deciding whether to do one of these programs they need to consider the long-term personal, financial, and time investment associated with the implementation. Your job is to help the parents sort through the information and make a decision based on what is best for their family and their resources.

- *What should I look for in a preschool for my child?* Again the best way to start the discussion is to ask the parents to make a list of the features they would like and what they expect from a pre-school. Suggest parents look for a good speech and language program, a social skills curriculum built into the program, and a behavioral specialist to address behaviors appropriately in the school setting. They should also look for a school experienced in working with children who have ASD and that wants to have a child with this problem in their program. Parents should never have to "talk a school into" accepting their child. In my experience this has always been a recipe for disaster. Finally, the parents need to feel comfortable with the amount of involvement the school encourages from their parents, and there has to be an open door policy for visits to the school and the classroom.

- *How can I access public services for my child?* For preschool before age 3 public services are available through state early intervention programs. County health offices or the state department of health will always have information on these programs and how to access them. Help your parents make those telephone calls or introduce them to parents or social workers who can help them. After age 3 the school system manages interventions, and contact can be made with the school system through the local school or through the school district's special education office. If the parents are stymied getting the school to help, refer them to parents in the system with special needs children or contact the state's department of education about access to services. Additionally, Internet resources such as http://wrightslaw.com or the names of local special education advocates or attorneys can help with advocating for access to special education services for a 3- to 5-year-old with ASD.

Our Experience

When Frankie was 3 years old we knew we had to change school placements, and it was not clear what the other placements would provide. We were at a point in our lives where a move was possible. We decided to move and looked at the options for school placement. Looking back on the move, there were many things that I should have examined more closely that related to Frankie's potential placements. I did not follow the advice I outlined above about talking to other parents and reviewing programs, but at that point, even though I had done this work professionally, I did not understand the potential problems. I was still naïve and believed that school placements would be available. I believed that the public school system usually did an okay job for our children. When we moved, I was not sure what we needed to do, but we decided to place Frankie in a summer program at a private school that felt they could meet his needs. It was a disaster. Within a couple of weeks it was clear that Frankie was not doing well. He withdrew, interacted even less, and seemed sad. The other children were not responding to him, and there was no facilitation on the part of the school staff to integrate him.

There was another placement I'd initially passed over because I thought it was a little too far away and believed incorrectly that the children at the school were more disabled than Frankie. I admit now that it was a prejudice based on my denial and my lack of understanding of that particular program. We were convinced to visit the program, and we decided to enroll Frankie. He stayed in that program from 3 to 5 years of age, and this was probably the period where he had the best and most appropriate school setting. The diversity of the children in the program and the quality of the staff made all the difference for him. The program was inclusive, with typically developing children and children with a variety of special needs. The school also utilized an ABA discrete trial approach to the children's learning and behavioral difficulties. It was a perfect match for us.

As a professional who works with families whose child has ASD, your input and assistance with the decisions about early placement are essential to the child and family getting off to the right start. It is important to be well informed about the resources and placements available. It is also necessary to confront the denial that many parents are still experiencing at this early stage in their child's life. This may be the most important task. I believe that it is better to overtreat and intervene at this point in the child's life than to wait and watch. While waiting and watching are okay for some children, for children who will ultimately be diagnosed with ASD it is a catastrophe. I know I was one of those parents who needed to be told things might be much worse than I wanted to believe. By following the advice of those who had a more objective view of Frankie, I was able to help him ultimately be more successful than he might have been. I believe he was certainly happier.

CHAPTER FOURTEEN

How to Talk about Elementary School

While many children with ASD have some interaction with the public school system before they reach kindergarten, many others attend public school for the first time when they are kindergarten age. Entering the public school system can be overwhelming for the child with ASD and his or her parents. Public schools generally are larger than preschool placements and much more bureaucratic.

While families often appreciate individual teachers and workers involved with their child, the school and system administrators are usually more removed. Ironically it is these administrators who often have the most say about what services are provided for a child and where he or she is placed. These decisions are made through an Individualized Education Plan (IEP). Many families will be familiar with this process of classification and development of an IEP or Individualized Service Plan (ISP) when their child turned 3 and the school system became responsible for providing services to him or her.

However, it is usually not until the child enters public school that these meetings increasingly become efforts to negotiate the most appropriate setting based not only on the child's needs, but also on the local, state, and federal laws, rules, and regulations. Although federal law requires the school to provide a "free and appropriate public education," the availability of school resources becomes a part of the discussion, albeit a usually unspoken and unacknowledged one.

Children with disabilities, including ASD, have rights to a free and appropriate public education in the "least restrictive environment" under the Individuals with Disabilities Education Act (2004). What does it mean to have a "free and appropriate public education?" FAPE is defined in the Individuals with Disabilities Education Act (IDEA) at 20 U.S.C. 1404 (9). Basically, it states that every child with a disability is eligible for an individualized education plan (IEP) that meets his or her special and unique needs. The IEP may include specialized programming or schooling that is provided in the public school system, but may also be found in other settings. These programs and services are publicly funded, and may include placement in a specialty school where room and board are required. Possible publicly-funded services for a child with ASD might include special speech services, social skills training, or residential placements for treatment of severe behavior problems (such as self-injurious behavior or aggression toward others). All educational services for children with disabilities should occur in the "least restrictive environment (LRE)" but it is not always clear, legally, exactly what this term means. It has generally be accepted that this would include an assessment of the unique educational needs of the child with disabilities, to determine what aids and supports would facilitate placement of the child in a regular education environment, for at least a portion of the school day.

This process is intimidating for most parents. The legal issues alone are often overwhelming. Parents are presented with an explanation of these rights at every IEP meeting that they attend. Nevertheless, I believe that many times rather than helping parents to feel empowered by the process, these rules and regulations are alienating. The parents begin to feel that they have no say in what happens to their child because they do not understand the process or the paperwork.

Some school systems will provide parent advocates on the IEP team. These advocates can answer questions and attend meetings, but even this often is not enough help for some parents. Also the parent "advocate" is often employed by the school system. I hear over and over again from parents that they feel overwhelmed and often "railroaded" into making decisions related to their child's placement and education plan. It can be a very difficult process. As a child with ASD begins kindergarten and the IEP process, parents should advocate for as much inclusion as possible. This is critical. It is important to push for inclusion with typical peers while a child is young to help with social modeling and to establish a community of peer support for the child. This is, at least in part, what the phrase "least restrictive environment" means.

I believe it is important for many reasons to have children who are diagnosed with ASD included in regular classrooms as much as possible, especially during the first few years of elementary school. The child with the disorder needs typical role models. Even more, in kindergarten children make friends more easily and more readily accept the child with ASD. As all of the children grow together these typical children will ultimately provide support for the special needs child as they go through the school system.

Not every child can tolerate inclusion, and some children certainly need levels of attention that can only be given in a separate environment. But if it is at all possible, push for an inclusive program. It is important for the child with the disorder and the typical children; even if it is more difficult and requires more resources, it is the law.

In addition to inclusion, every effort must be made to ensure that the child with ASD gets all the needed services. Sometimes getting these services also takes vigorous advocacy. Speech therapy is essential, and securing as much speech therapy as possible is very important. This can be accomplished by you or other professionals writing letters of support for the patient. You can also facilitate the parents obtaining evaluations from independent speech and language practitioners that clearly outline the therapies that would be beneficial, as well as recommendations for the amount of time necessary. The speech therapist should understand specifically the kinds of speech difficulties of a child with ASD and have experience working with such children. Speech therapy is where many of the social skills interventions will need to be made, and it is important to advocate for a social skills curriculum in the school setting for these children. The child with ASD might also require a social facilitator such as a specially trained school aide or paraprofessional to make suggestions in social situations or to set up play opportunities or interactions.

The child will usually need occupational therapy support as well to help with preeducational/vocational skills and sensory difficulties. As with speech therapy, parents may need help advocating for appropriate occupational therapy by getting similar letters and independent evaluations as discussed above for speech therapy.

Most children diagnosed with ASD also have learning and cognitive disabilities. They need special education support for these disabilities as well. These supports might include pulling the child out of the classroom for more individualized instruction.

Assuming that the parents, and you as a professional assisting them, are able to achieve all of the above in an IEP, you have just begun. Or as one parent was told by her practitioner, "Now the real work begins." The real challenge with a child in public schools is to ensure that the IEP is implemented fully and appropriately.

Each year all of these issues have to be readdressed. Most parents will tell you that each year brings a new situation. Administrators change, schools change, teachers come and go. Parents have little or no control over these changes, and don't know who the child's teacher will be from year to year. A new special education administrator might make widespread changes in the program or have a different philosophy of education that changes service provision. All of these changes can significantly impact a child's education from year to year. Given the vulnerability of any special needs child, especially the child with ASD, you have to help parents advocate for their child year after year and encourage them to be involved as much as possible in what is happening at the school. The more parents know about the school and the more people in the school system know the parents, the better the parents are able to advocate for their child each year.

What to Say to Parents

- *Your child has a right to a public education and to be included as much as possible with typically developing children.* Most parents of children with ASD will know that their child has a right to a public education but they may not know that the child has a right to be included in "regular" classes. They may not know that strong federal laws guarantee their child's rights, and that they can use this legal basis to advocate for their child. I believe that it is important to empower the parents of a child with ASD to vigorously advocate for their child, knowing the law is on their side. Parents of children with ASDs many times feel apologetic, bothersome, intimidated, confused, fearful—anything but empowered—as they try to deal with all of the day-to-day stressors of having a child with disabilities. Knowing the law may not eliminate the sense of relative weakness, but it helps.

- *You are the best advocate for your child.* Parents need to be reminded that they know their children best. Also, in the sometimes adversarial struggle for services, the parents are the only people who strictly represent the needs of their child. Everyone else in the system has other concerns to consider beyond the student. Parents of the child with ASD have only the child to consider. Parents should be encouraged to stand firm and not "think of what the school needs" or the problems of the school system in meeting the needs of their child. The parent's role is to advocate the absolute best for their child as they see it. If there is a difference of opinion, negotiations are possible, but the parents' power in the negotiations is based on the law. If a negotiation or difference of opinion is great, then parents can engage advocates or attorneys to help. Most communities have advocates or legal advisors experienced in disputes with the school over services. State and sometimes local advocacy agencies provide advocacy and legal services for free or at a reduced cost for families in need.

- *Stay as involved in the school as you possibly can.* Parents who are present in the school, befriend the teachers, get to know the administrators, and are involved in the classroom have an advantage when it comes to writing an IEP for their child. While involved parents may not always get all they want in an IEP, it can help smooth the way for good discussions about the needs of the child. I have also found that parents who are involved are less intimidated by the IEP and really feel more a part of the team educating their child. While it is theoretically true that parents of every child with an IEP are part of the team, parents who know all or most of the participants of an IEP meeting will feel more included. This helps the parents advocate more strongly for their children.

Questions Parents Might Ask

- *Should my child be in a special ASD classroom?* Many school systems and school districts have special classrooms for children with ASD. Sometimes these settings can be beneficial because they concentrate resources for these children and enrich service provision. The limitations arise when several students with varying levels of function are together in one classroom. This may lead to less service provision for one student versus another. Children in such classrooms may mimic undesirable behaviors of other students, leading to a new repertoire of maladaptive or inappropriate behaviors. Parents should visit the proposed classroom to see if the class is a good fit for their child. If a child is placed in a classroom specifically for children with ASDs, then parents need to ensure their child has as much inclusion with typically developing children as possible. The family may also need to plan more social activities with typically developing children outside of school.

- *What can I do if the school is refusing services I think my child needs?* As I stated above, the negotiations for services can often be at least somewhat adversarial and sometimes more adversarial. If parents feel that they are not getting what they need for their child, your job is to help do a reality check. This may mean getting other professional opinions or helping the parents to find paid or public advocates to help them decide exactly what their child needs, and advocate and negotiate for it. Parents do have recourse, but many times they need help asserting their rights to that recourse. Sometimes your job as the professional may also be to help parents accept that what they may be asking for is unreasonable, and to help them work through why they feel it is so important.

- *Can the school refuse to serve my child?* The school cannot refuse to serve a child with special education needs. In fact the school cannot even refuse to serve the child for a part of a day. I rarely get calls from a parent that a school is trying to expel their child, but I do get calls from parents stating that the, "school is calling me almost every day to come pick up my child." This is usually because the child has a problem behavior that is disruptive or threatening. While a very occasional call about such problems may be reasonable, calling frequently is not. If the school is calling often it's a good clue that the child is in an inappropriate setting or does not have the supports in place for him or her to be successful in the setting. It is time for an IEP meeting. If the school is not able to serve the child appropriately, the IEP team can talk about the nature of an appropriate setting and how the school can arrange to facilitate and pay for placement in that setting. This often requires help from an independent advocate. If the school is trying to expel a student with ASD for issues related to his or her disability, the same process would apply. The school should be forced to comply with their obligation to educate the child in a "free and appropriate" setting, whether in the school system or not.

- *What do I do if I am having a conflict with the school? Won't that make things worse for my child?* Sometimes parents are afraid to push schools because they believe that it will make things "worse" for their child. They believe the school will not provide for their child's needs, so they give in to the school's demands, although it conflicts with what they feel their child needs. My experience has generally been the opposite. Parents who are strong advocates for their children generally develop a more productive relationship with the school, and the IEP is followed more precisely. Of course, parents cannot be rude, disrespectful, or in any other way inappropriate. They must be patient, respectful, and determined. They can be strong and vociferous advocates without being obnoxious.

Our Experience

My experience both personally and professionally has been that the process of developing an IEP is, unfortunately, adversarial. The roles pit the parents as advocating for what is best for their child, against the school's advocacy for the child that is biased by what they *have* to do to be in compliance with budgets, rules, regulations, and laws.

In an IEP meeting for Frankie a few years ago I had the following exchange with one of the school system administrators attending the meeting. We were discussing the need for a trained one-on-one paraprofessional in the classroom dedicated to Frankie. I said, "I think that if we look at what is best for Frankie it seems clear that he needs the parapro to do his best." The administrator turned to me and said, "My job is not to do what is best for Frankie, but to do what we have to do to make sure his education is good enough." She could not have been clearer about where the lines of advocacy were drawn. That meeting showed me in a way I had not understood before that parents have to be determined advocates for their children because most of the time they are the *only* true advocates for their child. The corollary is also true, as I have stated before, regardless of the specialties or degrees of the others working with a child the parents are ultimately the expert on their child. That is a role that no one else fills.

Considering a Private School

For parents who are considering private school, there are several things to think about. Just as with public schools, parents need to be sure that the school has experience in teaching children with ASD. Ideally, there needs to be a mix of children with special needs and children who are typically developing. The private school needs to have services available for speech, occupational, and physical therapy. There should be small classrooms with time for individual instruction. There should be programming established to address problem behaviors. There should be services to help the child with ASD to transition back into the public school setting if that is a goal for the family. The goal of the private school, in addition to basic education, should be to help the child with ASD function as fully and completely as possible in typical social settings learning to interact appropriately with typically and nontypically developing children.

What to Say to Parents

- *Private school is definitely an option for your child.* In some places there are very good private schools that either specifically educate or include children with ASDs. These can be wonderful opportunities for families that live close enough and have the resources to take advantage of the opportunity. I encourage families to go through the checklist above when considering a private school and to weigh the pros and cons associated with the placement, including the impact on the family in both emotional and financial terms. Remember to tell parents that if they think they are being sold something they probably are.
- *Private school does not lessen the parents' responsibility to be involved in the school.* Private schools often require just as much, if not more, involvement on the parents' part as a public school setting. When families commit to a private school education they are committing to being part of that school's community. Their child

will need to have them involved as much as possible to ensure the child's needs are meet and he or she is succeeding. Again, it also helps when the time comes to advocate for things that may be more unique for their child.

Questions Parents May Ask

- *Will my child get as good an education in private school?* This is a very important question and one that has to be investigated closely. Families need to talk with other families that have had experience with the school. They need to talk with other schools about their impression of the school. They should consult with agencies like the Better Business Bureau to make sure the school has a reasonable reputation in the business community. It is even a good idea to check with the state department of education to see what information is available about the school. Finally, they need to ask for the accreditation status of the school and talk with the accrediting agencies about the school's profile and performance. Most importantly, the parents need to visit the school and directly observe classrooms and instruction. If possible, arrange for a trial visit for their child.
- *Can I still get services from the public school if my child is in a private school?* Children in private schools can get some special education services from the public school system. These services may be more limited, and there are more restrictions, but they are available. Parents should discuss the situation in detail with their local school and with local advocates and legal advisors. Of course, if a public school places a child in a private setting they are completely responsible for ensuring that provisions of the IEP are carried out and that appropriate services are provided.
- *What about home schooling?* I have worked with many families that have chosen to home school their child with ASD because the problems in and with the school have become too great. At times this is the most reasonable option, and in many communities there are great support networks for home schooling. The caveats to

home schooling are making sure that the parent is really able to educate the child in a way that makes the most of his or her learning ability. Home schooling must use some objective standard of measurement to help the parent to monitor the child's progress. Every state department of education has specific requirements parents must meet. There also needs to be lots of social engagement with typically developing peers.

Our Experience

In our case we had moved into a neighborhood close to a school where there was good support and an inclusive spirit. There were some struggles, but overall the environment was great. Frankie was happy and learning. Then a new superintendent was hired, and she immediately set about closing our school to consolidate resources. Our situation rapidly went from a safe, mostly secure, predictable school setting to what has become years of haggling and fighting for resources and appropriate placement. We struggle yearly to come close to what we need. As Frankie has gotten older, it has also been more difficult to maintain stable relationships for him with peers, but we have been able to do it, though with little help from the school that sees his social development as something secondary to what they "have to" provide for him.

We did pull him out of the public setting for one year and tried a private school, but like most families with these children, the placement was not really appropriate and the drain on resources was enormous. Most private special education schools cost nearly double other private settings. It became a debate over whether it was worth the resources to get the little extra that we were getting. Ultimately, we decided it was not and went back to the public school. The other factor that played into that decision was that Frankie himself wanted to go back to "regular school." He was then, and still is, quite adamant that he does not want to be "special" and wants to be with his friends from kindergarten and his early school years who started with him in an inclusive setting.

Other Concerns

Other issues that need to be seriously considered during elementary school, if they have not been considered before, are related to long-term care, both personal and financial, for the child with ASD. It may seem early, but by the time a child is in the middle of elementary school and certainly before elementary school's completion, there is a greater understanding of what the child's long-term functioning will be. Discussions with a financial planner or parents in a support group are very important to help parents understand how the family can prepare for the long-term care of the child once grown.

A reexamination of all of the services available in the community for family social and financial support is important. If finances allow, it may be important to establish a specific savings fund or a trust. Options related to educational saving should be explored. Elementary school is the time to get a better understanding of what will be necessary as the child grows.

As the child with ASD moves forward in the elementary school setting and more is understood about her abilities and her disabilities, it is important to continue to work to keep her as involved in your community as possible. Building friendships and skills through community sports recreation leagues and spiritual communities is important. It is also important to get to know other parents with children with disabilities including ASD and to try to create opportunities for friendship with children who have similar struggles and issues. Elementary school is the time to lay as solid foundation as possible for the turbulent years to come in middle and high school.

What to Say to Parents

- *It is never too early to be planning for the future.* I believe that it is important during the elementary years to get parents to start thinking about what the future will look like and what needs they and their child may have. During elementary school the ability to project the child's future level of functioning increases. Encourage parents to discuss with the professionals who work with their child the kinds of supports he or she might need later and help them start to plan to meet those needs. This will help parents and teachers set goals for the child as he or she moves through school.

- *Stay active socially.* Families need to resist becoming isolated during these years. Encourage families to get out into the community and be involved in activities for the community. Help them get their child with ASD out into the community so he or she can be known and be part of the life and fabric of the community. I know this can be difficult for many reasons, such as the effort involved in bringing some children into the community, or fear of being embarrassed. However, the more community exposure given a child with ASD, the better it will be for him or her, the family, and the community. These are long-term dividends that increase how successful and fulfilled a child will be as an adolescent and an adult.

Questions Parents May Ask

- *How do I get information to help me with planning for the future?* Many Internet sites can help parents think about what they need to do for their child's future. Working with families to write down their goals and dreams for their child is a good beginning. Then the family can begin to assess which goals are realistic and which are not. They can examine what the family and the child will need in order to realize those goals. Also professional planners can be helpful and many communities have a state funded advocacy office for people with disabilities that helps with beginning to look at these issues and meet with parents periodically to adjust and monitor progress on their plan. There are also nonprofit organizations that local service providers would know about who provide financial planning services.

Our Experience

We have been involved in planning for Frankie's future since he started school. We were able to hire an attorney to help us with wills and trusts to help ensure that Frankie would have access to some funds after our death but that he would also still be eligible for public assistance for the disabled. We have looked at the resources for adults with developmental disabilities and ASD in the community, and we have been involved in some of those organizations, although he is still not eligible for many services through these organizations.

We have also stayed very active socially. We keep Frankie involved in community activities. We attend a church where he has established friendships that will we hope last through his high school years and beyond. We have involved him in sports activities. The more active we are the more engaged Frankie is with the community and the community with Frankie. I have seen this engagement be very helpful for other children with ASD, and we intend to continue with it. I encourage other families to work as much as they can to lay the foundation early in a child's life for the support that he or she and the family will need as the child grows older.

CHAPTER FIFTEEN

How to Talk about Middle School

I think middle school probably strikes a little terror into every parent. For the parent of a child with ASD, the shift from a supportive, generally nurturing elementary school to a larger, more complex school is truly frightening.

Every year, starting in March or April, I watch the parents of children in my practice who will be entering the sixth grade become increasingly anxious about the increased social demands of middle school. There are issues related to increased responsibility on the part of students—they have to change classrooms between classes. There is textbook responsibility, lockers, lunches, all of which call for more independence and require increased self, food, and social awareness. None of these tasks is easy for the child with ASD.

Whether to Move on to Middle School or Spend One More Year in Elementary School

However, before even talking about middle school and its particular challenges, I want to talk briefly about whether children are really ready to move to middle school in the first place. At the start of the fifth grade year, I try to begin to talk with parents, and the children who are able, about the transition to the sixth grade and middle school. I want parents to start talking with teachers at the elementary school about the programming at the middle school their child will attend. I ask parents to set up an IEP meeting at the beginning of that fifth-grade year specifically for this discussion. I have them meet and talk with the system special education team about the impending transition. In addition to discussions related to programming, I want the team to seriously discuss whether the child is truly ready to move on or not.

I am not generally a strong advocate of retaining children in a particular grade or at a particular level, but at the transition between elementary school and middle school I sometimes think retention in elementary school can be best for the child. If the team believes they will recommend a retention in the fifth grade, I want that decision made early in the fifth-grade year so everyone will develop education planning and programming accordingly.

What should be the considerations in deciding to retain? The first is the child's level of social and intellectual function. If the child is moderately or severely impaired intellectually and has a similar level of social impairment, retention should be a consideration. For example, if the child is nonverbal, functioning at a second-grade level or below, and spending most of the day in a self-contained setting, then I definitely recommend retention in the fifth grade. If the child is functioning at a slightly higher level, but not at grade level, with few friends and very limited social skills, the decision is more difficult. I rely then on the teachers who know the child, and the parents, and even the child him- or herself to make the decision about whether to move on.

Many times the deciding factor is the strength of the child's social relationships and his or her desire to stay with a group of supportive peers. With children that are even higher functioning, the decision should definitely be to move on to the sixth grade but with supports appropriate for that child.

The second and third considerations are the programming available in the new school and the willingness of the new school's administration to work with the parents and the child to make appropriate accommodations. Of course these considerations for retention are mostly related to the middle group of children described above. These are the kids who are struggling intellectually and socially, but at a mild to moderate level. This group, if moved up to sixth grade, will need more comprehensive programming and the most accommodations. The programming needs to be available to provide support in a somewhat separate environment, but with plenty of opportunities to interact with typical children.

These children will need support because they are not ready for the freedoms usually given to middle school students. This is especially true in relation to matters of sex and sexuality, being bullied, and substance experimentation. There must be safeguards for monitoring the children with ASD, providing them with guidance, but giving them enough freedom so they can learn from experience how to take care of themselves. All of this needs to be accomplished in an environment with limited risks of being harmed.

Of course there should be discussions all the way through school and development about issues related to the body and sexuality, bullying and even substance abuse. Children should early on have been introduced to all of these issues by their parents and at times the school. All children, including those with ASD should have had discussions about body parts and sexuality, about safe and unsafe touch, and as they grow older what happens to the body as they mature. Some girls especially may start their menses before the end of fifth grade and they should have had some discussions about what to expect. Boys and girls both need discussions about attractions to the opposite sex, and based on the families' and the communities' standards and values, they should be given appropriate behavioral guidelines for handling these attractions.

There should be discussions about bullying that help kids know what to do when bullied. There are curricula that schools can use to help with bullying, and bullying is generally addressed more seriously these days than in the past. Also substance abuse curricula introduced early may have some beneficial effects on helping to decrease the problems with exposure once a child with or without ASD makes it to middle school. As I stated above, all of these issues, in addition to the academic and other social concerns, need to be considered when deciding whether or not a child should stay back one more year in an elementary school environment.

If the school administration seems willing to give the support necessary, whether in a more self-contained setting or with the addition of a parapro, and there is an understanding of children with ASD, with appropriate programming to meet the child's social and intellectual needs, then I recommend moving the child to sixth grade. Again, however, I would examine the strength of peer relationships for the child as he or she moves up and the child's own feelings about moving into middle school.

The key to making the best decision is to make as many inquiries with as many different people as possible to gain information about the middle school in question. Talk to administrators, teachers, district level employees of the school system, and parents. Sometimes even talking to the cafeteria staff, bus drivers, and janitorial staff is helpful. They will often speak candidly about the climate for students with disabilities. Parents should make trips to the school at unannounced times and ask to observe a classroom. If necessary and if the parents have the resources, they can hire a professional advocate to gather the necessary information to make the best decision and help them decide.

What to Say to Parents

- *In deciding whether to retain a child with ASD in the fifth grade remember that your child is eligible for school services until age 21.* Parents may be unaware or forget that their child can spend more time in school than the typical child. For higher functioning children with ASD, this may not be an appealing option. But for lower functioning children it should inform the overall educational plan. This sometimes gives parents a sense of breathing room to pace their child's progress accordingly and have adequate time to make decisions about posthigh school.

- *Retaining your child does not mean you have failed.* Some parents struggle with the notion that if their child is retained in a grade, they have failed somehow. It is important to help parents understand that if a decision is made to retain a child the retention is about what is best for the child, not about failure or success. As long as the child with ASD continues to learn and to grow, he or she is succeeding and so are the parents.

Questions Parents may Ask

- *If I allow my child to be retained does that mean I am giving up on academics?* Just because parents agree to retain their child in the fifth grade does not mean that they are giving up on academics. If they are able and interested, children with ASD still enjoy learning from the academic curriculum. Teachers should continue the emphasis on reading and mathematics. Challenging the children as far as they can go academically should always be part of the IEP. However, when the time comes to look at more daily living and community-based living skills then those should be emphasized.

- *What if I change my mind?* It is important for parents to be as clear as possible about the decision they make. It is very difficult to return to elementary school once a child has been enrolled in middle school. It is also equally as difficult for a child to transfer midyear from the elementary school to middle school. Help parents make the best decision for their child by encouraging them to do the work I outlined above regarding the transition. They should be satisfied with the decision they make. Beyond dealing with the school bureaucracy related to a change of heart, such a midyear change inevitably would be difficult for the student with ASD.

Middle School

Middle school is the time when children with ASD really begin to diverge from their peers in essential characteristics. This makes sense because so many of the tasks of the middle school age child are related to competencies in areas where the child with ASD has core difficulties. The child with ASD and the typical peers become increasingly aware of how they differ. This emotionally difficult time for any child becomes intensely more so for children with differences, especially a child with ASD who has limited social and language skills.

If the child is severely affected, middle school is also the time when parents are again forcefully confronted with their child's significant differences. Another period of adjustment and mourning may be required for parents, and for those children who are aware of their difficulties. This is a very tough transition, and these years in middle school will likely be difficult years. I urge parents to redouble their efforts to find appropriate peer group interactions for the child with ASD. Parents will certainly benefit from increased parent support from other parents of affected children. Many times, therapy either for the family or individuals within the family can be an important anchor through these years.

Middle school is a time when children with ASD, like other children, can learn to expand socially and practice for roles that they will have later in high school and beyond. It is, however, absolutely important that the children with ASD go into middle school prepared and continue to be supported. Parents have to be more, not less, vigilant of their children with ASD and their experiences at this point. Frequent meetings may be necessary to know clearly what is going on. In middle school no one person has responsibility for the child with ASD, so the parent must become the focal point and the driver for the team taking care of the child.

In the public setting, there might be resistance from some school administrators and teachers, but parents' involvement is essential for their child's success and safety. Because of this resistance to parent involvement and the increased difficulties associated with middle school, this is the time when families with the resources might look at private schools or even boarding school placements. Good private and boarding options are certainly available. These placements can also be wonderful experiences for a child who is different. Boarding schools or private schools that specialize in the care of children with special educational needs often have a mix of children with difficulties so that there is still a balance. This array of difficulties allows for the child with ASD to still be in a socially inclusive setting.

The schools have much smaller classrooms and there is generally closer supervision of students with facilitation of social interactions and support. The parents generally have greater access to school administrators and teachers to help with the educational planning for their child. Many of these schools even have vocational educational tracks in addition to the standard college preparatory curriculum to allow students to achieve greater success and feel they are learning what they need to for the future. More of these private school placements are available for higher functioning children with ASD, but there are private schools that serve more intellectually challenged individuals.

As outlined above, there are many things to consider related to placement in middle school. There are adjustments for the children and the parents. As a professional working with the families of children diagnosed with ASD, your job is to help the parents remember to consider the issues outlined above and to support them in their decisions.

What to Say to Parents

- *Your child with ASD deserves as much independence as he or she is competent to handle.* Many parents have a difficult time allowing their child with ASD enough independence. This can come from many sources. There is a natural desire to protect a child who seems more vulnerable than a typical child. This urge to protect may cause parents to be less aware of the child's strengths and skills than others outside the family. Nearly all of us parents see our children as less mature than they probably are or can be. While it is important to assure safety and to be involved in their child's life, parents should allow for as much independence as they can and deal with their own anxiety. As a professional working with the family, you can help the parents adjust to accepting a reasonable degree of discomfort related to their child's growth and development.

- *You may need more support.* As I outlined above when children with ASD get to middle school the child's difference is more apparent than before. Parents may need help dealing with their grief and sadness about their child's differences. They may need support to give their child more independence. They may need help in letting go of possibilities that are not realistic. Helping parents find support groups and counselors that can support them with these issues is very important.

- *Private school, even boarding school, may be an option.* Consideration of placements outside of the public school setting is always an option. As a child with ASD enters middle school and high school, boarding school is one of the private setting options. While these placements are not appropriate or even desirable for some children, they may be the most appropriate and helpful placement for others. The decision to enroll a child with ASD in a boarding school can be a very difficult one for parents. Boarding schools may be appropriate for higher-functioning children with ASD. There are specialty boarding schools throughout the country that either specifically cater to children with Asperger's and high-functioning autism, or have specific tracts for children with ASD. Finding the appropriate school can be daunting, and I advise families to consult with a professional educational consultant who has evaluated their child. While a child is away the parents need to stay in close contact with him or her, and with the school administration. Parents may want to make a surprise visit; they should also speak with parents of other children enrolled in the school. For children with ASD that are more moderately or severely impaired there can be residential placements as well; the same caveats apply. Usually children accessing these more treatment-oriented facilities will have a referral from health care professional or the school. Nevertheless, the same vigilance on the part of the parents is required to make sure their child is safe and happy.

Questions Parents May Ask

- *What can I do to get more support from the school for my child?* The first thing parents need to do about getting more support either collectively or individually for their child in the middle school setting is to ask. This can be accomplished by meeting with teachers and administrators informally or by calling an IEP meeting. If these meetings do not secure the needed support, then retaining a school advocate or an attorney might be appropriate. If a parent feels their child is not getting what he or she needs to succeed in middle school then they should advocate for that increased support.
- *How can I find out about private and boarding school options?* One way of finding out about private schools and boarding schools is via the Internet. Another way is to ask other parents via support groups and online forums. Parents can also retain private educational consultants to help with school placement. These consultants often know of specialty schools and can help parents evaluate the options with visits and discussions with school staff and parents of children enrolled in the schools. It is also helpful for the child with ASD to visit the school, talk with administrators if he or she will, meet other students, and talk with them about their experience at the school.

Sex, Bullying, and Substance Abuse

It is to be hoped that families have had some discussions with their children about sex, sexuality, bullying, and substance experimentation before they get to middle school: if not, middle school is the time to do it.

Let's start with sex and sexuality. Even though children with ASD by definition mature socially in a different way and cognitively at a slower pace (for many), their bodies' development of secondary sexual characteristics and sexual drive is similar to that of typical children.

When I am working with families, I ask them to start teaching about sexual issues as early as possible. From the very beginning, I talk to them about naming body parts appropriately with their child. I try to address issues related to masturbation when the issues first arise. I encourage families to redirect children to masturbate in private space and to answer children's questions honestly and simply about opposite sex issues and "where babies come from." Early discussions about boyfriends and girl friends, marriage and family are important. I discourage any activities that might send inappropriate messages about sex and sexual contact or conduct. I tell parents to be alert to their child's growing sexual nature as he or she matures.

During the final years of elementary school and when children enter middle school, discussions with girls must include the development of breasts and the onset of her menstrual period. Boys need discussions related to erections and ejaculation. Parents should discuss these topics in everyday, not clinical language, but avoid slang words with negative connotations about body parts or the opposite sex. Since children may hear words from peers, it may be useful to tell them the words and what they mean, while indicating that these words are not okay for kind or respectful people to use.

Discussions with the child need to include concrete statements and rules about what is and is not appropriate to say or do. There have to be rules about the do's and don'ts of physical contact and discussions of the topic of sex. There have to be clear discussions again about masturbation. There also should be all of the usual discussions of sex and sexuality that children this age receive about pregnancy and sexually transmitted diseases presented at a level the particular child with an ASD can understand. There have to be discussions that have become standard in helping children avoid sexual exploitation and abuse about good and bad touch. Parents need to ask children about any sexual content and monitor discussions and conversations, especially electronic exchanges. They need to be aware of who and where their children are and make sure that the school knows they are holding them accountable for helping to keep their child safe.

More than once I have been called by upset parents or middle school officials when a child with ASD said or did something interpreted as sexually inappropriate. Usually the child has simply talked about subjects not considered to be socially acceptable, because he or she does not know the appropriate context for discussion or questioning.

Parents have to be very direct about the "rules." If parents need help with these discussions then I generally recommend that the family meet with a therapist or social worker who specializes in issues of sex and sexuality with disabled people. For many social workers, especially those who work with adults and adolescents with ASD, who have extensive intellectual disabilities, this is a common request in their practice.

For children who are in the more severely affected group intellectually and socially, some of the above discussions will not be appropriate. However, that does not mean that there are not issues related to sex and sexuality. As I mentioned above, our children's bodies are still growing and maturing on a standard course, even though their minds are not. A frequent complaint that I hear from schools and parents of middle school boys and girls is about inappropriate masturbation. Frequent masturbation in this age group is going to occur, and it becomes a behavioral issue. The appropriate behavioral intervention is to redirect the behavior to a private setting, not to stop the masturbation. This task can generally be accomplished easily with the help of a behavior therapist. The other sex and sexuality issues raised for this lower functioning group of children are frequent or "inappropriate" erections in boys and problems with menstruation in girls.

For boys with frequent erections, the best recourse is to buy tight, appropriate underwear and to address any masturbation issues as above. There is not much else you can do. For girls coping with menstruation, problems can be more complicated, and beyond developing a behavior plan and frank discussions about the "rules," with or without the help of a health professional or social worker. Parents may need a referral to a gynecologist who has an expertise with disabled girls and women. Treatments for problems with menstruation can involve prescription of oral or injectable contraception that might stop or limit the menses. Of course these methods of control bring risks too.

Some parents may also decide at this point to start birth control to control pregnancy. This is an option that should definitely be considered if the parents have concerns about their daughter's potential sexual activity or inability to protect herself sexually. There should be a very long discussion with parents about these issues including the pro and cons from both a medical and ethical standpoint. We will discuss these issues in greater detail again in chapter 19.

There are many moral, ethical, and social issues inherent in discussions about sex and sexuality, but they are very important discussions to have with families of children with ASD. These include general concerns about safety and appropriateness and more specific concerns families have about sex and sexuality based on religious beliefs, concerns, thoughts, and feelings. If these topics have not been discussed before, the discussion at least needs to begin at the end of elementary school and continue during the middle school years.

Bullying also takes a new twist as the child with ASD attends middle school. The teasing can be much more subtle and hurtful. There also can be incidents of violence and aggression that are more severe. Both the higher and more moderately functioning children are susceptible to this teasing and need to be taught how to use the tools with which to handle it. I encourage parents to check into the school policies on bullying and to investigate what resources the school has to address any issues.

Parents need to talk frequently with their children about what is going on at school and to listen for any signs or discussion of bullying. Parents may have had quite a bit of experience dealing with these issues earlier because bullying probably more often starts in the fourth and fifth grades. However, in middle school some of the bullies from the early years increase their intensity, and it can become much more pointed and at times aggressive. Sometimes the school needs to do more to facilitate social interactions for the child with ASD, such as engaging a special parapro as a social facilitator or developing specific social skills groups and discussions about differences and bullying, to name a few. All of the teachers and other school workers need to be aware and mindful of what is going on if there is a suspicion of bullying. The child may ultimately need more protected classroom time in a noninclusive setting.

An issue very closely related to bullying is inappropriate peer pressure. Even though children with ASD have very poor social skills, they still often want to have friends. In their efforts to make friends, however, sometimes they are particularly susceptible to peer pressure. At times, peers may use the child with ASD to get a laugh or to do something that most typical children would recognize as inappropriate, but the child with the disability does not understand it to be wrong. In other words the child with ASD can be an easy victim, susceptible to being duped. Parents and school officials have to be very careful to investigate exactly what has happened when a child with ASD does something wrong that is out of character. Many times the child with ASD cannot even defend himself or tell the complete story. Efforts have to be made through social storytelling to teach the child how to say no to these sometimes very difficult to avoid situations. It is also important to help the student develop relationships with other students who will "look after" him or her and help to keep the special needs child out of the these kinds of exploitive situations. These can be students who have known the child with ASD for years or other good hearted students willing to lend a hand.

Exposure to children experimenting with substances also occurs in middle school. There will have been discussions about substance abuse before middle school, one hopes, but parents may have been reluctant to discuss the topic. However, higher functioning children with ASD can be especially vulnerable. Luckily, given the rigidity of the thinking of many of these children, simple, straightforward rules about what is and is not okay may suffice to keep them safe. However, you must have the conversations.

What to Say to Parents

- *We are all sexual beings and there will be some sexual expression.* Many parents do not always view their children as sexual beings and parents of children with disabilities, including ASD are especially disinclined to see their children as having sexual feelings and desires. Nevertheless all humans have sexual feelings and desires and generally will seek some outlet for those drives. Even in very low-functioning individuals masturbation and pleasure from self-touch is an important part of an individual's life. Parents may need to reconsider their own feelings about sex and sexuality in order to be comfortable with their children's drives and needs. They may also need support to talk frankly and openly with their children about these issues. I help parents talk about their thoughts and feelings about sex and their fears and anxieties about addressing these issues with their children. I also refer parents to social workers and other therapists who have specialized in working with families on issues of sex and sexuality. I also feel that it is helpful for parents to talk with other parents about these issues and to develop a healthy understanding of what it means to be sexual in a way that does not violate their moral or religious values.
- *Talk to your child about the school day and keep up with what goes on.* Adolescents by their nature are more secretive, and children with ASD have communication problems. Parents have to make an extra effort to keep communication open and freely flowing with their child through middle and high school. Encourage

parents to talk every day with their children about what is happening at school. Sometimes it is helpful to meet more verbal classmates or friends of their child with ASD to listen to their conversations about school and ask questions in a casual, conversational manner. Get to know the teachers as much as possible and try to establish a dialogue with them about what is happening in the school.

- *Stay involved in the school.* It is just as critical to be involved in the life of the school during middle school as it was in elementary school. Parents may feel more intimidated by the middle school or feel that they are inhibiting the growth and independence of their child by being as involved in the school, but my general sense is that this is not accurate. Parents can still be very involved in the school and with the school administration and teachers while giving their child room to grow and experiment. The involvement with the school allows parents to have greater access and credibility if and when they need to advocate for their child. The options for parents who wish to be involved with their child's school are not dissimilar to the kinds of involvement mentioned in the chapter on preschool. Parents can offer to volunteer for supervise activities and special events, attend school board meetings, or join the parent-teacher organization. Parents might also consider offering to make presentations for staff on being the parent of a child with ASD, or bring in representatives from local autism organizations to talk about ASD.

- *Learn about your school and the types of children that attend. Find out what kind of programs the school has in place for monitoring bullying and substance abuse.* Parents need to find out what kind of programming the school has that relates to bullying and substance use. They need to evaluate the programs as best they can, and if they are not satisfied they need to advocate for better programs. They can educate themselves on the Internet. They can talk with other parents in support groups about programs at other schools that seem to work well. They can engage other parents in the school about what needs to be done to ensure children are safe from bullying and illicit substances.

Questions Parents May Ask

- *What if my child can't understand sex?* Even children who cannot understand sex on an intellectual level still have sexual drives and will express them. Information about sex for children with ASD should be geared appropriately toward their developmental level. There are curricula available on the Internet and in books related to discussions about sexuality for individuals with developmental disabilities that parents can review and modify to fit their own beliefs and understanding about sex (see Appendices A & B). Professionals in the community often can help parents discuss sexual issues or determine whether it is appropriate to address sex and sexuality by talking about it or more appropriate to develop behavior plans to help keep a child with ASD safe and appropriate around issues of sexual expression.

- *How can I know if my child is being bullied?* The best way to know if your child is being bullied is to ask. If they are unable to communicate whether they are being bullied, then it is helpful to get to know other families in the school that have verbal children who interact with your child. Ask them to tell you about what goes on during the day as much as they can. Also parents can put teachers and administrators on notice that they have a responsibility to ensure that their child is not bullied.

- *What should I do if I discover my child has been exposed to illicit substances?* First of course parents should talk with their children about how to handle such situations. Ideally, parents will have had role plays with their children in the past where they have been given the social skills to say they are not interested. Parents should give children with ASDs a clear understanding of the rules about substance use so there is no question but that it is wrong to use substances. Parents need to be specific about what they are asking. The next thing parents need to do is to approach the school and let them know about their concerns. This can be tricky, and parents may need support to not hurt their child in any way by getting the school to address the problem. Lastly, parents can get in touch with other parents to help stop exposure to the substances in the school setting or in other settings associated with the school.

CHAPTER SIXTEEN

How to Talk about High School

In some ways, the transition to high school is not as traumatic for most families as the transition to middle school. In most school systems high school resembles middle school. Typical children have matured somewhat, and there is generally more tolerance of difference than in middle school. Teasing and bullying continue as serious concerns, but less so because children have settled more into their groups and roles. Since high schools often have more students, there may be problems with navigating a more complex environment.

For all children, the real task in high school is to prepare for the transition to adulthood. For lower-functioning students, training and education should teach functioning in day habilitation programs and learning skills for some form of group living setting. The emphasis for moderately functioning students should be on daily living skills and academic skills applicable to daily living. Vocational training should be a large part of the education at this point in the student's school career. There also needs to be an emphasis on relationships and social skills training. This training has been going on all along, one hopes, but specific emphasis and training at this point is important as it applies to living with roommates, and relating to coworkers, potential customers, and bosses. For higher functioning students, the goal is career development and education related to running a household, being part of a couple, and parenting. Some students will of course be following a typical precollege curriculum.

For those students who need it, from the start of high school parents and teachers should provide a plan related to transition from high school to adult services or work (I will describe some of these issues in more depth in the next chapter). Children who may be going on to college need a special plan. Consider what type of college the student can attend. Does he or she need greater support than is usually given in college settings? There are both colleges that specialize in assisting young adults with ASD specifically, and colleges that will make many accommodations for young adults matriculating with special needs.

In the first high school IEP meeting the team should discuss the anticipated year the student will transition/graduate from high school and what the student's post-high school life will be. Starting this process at the very beginning of high school helps the team teaching the student focus on preparing him or her for the post-high school world. Children with an IEP usually are able to continue in school until age 21. Most of the higher functioning students will not use the extended time, but moderate and lower functioning students and their families should be encouraged to take advantage of the additional time and training.

For most high functioning students, and even moderate functioning students, high school is the time when they really begin to look realistically at their differences and disabilities. At this point many children will really struggle with being different and their awareness of their disabilities or shortcomings. My clinical experience has shown me that this is the time when many children suffer depression for the first time. The most frequent stressor they talk about is their inability to find a boyfriend or girlfriend. Other than wanting a group of other teenagers to "hang out" with, this is the number one complaint of high school students with ASD, in my experience.

I encourage the development of social networks with other children with ASD. If there are groups for adolescents with ASD in the community, I encourage families to make use of those groups. If there are not, I encourage families to use online networking to help address that social need. Of course, the parents have to carefully monitor any online activity, given the inherent vulnerability of their children and their lack of social awareness or appropriateness. I have worked with one teenager with ASD who actually developed an online romance with another teenager with ASD. Even though the two of them lived in the same town, they were much more comfortable engaging in a romantic relationship through the electronic medium. The experience of actually meeting and talking with each other face to face was overwhelming. Eventually, after their parents called and spoke with one another, the teenagers met and had some interactions face to face; however, the mainstay of their relationship continues to be through e-mail and instant messaging. This arrangement has been very satisfying to my patient.

High school is also the time when parents of lower functioning children with ASD need to explore guardianship options. At 18 the child with ASD legally becomes his or her own guardian, even if the child is completely incapable of self care. Parents need to have discussions with other parents, legal advocacy groups, or an attorney to understand the best situation for their family and their child's needs. When the child turns 18, the family can apply for Social Security benefits for their child. Children who are moderate or lower functioning generally qualify. This assistance can be extremely helpful as the family looks at activity, work, and placement options after high school. Generally, Social Security eligibility also comes with some form of government-assisted health insurance either Medicaid and/or Medicare.

Some families experience continued emotional difficulties to overcome. Parents experience deeper and more disturbing recognition as their child with ASD approaches adulthood that he or she is different from typical developing children. Feelings of loss and grief arise again and again as the child fails to meet milestones or participate in activities typical for other children. Parents are struck that this experience is often vastly different from their experiences when they were in high school. Just as in earlier years, it may be important to look at family support groups or even some family counseling to help with the adjustments. The high school student with ASD may need support and counseling as well as outlined above.

If families have the monetary resources and will not be solely relying on governmental assistance, it is important to talk with an attorney or financial planner about the options that seem appropriate for the family's particular situation. There are also federally mandated legal advocacy programs available in every state for people who need legal services related to a developmental disability but cannot afford the assistance.

High school is the time to consolidate gains and to push for the services necessary for the child with ASD to make a successful transition to adult services and as independent a life as he or she can accomplish. High school is also the time to practice the skills necessary for independence, and for the young person to really try to be as independent as possible with a good safety net in place. Families should be encouraged to explore all of the options and to listen to their child about what he or she wants. Like anyone else, children with ASD should be allowed to follow their bliss—to do what makes them happy.

The years that a child with ASD spends in school allow the family to make a place for the adult with ASD. The work requires enormous emotional and even physical energy on the part of everyone involved, especially the child and the parents. Hard work put in during these years, however, will pay off in an easier transition to adulthood and a more fulfilling living experience as an adult. Above we have outlined a traditional interaction, mostly with public schools, but there are also private schools able to meet the needs of children with ASDs, and lately there are even specialty schools that are specifically designed to meet the needs of this group of children. Some of these are day schools, but there are some boarding schools. If families have the resources and these schools make sense to them financially, socially, and emotionally then they should be explored. The end goal is still the same: a solid foundation for a life as independent and fulfilling as possible.

What to Say to Parents

- *For families and children with ASD high school can be easier than middle school but you still have to push for an appropriate IEP.* There are many things about high school that are usually easier than earlier school years. This may not be as true for higher functioning children because of the desire to be in romantic relationships and be "normal," but even for them teasing and bullying decrease. There are usually peers with whom the adolescent with ASD is more comfortable. Usually it is clearer what the curriculum should be. Will the student be pursuing a standard academic diploma or getting a certificate of completion? There are options for curricula that focus on learning self-help skills, curricula for learning about living independently and holding a nonskilled job, curricula for specific vocational and technical training, curricula for general high school graduation, and curricula for college preparation. By the time a child with ASD makes it to high school, parents, teachers, and the student will have a better idea of his or her abilities. Parents still need to be very diligent about making sure the IEP outlines what the child needs in order to accomplish the goals that the parents and the student have established. Those goals, of course, depend on the student's level of functioning and can range widely. At one end the goal is to prepare the student to participate in a day habilitation program where staff are continuously present and the skills necessary are minimal. At the other end the goal may be college preparation and selection. Parents need to make sure that the supports are there to reach those goals. If they do not know what supports are necessary, they can talk with teachers they trust who know their child. They can ask their child what he or she wants or needs, or they can ask an independent educator or special education consultant to help with the development of the IEP. The family should place in the IEP specific goals about helping with the transition from high school to post-high school placement, regardless of what that might be. The IEP is the place to establish language that makes sure the school helps the family make that transition and secures the resources to make the transition as smooth as possible. This is the time to really push for what you need, and remember: the student with ASD will be able to stay in the school system through her or his 21st year if need be.

- *Stay involved in school.* Just as the parents cannot back away from being diligent about the IEP, they cannot step away from being involved in the school. Parents still need to be there as much as possible and they need to know the teachers, the special education support, and the administration as well as they can. Parents need to try and stay as engaged with the curriculum as they can so that they can step in if necessary to support their child. They need to work in school settings to continue to support some social connection for the child with ASD and be there for some facilitation while still giving the child as much room as possible. For example, they can volunteer at dances or other socials. They can help the child with ASD secure a role on a sports team or in a club. Again, much depends on the student's level of functioning, but the continued engagement of the community is still very important to support the student through high school and beyond.

- *It is imperative to decide the most appropriate goals for your child's future.* Parents should be encouraged to think deeply and carefully about the goals they will set for their child, ideally with their child's input and help. Envisioning life after high school and then using high school to get ready for that life is the most important thing to do. Finding and talking with people who know the student with ASD and understand what adult life is like for peo-

ple with similar struggles can be a great place to start. Your job as
a professional working with the family may be to help the family
set realistic goals. Some families may be too optimistic about what
their son or daughter with ASD may be able to accomplish. Some
families may be too pessimistic or too protective. Both of these
scenarios have to be addressed and a realistic appraisal of the child's
potential should be the main measure for determining the goals
post-high school and setting the goals during high school to meet
them.

- *Allow your child as much independence as possible.* So much of
  the determination of the level of independence of a child with
  ASD depends on that child's level of function. However, even the
  most severely impaired child needs to be encouraged and taught to
  be as independent as possible. My experience has been that when
  I can encourage parents to stay involved but back out as much as
  possible, they will be surprised at how much their son or daughter
  can do. The same is true for teachers as well. One of the potential
  positives or negatives in high school is that often the student with
  an ASD will have the same teacher or teachers for several years. If
  the match is good, this is great—and if the teacher is committed
  and not too protective. But it is not so great if the opposite is true.
  Sometimes as a professional working with the family you may need
  to step in to help them advocate for greater independent living
  skills for the student with ASD. Children will almost always surprise
  people with what they can do.

- *Keep up with the deadlines and important dates.* During high
  school, especially as the child with ASD approaches 18, there will
  be a lot of things to be done to help smooth the transition from
  school. When lower functioning children reach the age of 18 families need to apply for Social Security benefits. They will need to
  apply for the special programming all states provide to one degree
  or another for adults with developmental disabilities. They may also
  need to apply for guardianship of their child, if he or she cannot
  make decisions related to their disability. For children who may be

going on to vocational training programs or to college of some sort, the options for this post-high school training need to be explored. Pay close attention to deadlines for admissions applications and for accommodations and funding. For children going into day habilitation programs or supportive workshops or employment, families need to plan on doing the legwork necessary to plan that transition. We will talk about all of these to a greater degree in the next chapter on transitioning from high school, but these are all issues that the family needs to be aware of even as the child is entering high school and beginning the final years in school.

Question Parents May Ask

- *What about academics?* If a child with ASD has an average, above average, or very near average intelligence, then pursuing academics through high school should be a priority. Families should be encouraged to help put into place all of the resources necessary to make typical academic success possible. However, if a child with ASD has mild to moderate intellectual difficulties, then the best decision a family can make is to have their child take the track of learning community-based and survival living skills. All schools have these programs, and they are based on helping young adults learn what they need to care for themselves in the community as independently as possible. This track teaches money management, cooking, housekeeping, looking for employment, applying for jobs, learning how to be a good employee, and other self-help skills. The students will be learning basic academics like math and reading, but in the context of what they will need to know to take care of themselves. Many parents have a difficult time facing the reality that their child is unable to earn an academic diploma. However, the relief children and families feel when they finally accept the community-based learning, if it is appropriate, is immense, and life for the child with ASD and the family almost always is easier and more rewarding. They find energy freed to pursue other interests, including social interactions that may have previously been difficult because of the academic pressures. Children with more significant intellectual disabilities will continue to learn self-help skills as they gear toward doing well in group home settings and day habilitation programming.

- *What do we need to do about college?* If a child with ASD is intellectually and academically capable of pursuing college, then every effort should be made to get him or her to college. Serious social skills problems most often continue to be challenges. There are strategies for accommodating the disabilities. Some children need to start out at a nearby two-year college while still living at home or very close by. Some children need to stay in high school a bit longer to consolidate both academics and social skills to make the transition smoother. There are specialized programs in some communities for graduating students with ASD to help with the transition, and there are specialty schools that have a one- to two-year transition program or even four years devoted to educating young adults with ASD and helping them get their college degrees. These programs tend to be very expensive, but if families have the resources, they are great supportive options. Students with fewer social skills problems can also do well in a regular college setting if arrangements are made with the school where the student will matriculate to make appropriate accommodations for the disabilities as the public school did through the IEP. In fact, many of the same accommodations will apply. Some families have even been successful in securing some money from the state public education system to offset the cost of accommodations in college, if a student is not yet 21 years old (since the public school system is theoretically still responsible for educating a child with ASD until age 21). I would recommend consulting a lawyer specializing in education law about this possibility if it is not available in your school system or state. Ultimately those funds may not be an option for students with an IEP.

- *Who can help me with questions about Social Security and guardianship?* Parents with questions about Social Security and guardianship should start by contacting their local Social Security office and the community that works with adults with developmental disabilities. Some private attorneys specialize in issues related to disability, including guardianship and Social Security. Also, every state has federally mandated legal advocates who provide this information for families. Contacting the state division, department, or commission for developmental disabilities should help you access these free or low-cost legal services. Another good source, of course, is always other parents who have been down this path before. Schools and school social workers can also be of great assistance.

- *How do I find out about publicly funded supports for adults?* Probably the best source of information will be other parents and school officials, but contacting the agencies directly is also a possibility. Contact local community mental health agencies or talk with the state offices mentioned above that work with people with developmental disabilities. Many communities are home to private advocates who will do this work as well for a fee.

CHAPTER SEVENTEEN

How to Talk about Transitioning from School

I would wager that parents of children with ASD wonder every day, at least once a day, about what life will be like for their son or daughter when he or she grows up. The imagined problems to be faced undoubtedly vary depending on the child's level of functioning, but the question remains: What will life offer my child?

For parents with a child who is moderate or low functioning, these thoughts and worries are constant. It is difficult to envision what life will bring. While it is good to try to take one day at a time, when you have a child with a lifelong cognitive and social disability, you cannot afford to be short-sighted. Parents with any child diagnosed with ASD need to start considering early what the options will be for them and their child.

For parents with children who are higher functioning the need for direct care will be less, but there are always concerns about how a child with a social disability will navigate the everyday world of work and relationships. These children will probably have greater need for parental or other caretaker support than a typical child. However, if they are capable, higher functioning children need to be given their freedom to choose and shape their own lives. Even moderate or low functioning children need as much freedom as they can handle. I have been told by more than one person with disabilities that all individuals with disabilities have the right to fail, like anyone else. My job as a parent and a professional is to try to help him or her succeed or to figure out "what next?" when there is a failure.

Transition from School

Most children with ASD will transition from school between ages 18 and 22. Schools are required to keep students enrolled through their 21st year and to provide services. Some higher functioning children with ASD will not need to stay in school that long and may go on to different kinds of post-high school learning, including college, but for moderate and lower functioning students those extra years are important to help prepare them for life outside of a sheltered school setting.

For these low functioning children, the school needs to work diligently on their transition plan during the final years of high school. The school should focus on the most appropriate programming for the student once she or he is no longer able to attend school. For moderately functioning individuals or those on the mildly to moderately impaired spectrum, these last few years in school should focus on job training and all that is necessary to maintain a job in the workplace.

As noted in the last chapter, most schools have programs known as "community based learning" or some similar title. These programs teach basic academic skills, everyday life skills, and work skills at school for part of the day. The student then spends part of each day on a job site. During the early years of the program the student may spend time at a variety of job sites. The teachers and job coaches evaluate skills and vocational aptitude. Then as the student gets older, he or she will spend more time at a particular job site or kind of job.

This helps to teach the kinds of specifics necessary for a particular job.

Parents should push the school to provide this kind of programming for their child if he or she is capable. Students need to learn about all of the day-to-day skills that they will need to live as independently as possible. They need education on hygiene. How to function in an apartment or house is essential. They need to know how to wash dishes, cook, wash clothes, clean the house, and how to make simple repairs (like using a plunger or changing a light bulb). They need to know how to purchase household items, clothes, food, and cleaning materials. They need to know how to write a check or use a debit card and keep a checkbook or record of money spent. They need to know how to deal with the bank and pay bills. They need to study to take a driving test and learn to drive in a driver education class, if there is one available. If they are unable to learn to drive then they need to learn all about public transportation available in the area.

Young people with ASD in this moderately functioning range that I am familiar with have worked in a variety of jobs, including child care or animal care, in plant nurseries, grocery stores, offices, janitorial service, and many other positions. Generally there are many jobs available for the young adult with ASD who can read and do math at about a fourth to sixth grade level.

Usually state vocational rehabilitation staff are also involved during these last years of schooling to evaluate the student's abilities. In many states, if a student is not ready to transition to a particular job after high school, state vocational education facilities provide free training. These facilities usually require living on campus from six months to a year while the student is more specially trained for employment such as childcare, hair care, automobile or truck mechanics, air conditioning and heating assistant, or even healthcare assistants of different types. The training is based on the aptitude and interests of the student and assessments that the facilities generally complete on site.

I have found this break from the family is often a good thing for the family and for the young adult. Almost always the family and the young adult learn that he or she is far more capable than anyone realized and enjoys being challenged. Sometimes social difficulties or anxious feelings must be overcome, but these are usually managed by the staff at the facilities. Generally, students come away from the vocational training programs much more confident and capable.

Before the student leaves the vocational training school, staff work to place the student in a job or with a job coach service, run privately or through the state. It is important to help the families work with the state and local agencies to find the services most appropriate for the student returning home.

All of the young adults in the moderate range of functioning should have had help applying for Social Security disability at 18, so some funds should be available for housing expenses. Most states have programs to support individuals in the moderate to severe range of disability, including some housing, community, and job support according to the individual's abilities. These services, of course, are available whether the student has been away to vocational training school or not. If a student has been away, it is important to continue the move toward independence and as much self-sufficiency as possible. Parents sometimes have emotional work to do in order to relinquish some control over their child's life and encourage greater independence.

Over just the past few years a new trend at certain colleges and universities has included programs for individuals who are moderately affected by ASD and have mild intellectual disabilities. Perhaps this growth in programming is a product of the inclusion movement of the past two decades. Young people in these settings will have been more used to studying and being involved with students with developmental disabilities. I certainly believe that it is worth exploring these programs as possibilities for individuals who are moderately affected by ASD. I am sure over the next few years the number and scope of these programs will grow.

For individuals who are higher functioning and are intellectually capable of pursuing a college degree, this transition from high school to college can be very difficult. Some families are better than others at facilitating the process of their children leaving home. Some schools are better than others at preparing students for the transition. Some communities offer resources to make this transition easier.

When I work with families making this transition, I try to help them start preparing for the transition two years before the student is ready to leave high school. We work with the teachers and counselors at the high school. Parents and the student explore local resources, including community colleges and technical schools. I ask them to learn about living situations away from home, or we talk about how living space in the home might be modified to provide more independence. As an aside, I have found that families whose children went away to camp as youngsters do a better job anticipating these transitions. These days there are excellent camps for children with all sorts of difficulties or issues including high-functioning ASD.

I also have families who begin to explore colleges that might be appropriate for the student. Just as there are more programs in colleges and universities these days that provide specialty programming for individuals with moderate autism and mild intellectual disabilities, there are programs for individuals with high-functioning ASD as well. So it is worthwhile looking at those programs. Sometimes there may even be scholarship money available for such placements.

I have worked with several people with higher functioning ASD who have made a successful transition to college; some have even completed postgraduate work. Certainly there are difficulties, and these students definitely needed more support than non-ASD students, but they have been successful.

The most difficult part of the process for the students has, of course, been the social difficulty. However, I have noticed that in college individuals with ASD often have an easier time making friends and even dating than they did in high school, because there is more freedom and everyone is more mature, including the student with ASD.

For more severely affected, more intellectually disabled young adults, there are fewer options after graduation from the public school setting. However, most communities provide continued day services for these individuals, very similar to the school placements they have been attending. Families must start investigating all of the options for postschool placement about two years before the anticipated transition. This is important because it sometimes takes that long or even longer to work through the bureaucracy involved in achieving a placement.

When I talk about looking at options for day activity placement and day habilitation options for young adults, I mean that the parents should really visit (more than once) and spend time at every available placement, talk with the staff, talk with residents there who are conversational, observe how the staff and the residents treat one another, and talk with the parents of the residents.

Some communities may be fortunate to have several options, and there may be one placement that seems to fit better for one young adult versus another, even solely on the basis of the other residents. I encourage parents to look especially closely at the sense of life in a placement. Do the people there seem happy? Is there conversation and engagement? Are people doing more than just sitting around? Does the staff seem responsive to individual preferences and interests or is it all just one-size-fits-all?

Additionally, as families do the exploration necessary to find appropriate day placements, they sometimes find appropriate out-of-the-home living arrangements for their children. Considering placement outside of the home is often traumatic for families with a severely affected child; however, there are often many options that are good for the young adult and for the family. Considering the long-term issues of life with a severe disability, long-term care placement outside of the home early in adulthood is often a very good choice. Such a placement allows the family to be very involved in the care of their son or daughter for many years before their deaths, when the need for care outside of the home is no longer an option but a necessity.

An earlier placement also allows for individuals outside of the family to develop strong, loving relationships with the person with severe ASD, and this in turn ensures a richer, fuller, and safer life.

I have been working with several families over the past few years who have banded together to pool resources to create a group home for their children. Three or four families have formed a small nonprofit corporation that bought a house and staffed it with caretakers to look after their three or four children. The families stay very active in the day-to-day running of the home, and they manage many of the aspects of the group home. This sharing of the burden places the families, and ultimately their children, in safer, more rewarding settings. One family took a vacation for the first time in almost 20 years, finally feeling comfortable that other people who cared about their son would look after him in a safe, stimulating environment.

Two intentional community movements provide options for living away from home for young adults and older adults with moderate to severe ASD. These are the L'Arche Communities (http://www.larcheusa.org) and the Camphill Movement (http://www.camphill.org). Although I am not an expert on either one of these organizations, what I do know of the residential placements is impressive. Both of these organizations offer individuals with developmental disabilities and people without developmental disabilities an opportunity to live together in intentional communities. Each organization or movement is concerned with providing both the individual with developmental disabilities and the people without a disability a purposeful, engaged life that is physically and spiritually fulfilling. I also know that in many communities there are similar living situations, but they are more locally sustained.

I stress to the families I work with the need for this kind of constant reflection on the future. No place will be perfect, and we all need to take care we don't spend so much time looking for the perfect answers that we miss the good enough opportunities that are with us all along. But parents owe it to themselves and their children, both with and without disabilities, to look at all of the options. My experience has been that this keeps families from feeling that they made the wrong choices when they make decisions about transition and placement.

What to Say to Parents

- *Develop a solid transition plan over the course of high school, and then work the plan to make your child's transition a success.* I encourage parents, with their child if he or she is able, to write down all of the things needed to be done to accomplish the goals for the time after high school. I ask them to start doing this before their son or daughter's 18th birthday. I encourage them to break down the overall plan into small tasks. Then I ask them to commit to accomplishing just one of those very small tasks each day. A task might be a telephone call or to fill out the first page of an application or some other job that is achievable one day at a time. There will be days when bigger jobs are required, such as trips to Social Security or visits to potential post-high school placements, but those seem less challenging if they are accomplishing the small tasks each day. One of the other benefits to having the small tasks list is being able to get other people to help you. Some of the tasks are things that the child with ASD might be able to do. As I outlined before in the high school chapter, it is important to have input from people working with the student with ASD to create a solid and reasonable transition plan that reflects the goals everyone has helped to establish for after high school.
- *Consider as many of the options for placement for your child as are appropriate.* When looking at the different postplacement options, whether college or day habilitation, ask parents to consider as many options as seem appropriate. Encourage parents to not "just settle" for the first placement possibility they find. There are almost always others to consider, and helping families to talk with other families who have recently experienced the transition process

can help greatly. If the family is looking at colleges, look at as many as seem reasonable given the time, resources, and appropriateness of the college, based on what is known about the institution. The Internet can provide enormous amounts of information about colleges, before you ever e-mail or pick up the phone. If the placement is post-high school vocational educational training, look at all options. The same is especially true for day habilitation programs, because the individuals attending those programs may be unable to easily solve problems that arise there. Encourage parents and individuals with ASD to explore so that they will not feel trapped and resentful further down the road.

- *If he or she is able, work with your son or daughter to decide about placement.* As I stated above, help parents find some role for their child in the transition plan, to the extent he or she is capable. Not only are you then helping the parents to foster necessary independence, but you are also helping them to ensure that the transition placement is successful. Participation, of course, is no guarantee, but it is a good start.

- *Think about the best living situation for your son or daughter.* Another decision point that comes at this time and somewhat later for some families is whether staying in the home with the parents is the best long-term living arrangement for the person with ASD. Many parents and some children assume that living with parents is the best option, but perhaps it is not. As a professional working with the family, part of your job may be to help them sit down and sort out other options. They may feel guilty or overprotective, and you can talk with them about this. Especially for higher functioning individuals, living as independently as possible is very important. But even for moderately and severely affected individuals there are other options, from supported apartment living for the former to group homes with around-the-clock care for the latter. Talk with families to help them explore all of the possibilities. Making those transitions earlier rather than later can be helpful, if later on parents (being older or absent) lack the energy or may be unavailable to help with moves or decisions. Helping individuals make the transition away from the home earlier, when there is lots of support and energy, as well as time to plan, keeps it from being rushed and traumatic if a necessity arises later due to problems associated with the parents' health problems or death.

Questions Parents May Ask

- *What if I am overwhelmed and I can't do all of this planning?* Parents often feel completely overwhelmed by this process. Many times they are tired from years of demanding care of their child. They often just want someone else to handle everything. Of course, you can work with families where there is the opposite problem: despite the fact that they are seriously overwhelmed, they want to do everything and handle every detail of every task. Agencies and other people will help with some of these transition tasks on a fee basis. Some state and local governments will even provide care managers to help at no cost. It is important to talk with other parents and school officials about resources available in your community to help with these issues. It is also important to help the families feel as supported as they can be and to offer to help find counseling and support as needed to deal with all of the difficult feelings engendered by transition planning. Issues associated with guilt, hopelessness, helplessness, and feelings of failure and loss are common. Helping parents work through these issues will help to make the transition process healthier, more successful, and more productive for everyone involved including the son or daughter with ASD.
- *How do I know a placement is safe?* Insist that families visit any placement before agreeing to it. Once a decision is made about a placement, encourage families to visit and stay involved in much the same way they were during school. Higher functioning individuals may need less supervision because they can tell parents what is going on. But for more moderately or severely impaired individuals,

frequent, even unannounced, visits are important. Also, developing relationships with other families using the placement and developing relationships with workers at the placement can help to ensure good information, leading to better odds for safety.

- *How can I afford college, day placement, or out-of-the-home residence for my son or daughter?* For private, nongovernmental placements money is often a major concern. For most individuals who are more seriously affected, especially with a diagnosis of mental retardation as well, there will be governmental support for placement and housing. These funds are more generous in some states than others, and some states have long waiting lists of individuals waiting for these placements. These governmental funding sources also oftentimes come with multiple rules and restrictions, so it is important to seek help from other families and government officials to decipher them. Colleges that serve higher functioning individuals with ASD are generally private, and almost always many times the cost of standard postsecondary education. Sometimes scholarships are available, but many times they are not. For some families and individuals these simply won't be options, but for families that might be able to send their son or daughter to such an institution, and it seems appropriate, then it is important to sit down with them and do a careful cost–benefits analysis for the family. Sometimes it will make sense to spend the money, and other times the burden on the family or the benefit for a particular individual might make the extreme cost unreasonable.

Our Experience

For Frankie, whose disabilities are more moderate than mild, we have already started considering the types of services he will need in order to make the transition from school into the workplace. We are constantly evaluating our community and reviewing the options in other communities that might provide a wider array or higher quality of services. There are times when we have considered moving in order to ensure that appropriate services will available for him when he gets older. Of course, we have to consider all of the factors involved in such a move, including our current support system and the needs of each family member. We also must consider whether we would be able to create opportunities not already available for Frankie.

PART 5

ENTERING ADULTHOOD AND PLANNING FOR THE FUTURE

CHAPTER EIGHTEEN

How to Talk about Further Planning for the Future

When parents have a child with moderate to severe ASD and related intellectual disabilities, they are going to be caring for that child in one form or another for as long as they live. This may not be as applicable to parents of higher functioning children, but it still concerns them more than it does the parents of typically functioning children. Either way, some sort of comprehensive plan needs to be put into place to accomplish the tasks necessary for this care both during the parents' lifetime and afterwards.

Caring long term for a person with disabilities, whether in the home or in some other placement, are concerns families need to consider probably from the time their child is diagnosed. During the early years families need to talk about the issues anyone with children should consider: for example, wills and consideration of who will take care of the children if anything were to happen to either or both parents.

Families have to consider carefully whether the arrangements they make will be a good fit for their child with ASD. What does the designated caregiver know about the disorder? What does the proposed caregiver know about the son or daughter with ASD? What kind of resources does the designated caregiver have? What are the resources for people with disabilities where they live?

All of these questions and probably many more are important considerations. I have patients who are now wards of a family member because the parents died or were otherwise unable to care for them. It is difficult enough to piece together what needs to be done to care for a person with ASD when one starts from the diagnosis, but some of these new caregivers are completely overwhelmed by the child or adult's disability and the information needed to care for the individual now in their charge.

As a professional working with families with children diagnosed with ASD it is important to help them think about these issues, look at the possible caregivers for their children/adult children, and start the process of education as soon as possible. Preparing scrapbooks or workbooks with materials associated with the disability, including specific information about the individual with the diagnosis, would be helpful and important to the proposed guardian. As a professional you can tell parents to inform all of the professionals involved with their child about their plans in case they are unable to care for their child.

If you are working with a family with economic resources, then discuss with them how those resources will be preserved to care for the child. Don't limit this to a will, but ask questions about a trust or other mechanisms for ensuring that resources are available for the care of a child with ASD for life. How such arrangements will impact public funding and resources also needs to be considered in the decision-making process. Sometimes as the professional working with the family, you have to raise difficult questions about whether resources are divided equally if there is more than one child. What is the responsibility of the family to the child with the disability?

Issues to be explored in the will or other documents related to the long-term care of a person with ASD should include who will make decisions related to health care. Who will make the decisions related to money and economic resources? Who makes the determination about where the person will live? Will there be a full guardianship, a partial guardianship, or no guardianship? Will the caregiver arrangement be a formal or legal one or just an informal arrangement where the designated person accepts responsibility for the individual with ASD, although the individual is more or less capable of making decisions with some guidance?

Parents also have to examine issues associated with long-term care. Many of the questions raised above are still pertinent. There should be documentation of the wishes of the parents for long-term care of their child. Discuss these wishes with all involved. The same consideration should be shared about knowledge of the disorder and about the special needs person. Also, even more important in older individuals, especially those who are able to speak and relate their needs and concerns, are the feelings and concerns of the person with ASD about the plan and the proposed caregiver/guardian.

If parents have adult children with ASD living with them, what are the plans for where the adult child will live after the parents' death? Have there been arrangements made for some group or institutional living setting? Have these options been reviewed and visited? Has the family asked the questions related to these residential placements that I posed above for day habilitation options? All of those questions and others related to health care, food, comfort of facilities, opportunities for outside involvement, and community interaction must considered.

Families need to find placements that are integrated into the community, not isolated. Are local schools involved with the facility? Are local churches or other religious or civic organizations part of the everyday fabric of the residential facility? What kind of freedoms will the resident have? Who handles discretionary money for the person with ASD? What access does the person with ASD have to his or her money?

If an adult child is already living independently or in a residential setting away from the home, everyone involved in day-to-day care and protection of the person needs to be aware of the plan should something happens to the parents. Questions related to guardianship need to be addressed again. If there is no guardianship in place, does there now need to be a guardianship? If not a guardianship are there other legal instruments that might help ensure things are taken care of? Should there be powers of attorney for various functions related to the person, such as power of attorney for health care or for financial concerns, or both? Many times a lawyer can help sort out these questions. Of course the more resources that a family has, the more complicated some of these questions become.

For families with resources, it is essential that they involve an experienced attorney knowledgeable about issues of caring for individuals with ASD. Families that either do not look at these issues or do not consult an attorney put their adult child with ASD at serious risk of not having what he or she needs after they are unable to continue as caretakers.

Professionals working with families that have any disabled child should continuously raise these questions in a supportive and encouraging manner. Despite the power of denial and the wish to avoid difficult subjects and decisions, these are issues that must be considered and reconsidered. The specifics of a particular family's situation changes and evolves over time. Each time the situation changes, the decisions made previously about such issues as caretaker, placement, guardianship, or resources, will have to be reexamined.

What to Say to Parents

- *Make a plan for when you are no longer able to care for your son or daughter with ASD.* For most parents just thinking about not being able to care for their child is so terrifying it may paralyze them. To sit down and actually plan for that eventuality may be more than they can do at first. Begin by simply raising the issue gently and firmly, being sensitive to the emotions associated with the subject. Gradually, engage them in conversation about small, then progressively more important issues. As a professional working with the parents, part of your responsibility is to help them consider the need for a plan of care and then work with them to see that a plan is put into place. Parents must have a plan. Leaving any child without a plan creates a crisis for all involved. Leaving a vulnerable child without a plan is not an act of love.

- *Talk with other parents and with professionals to help you make a good plan for your child.* Encourage families to listen to what other families have done to ensure a plan for their child after they are unable to care for him or her. Encourage families to find an attorney who specializes in issues related to estate planning, especially for families with a special needs child. If the family is unable to afford an attorney, help them to access legal advocacy agencies for individuals with developmental disabilities where legal advice is available at no cost in most states. Encourage families to talk with their clergy, if appropriate, because this can also be helpful in sorting through all of the emotional issues related to making a plan for care after the parents are incapacitated or dead.
- *Talk with your family and friends about your plan.* After families have developed a plan, they need to let other people know about the plan, its directives, and location. Encourage the family to let everyone who has a specific role in a plan know their role. Work with families to get them to talk especially to all of the individuals who would play an important role in their child's life. Have them share the plan with anyone with any interest in their son or daughter's life to avoid misunderstandings or other significant difficulties, especially if the parents die. These kinds of discussions are especially important with extended family members so any hurt or conflicted feelings can be dealt with before and not during the crisis.
- *Include your children, including your child with ASD as he or she is able, in the plans for the future.* If children are able they should play a role in planning for the future. They should have a say in

who continues to take care of them. If they are able, talk with them not only about who would care for them, but where they would like to live, what they would like to see stay the same (if possible), and other issues as they are able. Of course issues related to care after a parent's death or disability should not be raised with children who would have serious anxiety or fear associated with such discussions. But if they are able developmentally and psychologically to deal with the issue, I believe that it is very important to include the affected child. You can talk with the family about your own estimation of the appropriateness of such a discussion. And of course include the siblings in the discussions about the future. Listen to their concerns and opinions. They are often great sources of knowledge about strengths and weaknesses of various plans and their affected siblings' strengths and vulnerabilities.

Questions Parents May Ask

- *How do I make sure my child with ASD is cared for once I am no longer able to care for him or her?* The best way to have as much certainty about care after your disability or death is to make a plan and talk with everyone about it. Also, it is never too early to start planning for financial security if that is an option for the family. While many families struggle to make ends meet, others have the capacity to take actions now that help with the virtual certainty that the child with ASD at some point in time will have to be without the parents' support.
- *Won't there be government funding to take care of my son or daughter with ASD?* Generally, for most children with ASD who are moderately or more severely affected, there will be government funding for care through Social Security Supplemental Income and in some communities other public funding sources, too. However, these may not always be available, and it is best to plan as much as you can on the assumption that there will be few other re-

sources. The family really needs to be very diligent about discussing these issues with other families and with government officials who work in their community. While I would hope there would always be some governmental funding available for individuals with ASD, it probably will be less available or unavailable for higher functioning people. Availability to others may vary according to government budgets and the policies associated with the different governmental funding sources.

- *Where can I get the help I need to make sure my child is cared for once I am deceased?* The first thing to do is to have the family talk with immediate and extended family members about their obligation to care for the child if a parent is unable to care for him or her. Second, talk with a legal or financial planning resource, either privately or through public resources, about how to make the family's plans secure in the community where they live. Each state has different rules and regulations related to wills and individuals with developmental disabilities, so it is critical to talk with someone who knows the specifics of resources, rules, and regulations of your particular state and community.

Our Experience

I know the weight of considering these issues. I am an older parent of an 11-year-old child with moderate disabilities associated with his diagnosis of ASD. I will be 58 years old when Frankie finishes high school. I know that for a substantial part of his life, Frankie is going to have to live without me. I have concerns about how much he will need from us as he gets older. I know now how much more he depends on us just day-to-day than his younger, typically developing brother. As he gets older it is clearer to me with each passing year that Frankie is never going to be able to fully communicate his needs and desires to people who do not know him very well. Even with those of us who know him it is sometimes difficult for him to clearly express his concerns.

Not long after Frankie was diagnosed, we began to set up specific wills and trusts outlining our plan for him and later his brother should something happen to us. We have revised those documents as time has passed and our situation has changed. Increased knowledge and awareness of Frankie's specific problems have also informed our alterations to these plans. I am sure that as we all get older we will revise the plans even further.

We have also discussed with Frankie and with his brother their lives with one another after we are unable to care for Frankie. McCrae, Frankie's brother, although still young, is beginning to understand Frankie's disabilities. He and Frankie both are aware that they have a responsibility to love and care for one another. We have talked to Frankie and let him know that one day he may need to depend on his brother to help him out. We have let McCrae know that he may need to keep helping his brother when he grows up, just like he does now. We encourage Frankie to let McCrae help him with people and situations, so that he will feel comfortable with the help. We talk about him needing help with his "troubles" as he calls them, and we have let him know that we are here to help him and so is his brother. We have also included our extended family in these discussions, and we have a group of old and very trusted friends who are also part of the caregiving team should anything happen to us.

CHAPTER NINETEEN

How to Talk about Community, Relationships, Romance, and Sex

In many ways this chapter may relate more to higher functioning people with ASD, but there are also issues related to those who are more moderately and severely affected. All of us need relationships and community. Granted, many individuals with ASD seem to have no desire for community. However, for anyone who has ever developed a relationship with a person with ASD it is clear that it is not necessarily lack of desire to be part of a community that is the problem. It is simply a problem of knowing how or feeling comfortable with engaging the community.

Acceptance

As we discussed above, many higher functioning individuals with ASD experience significant emotional distress about relationships when they enter puberty. The need to find a girlfriend or boyfriend is often very powerful. Sometimes for the first time, the adolescent with ASD is aware that he or she is very different. The adolescent understands that his or her differences create problems in developing a romantic relationship. For many adolescents with Asperger's or high-functioning autism, this growing self-awareness is very depressing and extremely frustrating. Some will deny the problem and continue to try to be like everyone else; others will become severely depressed and withdraw into their own world. Still others will embrace being different as part of their identity and move forward looking for other individuals who will accept them with all of their differences. Of course, the latter group seems to make the best adjustment. Some adolescents come to a place of acceptance without much difficulty at all. For others the road to acceptance is very difficult and many never achieve a level of acceptance that allows them to be more comfortable with themselves.

Fortunately, these days there are more opportunities for adolescents and young adults with differences to meet. This way they have a chance to help one another with differentiation from family, the primary developmental task of these years. Many adolescent patients I work with have found support with other high functioning adolescents or young adults with ASD on the Internet. Sometimes they have found others with high-functioning ASD in their communities. Others have chosen to be part of a group of adolescents or young adults who are different themselves from "normal" or at least more accepting of diversity and difference. All who have been successful have found a place where they can be themselves without changing who they are fundamentally. They may have to continue to work on and improve their manners and other social skills but they do not have to disown the parts of themselves that are more difficult, if not impossible, to change.

In fact, I have been to a few conferences where there are groups of people with high functioning ASD who assert that they are proud to be who they are and state the benefits to being "on the spectrum." The adolescents and young adults in the group will even look at those of us not "on the spectrum" and disdainfully and dismissively call us "neurotypicals." While not exactly embracing of diversity, I view these efforts at group identification and pride as important and helpful for the individuals with ASD as they move forward beyond their diagnosis, owning their gifts and disabilities, and refusing to be stopped by any perceived limitations.

For those who withdraw or become increasing depressed or both, life is much tougher. Many individuals in this group may need pharmaceutical assistance to overcome what can be diagnosed as a major depression. All who struggle certainly need some psychotherapeutic process. The goal of the process should be to help the individuals move to a place of self-acceptance.

The adolescents and young adults with ASD who I find make the best transition are those who have been accepted and supported all along with all of their differences and celebrated for the unique individuals they are. The adolescents and young adults who struggle most are surrounded by family and other people in their community of support who want them to be as "normal" as possible and deny their differences—almost at any cost. This stance implies that the person is also a problem that needs to be "fixed." I try to help parents and individuals with ASD to understand that the differences are not the problem. Instead it is how the differences and symptoms may be viewed negatively by those around them and how the differences or symptoms impact the individual's ability to function.

I know this may not seem like much of a distinction, but I think it is very important. Considering the problem in this way helps individuals with ASD to accept and even embrace the differences, especially those that do not inhibit their ability to achieve life goals. Subsequently, everyone develops a more content and successful life.

A point I make repeatedly to people with ASD and their families is that there is no cure. However, what can be changed is how the symptoms are managed by the individual affected and the people around them. The attitude of individuals with the disorder and the people around them regarding the symptoms and differences they create can also be changed. These changes lead to a greater chance for success and psychological peace.

The individuals mentioned above who are successful generally embrace their diagnosis, while not necessarily being happy about it. Nevertheless, they go on to figure out, "What can I do about this symptom?" "Where can I go or what situations can I be in where this or that symptom will not be a problem?" "Where are people who will accept me?" "How important are other people's responses to this or that symptom anyway?" Successful individuals with ASD ask these and similar questions to navigate the world of the "neurotypicals." People with ASD who take this approach continue to grow and learn from their experiences of living with their diagnosis and its symptoms. They create the opportunity to thrive.

Of course I am not saying that we should not continue to look for a solution to ASD, especially in people who are more severely and profoundly affected. However, I am saying that we should accept our children and neighbors with ASD as they are, while helping them to continue grow and develop into the best people they can be. We should also help them to accept themselves. I believe that part of your role as a professional working with people with ASD and their families is to help further these goals by bringing up these issues and discussing them with the affected individual and the family.

What to Say to Parents

- *Acceptance of the diagnosis is essential to long-term contentment and success.* Helping parents to accept their child with his or her ASD, while keeping them motivated to do necessary things to lessen the impairment caused by the symptoms and better manage them, is a difficult balance. I have found success in helping parents through this task by having them list the gifts of a child with ASD and then list the child's struggles. This exercise helps the parents see the whole child. Next I ask the parents to make another list that can be much more difficult. I ask them to list the ways their child is gifted because of the disability. In other words what gifts or positives does the ASD bring into the child's and family's lives? Over time, families and higher-functioning children with ASD many times come to recognize that there are positives and negatives to living with ASD. I hope over time it helps families and individuals with struggles to separate the person from the disorder, recognizing that the disorder brings struggles and gifts but does not represent the whole person. In other words people with ASD are not just the disorder but whole people. Moving to this acceptance, and moving beyond seeing a child (or the child seeing him- or herself) as the disorder leads to a serenity about the disorder that allows for work on the struggles of the disorder and a pursuit of the joys and gifts the child has as well.

- *As parents you should work through your own issues related to the diagnosis of ASD through your own therapeutic process.* If parents are struggling with their own issues related to the diagnosis and are unable to move beyond feeling overwhelmed and trapped by it, then they should seek their own counseling. Parents may actually from time to time be at a point of acceptance and peace with the disorder only to have the grief and fear associated with the diagnosis resurface. Sometimes parents are able to work through these feelings themselves, but other times they need the help of family support groups and other parents, or even professional counseling. Helping parents continue to work on their own issues will help the child with ASD better manage his or her own struggle for acceptance.

- *Encourage your child to do his or her own psychotherapeutic work related to accepting the disability.* If parents are doing well, but they see their son or daughter struggling with issues of acceptance, then they should offer to find the psychotherapeutic support he or she might need. By continuing to build acceptance of the disorder, its struggles and its gifts, the child will be able to move more freely in the community and be more open to community engagement and involvement. Children and their parents who have moved to this level of acceptance are also better able to create a community for people with ASD.

- *Building community for yourself and your child with ASD is an important part of your role as a parent.* Parents who are open and engaged about their children this diagnosis can better create a community for their child and others. Coming out of the shadows and claiming a place in the community can be difficult, but it is essential to people with ASD to have a place in the community, an opportunity to share themselves and their gifts, regardless of how affected they may be by the disorder, and an opportunity for the community to benefit from the gifts they bring.

Questions Parents May Ask

- *If we "accept" the disability won't that send the message that there is no need to get better?* As a professional you can help the parents separate accepting the disability from accepting the disability's limitations. Parents can understand the particular struggles of their child and help him or her to change the impact of those struggles, while still accepting that their child has a disorder that will not go away—nor does it have to go away in order for the child to be an accepted and important participant in the family and the community.
- *Won't people tease and hurt my son or daughter if they know about the disorder?* Higher functioning individuals with ASD often find it helpful to explain their difficulties by stating that they have a disability or even saying they have ASD. Parents of such children often worry that this will set them up to be teased more. My experience has been that this is not the case. But if parents or children are afraid, this usually can be overcome by having a counselor or teacher work with the child to introduce him- or herself to the

school. I recently worked with a student who is a rising sixth grader who taped a television special about autism and Asperger's. Then he asked to make a presentation to several middle school classes before he entered middle school. The administration embraced the idea and helped to facilitate the different classes where he made the presentation. By all accounts it was a great success and paved the way for a successful transition that could otherwise have been very difficult. He told me now people can get to know him without just seeing him as "weird" and trying to figure out why he acted the way he did. Now they know, and they can approach him and talk to him about his interests such as videogames and electronics.

Our Experience

Frankie is currently struggling with many of these issues around acceptance, what can be changed and what cannot. We were driving to his karate lesson one evening, and he was discussing an examination at school. He told me that he hoped he earned an A+. I knew from having worked with him over the week studying for the exam that he probably had not earned a perfect score. I told him that he had studied very hard, and that I was sure that he did his very best and that was great. We also talked about all of the new things he had learned in studying for the test. After we talked for a few minutes he sat there quietly and then said, "Daddy, I need an x-ray to fix my brain. I don't want my brain this way."

After I caught my breath, we talked about his brain and what he calls his "troubles." We discussed that there is nothing I know of that can fix his brain. I told him that even though we cannot fix his brain, we will continue to work as hard as we can to help him do what he wants to do and to have the life that he wants. He is not always able to articulate it clearly, but he has let us know that what he wants most is to have friends, be loved by his family, and to do his best. I assured him that we will always help him to reach those goals.

Romance, Relationships and Sexual Expression

I also want to explore the need for romantic relationships or sexual expression for people with ASD. Of course a romantic relationship is not a realistic option for someone who is severely affected by ASD, but for those individuals who are more mildly or moderately affected, romantic relationships are often very important. Even for some older adults with ASD with whom I work, finding a romantic partner is a priority.

The ability to be in a reciprocal relationship, however, is often difficult. Sometimes novel approaches to romantic relationships are the answer, as with the adolescent couple I mentioned earlier who carry on most of their relationship via e-mail and instant messaging. As is true for most of us, finding groups of individuals with like interests can be a way to meet a romantic partner, especially when the interest may be one of the restricted interests of the person with the ASD.

Of course many people with ASD will meet potential romantic partners in their everyday lives. They might meet someone at their place of work or in their religious or other social groups. Your task, as the professional working with the family or individual, is to help the family or the person with the diagnosis make sure the relationship can be reciprocal, appropriate, and that barriers to the relationship are lifted when appropriate. As a professional you can also help the family and other professional staff who may be working with more moderately impaired individuals to understand that it is a good thing to have a romantic partner. It is important to the growth and happiness of the individuals who want a romantic relationship.

Of most concern to families and helping professionals is the prospect of sexual involvement for the young person or adult. However, there are times when the goals of individuals with ASD who seek a romantic relationship do not even include sexual involvement. So it is important to clarify what the relationship is about. If there is a desire for sexual involvement, then it is important to explore what that involvement will be, and whether it is appropriate and in keeping with the individuals' values. The family's values are also important, but it is important that their values alone not determine the level of involvement. The values of the professional staff working with the individual with ASD should not determine the level of involvement either.

There should be efforts to work out all of the issues and concerns, but in the end, if the individuals with ASD are competent to make their own decisions as determined by whether there is a guardian appointed or not, then their say in the matter should be final. They certainly have the right to make mistakes in romantic and sexual relationships like the rest of us.

The issue of birth control, both voluntary and involuntary, often comes up in these discussions of sexual involvement. Certainly there need to be appropriate discussions about birth control in a clear, simple manner. As to the issue of forced sterilization, I do not believe that it is generally ethical or moral to sterilize anyone without their full consent and knowledge. However, some families will think differently. Some doctors and judges allow families to make these determinations for people with ASD in their care. This is an issue that has to be approached and considered carefully in any discussion about sexual involvement between two people.

With individuals who are more seriously impaired in their symptoms, the prospect of a romantic relationship with sexual involvement is not viable. However, many of these individuals will have sexual drives and will attempt to engage in sexual behaviors. Sometimes these are more appropriate than others. As a professional involved with the care of the patient with ASD and their family, it is your role to help the young person or adult find an appropriate and acceptable, noninjurious expression of their sexual urges. With severely impaired persons the acceptable sexual activity will be some form of masturbation. Individuals severely affected by ASD may still try to engage other people sexually by grabbing or touching breasts or other private parts of the individuals around them. Such behaviors involving others should be addressed by finding a behavior specialist to develop specific behavioral interventions to decrease these inappropriate behaviors and reinforce sexual behaviors that are satisfying and private.

Discussions about romance, sex, and masturbation are often difficult for the people involved but they are essential to helping people with ASD live as fully and completely as possible. As the professionals working with these individuals and their families we have to be willing to bring up these topics and encourage open, frank discussions.

As I stated at the beginning of this section, the need for community, relationship, and sexual expression are all part of being a whole person. To deny an individual the opportunities for these pursuits is to deny their personhood. These needs are as important being cared for. We need to spend as much time cultivating these needs as establishing appropriate living situations and work or day habilitation placements. If parents or families lack the ability to conduct these discussions alone, professionals can be important advisors and facilitators.

What to Say to Parents

- *Special romantic involvement is possible and desirable for some people with ASD.* Many of these individuals would like to have a romantic involvement. Some moderate to higher functioning individuals may even wish to marry. I help parents and other people working with these individuals to acknowledge how important and fulfilling the pursuit, discovery, and commitment to a romantic relationship can be. These relationships often have a therapeutic benefit that helps to lessen the symptoms of the disorders. Of course the opposite can be true at times, and the pursuit and engagement in romantic relationships can lead to increased difficulties and an exacerbation of struggles. But isn't this true for anyone who engages romantically? Sometimes things are great, and we are better for our involvement, and sometimes things go very wrong and we struggle with our choices. There is living and learning to be found in both experiences.

- *Sex is not always a part of romantic involvement.* Sex is not always what an individual with ASD seeks in a romantic involvement. Sometimes sex can be too much, too close, and too personal. It is important to clarify the intentions if that is a concern for family members of moderately affected individuals. However, sex is sometimes a part of their desire. Ideally the groundwork has been laid down to make sure the person is protected and safe, is not exploited, and doesn't exploit. Helping families to talk about their concerns and issues and keeping an open dialogue about relationships and sex is very important. If it is too difficult for the parents to do it themselves, but if they have significant concerns, then they should ask a professional to help—perhaps a counselor, advisor, teacher, or clergy person.

Questions Parents May Ask

- *How can I know that my son/daughter is safe and not exploited in a romantic or sexual relationship?* The best way for parents to help their children remain safe in a romantic or sexual relationship is to keep the communication open either with them or with another trusted adult as outlined above. As the professional working with the family you can help make sure that the openness is there and that issues associated with discomfort are discussed and overcome as necessary to provide for the openness.
- *What if there are children?* One of the main concerns for parents of any developmentally disabled person relating to romance, sex, and marriage is the possibility of children. Let me first say that living in communities throughout the country there are many individuals with higher functioning ASD who are married or have children. They do as good a job as anyone else in raising their children. Part of the fear behind this concern is that the parents may not trust their son or daughter to be able to raise a child (this would be especially true for moderately or more severely affected individu-

als). There may also be a fear that the parents will have to raise the grandchild. If there are concerns about children, then these concerns need to be discussed, and perhaps a professional should be involved in the discussion. If the person with ASD has no desire for a child, then there needs to be frank and open discussions about contraception. All of the concerns should be raised and talked through, so that everyone has a clear understanding of the issues involved in sexual engagement, marriage, and the possibility of children. As the professional working with the family, you can help to make sure those discussions take place, and you can mediate or help find someone with experience to mediate as appropriate. Families, too, can sometimes find help by talking with other families in similar circumstances as I have discussed before.

That brings me back to the original point of this chapter. Every individual, no matter how affected by a disability, has the need for community and relationships. These relationships may be different from the relationships of more typical individuals but the need is still there. Professionals working with families of people with ASD should help the family do what is necessary to ensure community and the opportunity for relationships.

This can be accomplished by helping families to find support for themselves. Encouraging families to foster friendships for their child from the very beginning, regardless of how disabled the child may seem. This effort should continue for as long as the child needs help developing those relationships, even into adulthood if necessary. Many times helping families make these connections means helping them and the affected child, if they are able, deal with the grief and sense of loss that often comes with a chronic, incurable disability like ASD.

Conclusion

Few people realize how tremendous and consuming being a parent is when they decide to become parents for the first time. We did not. Looking back on the decision there are times when I wonder how things would have been different if we had decided not to parent. Then I look at our boys, and I cannot imagine having made a decision that would not put me exactly where I am right now.

I believe that most parents of children with ASD feel the same way about their children. They realize the enormity of the tasks before them. They are aware of the heartache and pain that may lie around every turn. But most of them experience deep joy and understanding that comes from loving and honoring a child, especially a child with ASD.

I do not like the fact that Frankie has disabilities, and there are days when, if I could, I would "get an x-ray and fix [his] brain." Nevertheless, I love my son as he is, with all of his joy and life, as well as his struggles and pain. I am a better parent, physician, and person because Frankie is in my life. Being a parent is always a mighty developmental and spiritual undertaking. Being the parent of a child with any disability, including ASD, is a journey that requires even more—more courage, more strength, more stamina, more understanding, and more humility.

As you make this journey with parents for a short way or for an extended part of the path, remember to listen, challenge, and support them as they do their best to help their child to flourish. Help them to see the journey as an opportunity for them to grow, even when they desperately want to retreat into the safety of denial. Listen and try to empathize with them when they tell you how hard it really is to be a parent of a child that at times can show you no noticeable semblance of love or attachment. Comfort them when they cry in pain from watching their child suffer. Mourn with them when they cry in grief for all that is not and will not be. Help them to find a good path, if not the best path for their family.

How do you talk to parents of children with ASD? You listen and understand that we want our children to be safe and loved. We want their lives to have meaning and purpose. You can help us find the resources to do our best to make those dreams a reality.

References

American Psychiatric Association. (1994). *Diagnostic and Statistical Manual of Mental Disorders, 4th edition*. Washington, DC: American Psychiatric Association.

Asperger, H. (1994), Die'Autistischen psychopathen'im kindesalter. *Archiv für Psychiatrie und Nervenkrankheiten*, 117,76–136.

Findling, R.L., Henderson, R.L., & Posey, D.J. (2007). Enhancing patient care and providing caregiver support. *Counseling Points*, 1, 4–11.

Fombonne, E. (2005). Epidemiology of Autistic disorder and other pervasive development disorders. *J Clin Psychiarty*, 66, suppl 10, 3–8.

Kanner, L. (1943). Autistic disturbances of affective contact. *Nervous Child*, 2, 217–250.

Kingsley. E.P. (1987). "Welcome to Holland." Essay.

National Autistic Society. (2003). *Approaches to Autism*. London, U.K.: The National Autistic Society.

National Institute of Neurological Disorders and Stroke, National Institutes of Health. (2007). *Rett Syndrome Fact Sheet* (Publication No. 04–4863). Bethesda, MD: Office of Communications and

Public Liaison, National Institute of Neurological Disorders and Stroke, National Institutes of Health.

Owley, T., McMahon, W., Cook, E.H., Laulhere, T., South, M., Mays, L.Z., et al. (2001). Multisite, Double-blind, Placebo-controlled Trial of Porcine Secretin in Autism. *Journal of the American Academy of Child and Adolescent Psychiatry, 40,*1293–1299.

Remen, R.N. (1997). *Kitchen Table Wisdom.* New York, NY: Riverhead Books.

108th Congress. (2004). *Individuals with Disabilities Education Improvement Act of 2004.* Public Law 108–446.

Appendix A: Helpful Web sites

http://www.autismspeaks.org: Information, advocacy and grants.

http://www.autism-society.org: Information, parent support and advocacy.

http://www.autismresearchcentre.com: Research facilitation and information.

http://www.nimh.nih.gov/healthinformation/autismmenu.cfm: Information.

http://www.cdc.gov/autism/index.htm: Information.

http://home.san.rr.com/autismnet/index.html: Autism network resources for physicians.

http://www.cureautismnow.org: Information and research facilitation.

http://www.autism.com: Defeat Autism Now (DAN) Web site.

http://www.udel.edu/bkirby/asperger: Comprehensive information about Asperger's Syndrome.

http://www.BCBA.com: Information about Board Certified Behavior Analysts.

http://www.wrightslaw.com: Information related to special education services.

http://www.sexualityandu.ca/teachers/tools-10-1.aspx: Information about sexuality.

http://www.achievableconcepts.us/usa_sex_resources.htm: Information about sexuality.

http://www.nas.org.uk: Information and advocacy.

Appendix B: Helpful Books

Baker, J. (2005). *Preparing for Life: The Complete Guide for Transitioning to Adulthood for Those with Autism and Asperger's Syndrome*. Arlington, TX: Future Horizons, Inc.

Batts, B.M. (2004). *Road to Independence: Independence Skills Training For Special Needs Children*. Lincoln, NE: iUniverse.

Bettison, S. (1982). *Toilet Training to Independence for the Handicapped: A Manual for Trainers*. Springfield, IL: Charles C. Thomas Publishers.

Coleman, M. (2005). *The Neurology of Autism*. New York: Oxford University Press.

Fiona, B. (2001). *Everybody Is Different: A Book for Young People Who Have Brothers or Sisters with Autism*. London: The National Autistic Society.

Grandin, T. (1995). *Thinking in Pictures*. New York: Doubleday.

Greenspan, S. (2006). *Engaging Autism: Helping Children Relate, Communicate and Think with DIR Floortime Approach*. Cambridge, MA: Perseus Books.

Greenspan, S. (1998). *The Child With Special Needs: Encouraging*

Intellectual and Emotional Growth. Cambridge, MA: Perseus Books.

Gutstein, S.E., and Sheely, R.K. (2002). *Relationship Development Intervention with Young Children: Social and Emotional Development Activities for Asperger Syndrome, Autism, PDD and NLD*. London: Jessica Kingsley.

Harris, S.L., and Glasberg B.A. (2003). *Siblings of Children With Autism: A Guide for Families*. Bethesda, MD: Woodbine House.

Hart, C. (1993). *A Parent's Guide to Autism*. New York: Pocket Books.

Jepson, B. (1994). *Changing the Course of Autism: A Scientific Approach for Parents and Physicians*. Boulder, CO: Sentient Publications.

Kaufman, B. (1994). *Son Rise the Miracle Continues*. Tiburon, CA: HJ Kramer.

Maurice, C., Green, G., and Luce, S.C. (1996). *Behavioral Intervention for Young Children With Autism: A Manual for Parents and Professionals*. Austin, TX: ProEd.

National Autistic Society. (2001). *The Autistic Spectrum*. London: The National Autistic Society.

Newport, J., and Newport, M. (2002). *Autism – Asperger's and Sexuality: Puberty and Beyond*. Arlington, TX: Future Horizons.

Robledo, J., and Ham-Kucharski, D. (2005). *The Autism Book*. New York: Penguin Group.

Schopler, E., and Mesibov, G. (1988). *Diagnosis and Assessment in Autism*. New York: Plenum Press.

Schwier, K.M., and Hingsburge, D.R. (2000). *Sexuality: Your Sons and Daughters with Intellectual Disabilities,* Baltimore: Brookes Publishing Company.

Sherman, D.A. (2007). *Autism: Asserting Your Child's Rights to a Special Education*. San Francisco: Oxford Churchill.

Sicile-Kira, C. (2004). *Autism Spectrum Disorders: The Complete Guide to Understanding Autism, Asperger's Syndrome, Perva-*

sive Development Disorder, and Other ASDs. New York: Perigee Books.

Vermeulen, P. (2000). *I Am Special: Introducing Children and Young People to their Autistic Spectrum Disorder*. London: Jessica Kingsley.

Wall, K. (2004). *Autism and Early Years Practice: A Guide for Early Years Professionals, Teachers and Parents*. London: Sage.

Wheeler, M. (1998). *Toilet Training for Individuals with Autism and Related Disorders* Arlington, TX: Future Horizons, Inc.

Wrobel, M. (2003). *Taking Care of Myself: A Hygiene, Puberty and Personal Curriculum for Young People with Autism*. Arlington, TX: Future Horizons, Inc.

Index

parents' questions about, 32-34
prognosis for, 33
range of severity of, 30, 31
symptoms of, 25, 30
tolerating behaviors associated with,
31-32
what to say about, 31-32

Behavior Analyst Certification Board, 111
behaviors, tolerance for
Asperger's disorder, 36
autistic disorder, 31-32
obsessive compulsive disorder, 60, 61
repetitive/rigid behaviors, 98
Tic/Tourette's, 64
benzodiazepines, 148
beta-blockers, 146
Better Business Bureau, 206
bipolar disorder, 66-67
birth control, 222, 269, 272
blame, 9, 24, 36, 139-40
blood pressure medications, 55, 102,
144, 146
board certified behavior analyst (BCBA),
111
boarding schools, 217-19
brain injury, 16
bullying, 213-14, 222-23, 225-26

Camphill Movement, 244
camps, 242
causes
Autism Spectrum Disorder (ASD),
15-16
autistic disorder, 32
Rett's disorder, 38
Celexa, 148
Centers for Disease Control, 3
cerebral palsy, 19
chamomile, 119
child psychiatrists, 152
childhood disintegrative disorder, 39-40
childhood schizophrenia, 14
childrearing, by ASD individuals, 271-72
children with ASD. See also adulthood,
for ASD children; prognosis
and acceptance, 261-67

depression in, 263
following lead of, 71, 80, 231
high-functioning, 238-39, 242, 261-72
independence of, 217-18, 231, 234
parent's relationship with, 172
self-awareness of, 229, 262-63
support system of, 262
typical peers versus, 216, 230-31
what to say to, 51
chiropractic care, 154-55
chromosomal abnormalities, 16
clonidine, 119
coexisting diagnoses/labels, 43-71
ADHD, 56-59
ASD and, 43-44, 45t
mental retardation, 44, 46-51
mood disorder, 65-68
obsessive compulsive disorder, 59-62
sensory integration dysfunction, 51-
56
Tic/Tourette's, 62-65
college, 229, 236, 241-42
communication, 76-84. See also language
assistive technologies for, 77, 79
autistic disorder and, 30, 31, 33-34
family engagement in, 33-34
importance of, 76, 79-80
interventions for, 31, 33-34, 76-83
language versus, 80
as lifelong process, 81
medication and, 82
parents' questions about, 81-83
school services for, 199-200
sign language, 77
social skills and, 82-83
what to say about, 79-81
community-based living skills, 235,
239-40
community, involvement in, 208-9,
266
computers, evening restrictions on, 115
contraception. See birth control
corporal punishment, 111
costs. See also financial planning
of adult placements, 248
of alternative treatments, 156-57